THE
NEW YORK
TIMES
GARDEN
BOOK

THE NEW YORK TIMES GARDEN BOOK

Edited by

JOAN LEE FAUST

with a Preface by HAL BORLAND

Revised Edition

BALLANTINE BOOKS · NEW YORK

Library of Congress Catalog Card Number: 72-11016

ISBN 0-345-25682-4-495

First Ballantine Books Edition: March 1977

The Green Miracle

HAL BORLAND

EVERY SPRING I think how much simpler life would be if we were still content to eat wild herbs and pluck the lilies of the fields. The wildlings have their truce with wind and weather, bug and blight. But since we are no longer savages, in diet at least, we have gardens as well as wild meadows, and pay the price in sweat. True, lettuce was once a weed in the Indies, the tomato was an acid little Central American berry and the zinnia grows wild in Mexico. But we civilized them to our needs and our desires long ago, and now we are trapped. Tame a wildling, bird, beast or plant, and you become a caretaker. Tame a piece of land and you are a gardener or a farmer forever after.

I happen to be a countryman, one who spent his time in the cities and returned to the land because it seemed important to set my clock by the stars and measure my thoughts against the hills. But I am sure I am not alone in listening for the first April peeper and the first southbound goose in October. Hosts of others watch as eagerly as I do for the first crocus and the first green shoot in the chive bed. We all respond to the great rhythms of the universe and marvel at the miracle of the root, the seed, the bud and the blossom, the succession of growth and harvest.

Veneer man as you may with urbanity, he still yearns for his eternal

(v)

heritage, the earth and growing things. City planners make room for trees and grass, a park. The tenement dweller cherishes a window-sill geranium and the penthouse resident coddles a tree in a tub. Move a family to the suburbs and they revel in green grass, gay tulips and home-grown scallions. Loose a man in the country and he wants a meadow, a woodland, an orchard and half an acre of sweet corn.

The green world is a comfort not only to tired eyes but to jangled nerves. Man's haste and tensions have not altered by one iota the pulse of a maple's sap or the deliberate growth of a carrot, and his loud disagreements have yet to change the relationship of a bee and a blossom. Man gets so busy with his own affairs that he sometimes forgets these things. The noise of his machines tends to drown out the quiet, fundamental voices. But if all the machines rusted away, the green world would still be there, quietly going about important business and waiting for man to look and listen and learn.

Each week when I pick up the Sunday edition of *The New York Times* I can hear whispers of those quiet voices down inside the vast bulk of news and opinion about man's follies and his triumphs. Somewhere among those pages is a section devoted to the cultural arts, and back beyond the news of the theater, the movies, television, the concert halls and the museums, is news of the oldest cultural art of all— gardening. I turn to the Garden Pages, and the world begins to fall into perspective. Even if I happen to be in Manhattan, I can see the green hills beyond.

Now those Garden Pages from *The Times* have been summarized in a book. Garden Editor Joan Faust has sorted the seedlings, arranged the flowers, gathered the harvest. In a sense, this book is a garden itself, complete with hoe and trowel, hotbed and duster. There is even crabgrass in the lawn. I thought I saw a cutworm there among the beans, but maybe not. *You* look for it. I have a date this morning with the brown thrashers nesting in that lilac bush right over there.

Introduction

ENDING THE GREEN THINGS that grow keeps the gardener in touch with the unlabored way that nature governs. An awareness of the ease with which the seasons unfold and plants mature to harvest is perhaps one of the deepest rewards to be gained by those who plant and sow.

Spring's arrival never is doubted. One day winter's snow melts and all the ground becomes new. It opens to free treasures from bulbs, seeds and roots; greening buds spread and flowers in infinite variety begin to show themselves.

Nature's timing is unfoldment. Summer surely follows spring. It brings those "perfect days" with blue skies, fragrances, buzzing bees and sudden showers. The plantings of springtime flower; strawberries and raspberries ripen. Pride and satisfaction are high in the happy gardener's heart.

Too soon fall blows in with nips of frost and spicy, refreshing days. The hills reply with bizarre foliage displays, and baskets overflow from the abundance of harvest. The time for Thanksgiving comes. And then a gentle hush; the blanket of winter descends.

Those who work with trowel and hoe become familiar with the minute details of the seasons. Plants, flowers and fruit appear as if on whispered cue; the gardener learns to stand by, to appreciate, to observe. There develops within him a plant sense, a trust that the seeds he sows and the bulbs he plants will prosper and grow.

And this is where this book steps in. It is hoped that the material presented here will broaden the gardener's view and lift him above a sense of day-to-day puttering to a realization of accomplishment. The articles gathered here have been selected to emphasize the "what" of gardening even more than the "how." The book goes beyond the general reference manuals on workaday chores to present a rich collection of ideas, both new and tried-and-tested. These ideas encourage the gardener to discover the vast quantity of fine ornamentals available to him and to learn ways they can be used.

The book includes suggestions for adaptable landscape designs to refurbish old lots or give color and warmth to the still bare grounds of a new home. The special problems of planting by the seaside or in the city are brought into focus. Schemes for youngsters, outdoors and in, invite them to share the pleasures of gardening as a hobby too.

There are ideas for flowering plants for cutting and for drying, as well as hints about friuts, herbs and vegetables that will appeal to the gourmet gardener. And for the apartment gardeners, there are multiple schemes for growing plants indoors.

Generally, plant recommendations apply to the hardiness zones numbered 5, 6 and 7, as represented on the United States Department of Agriculture Plant Hardiness Zone Map on pages xxvi–xxvii. Gardeners living north of these zones should consult local recommendations for the suitability of particular plants.

All of the articles have appeared on the garden pages of *The New York Times*. The writings are the efforts of a fine roster of professional and nonprofessional horticulturists, many of whom are authorities in their respective fields.

Among the authors represented are faculty members or extension specialists at many of the country's leading agricultural universities. Others are engaged in plant research, and some are landscape architects. A number of the articles have been written by business people and housewives who in their spare hours are good gardeners and writers.

It is with deep appreciation to these people for their prompt and loyal response to assignments and their willingness to have their articles reprinted that this book has been assembled.

Joan Lee Faust

Contents

Contents

PART II : TREES AND SHRUBS

PART IV : LAWNS

PART VI : FRUITS AND VEGETABLES

PART VII : PROPAGATION

PART VIII : HOUSE PLANTS

PART IX : AROUND THE GARDEN

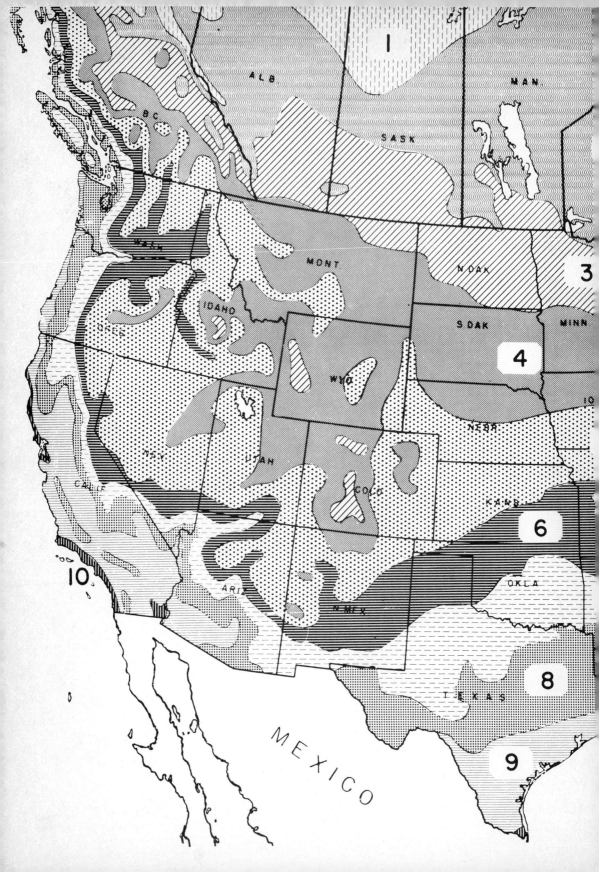

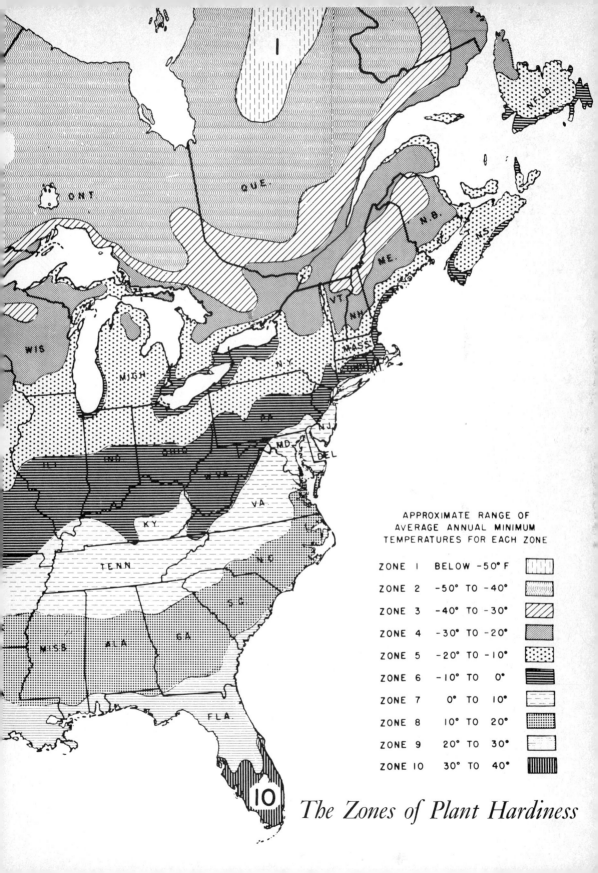

APPROXIMATE RANGE OF
AVERAGE ANNUAL MINIMUM
TEMPERATURES FOR EACH ZONE

ZONE 1   BELOW −50° F

ZONE 2   −50° TO −40°

ZONE 3   −40° TO −30°

ZONE 4   −30° TO −20°

ZONE 5   −20° TO −10°

ZONE 6   −10° TO   0°

ZONE 7   0° TO 10°

ZONE 8   10° TO 20°

ZONE 9   20° TO 30°

ZONE 10   30° TO 40°

The Zones of Plant Hardiness

PART I

LANDSCAPING

P LANTS AROUND THE HOME and garden are not meant to be mere decoration. If selected and arranged tastefully, they can create a harmonious setting in which each tree, shrub and groundcover fills a definite role. For example, a well-placed flowering tree can stop the low line of a rambling house and provide a sense of height, while a group of evergreens can soften angular corners. Hedges will screen or define areas and shade trees will provide cool cover. A lawn always is an inviting carpet.

The family that can start its landscape planning from the ground up, with a new lot and house yet to be built is fortunate indeed. Then the plantings can make the most of the site's features. Play needs, a kitchen garden, outdoor living space and service areas can be placed logically.

Sometimes a garden merely needs rejuvenation. It may have been growing along for so many years that the plants are ungainly and overcrowded. Or a family's habits may have changed and the landscaping needs revision to suit new needs. No matter what the problems may be, there is wide latitude for individuality within the framework of good principles of landscape design. The following pages outline some of these basic principles and suggest ways to brighten new or established properties.

ABOVE: An unusual fountain, set in a stone garden wall, serves as a focal point. Petunias, marguerites and geraniums add charm.

Roche

ABOVE: Ornaments add charm to a garden and give a property individuality. A bell, placed strategically, will ring a welcome invitation to meals.

Molly Adams

BELOW: If set properly, the sundial can record the garden's hours.

Gottscho-Schleisner

LEFT: There is a homey friendliness to an old-fashioned lamppost which lights the way to a garage.

Gottscho-Schleisner

Wise Landscaping for Family Use

CARLTON B. LEES

LANDSCAPING does not begin and end with foundation planting, which merely provides a pretty picture from the street. The real purpose of good landscape design is to achieve useful and decorative outdoor space around the home.

As families grow, every bit of house space becomes important. To relieve this crowding, indoor living areas can be extended outdoors for the warmer months, May to October.

To do this the home owner must think of the outdoors as a space which differs little from the indoors except in the materials defining it and the furnishings. A back yard is truly three-dimensional, having a lawn, paved areas, carpets of groundcover and low-growing plants for a floor. The walls are the sides of buildings, hedges, fences, tall shrubs and low-branched trees. A ceiling is provided by overhanging tree limbs or arbors draped with vines.

To make this outdoor space useful, it should be connected directly with an indoor space such as the living room, dining room or family room. In many cases a screened porch can serve as an intermediate area.

To develop an outdoor living space, the needs of the family should be taken into consideration. Families vary in size, and interests. A rose hobbyist may like to have a setting where roses can be seen. Those who are not particularly interested in gardening may like a private retreat arranged with plant materials requiring low maintenance.

The screened porch or paved terrace requires the greatest degree of privacy. These are the areas where the family relaxes, dines and entertains. By standing on the porch or terrace and looking toward

In a well-planned landscape, each plant has its purpose. In the plan shown here a dogwood is set some distance from the corner to blend the vertical house line with the horizontal ground line. A slow-growing grouping of holly and rhododendron will remain in scale for many years. Complementing the attractive entrance is a 40-year-old dwarf white pine. Water worn stones at the base accentuate its artistically contorted branches. Between the front walk and driveway, an espaliered yew provides height without bulk. The crabapple placed at the left of the drive anchors that corner of the house and gives privacy to the back yard. Beneath it is a heath groundcover. Plants corresponding to the numbers are:

1. White dogwood (*Cornus florida*)
2. Dwarf white pine (*Pinus strobus nana*)
3. Rhododendron Boule de Neige (dwarf white)
4. Small-leaved Japanese holly (*Ilex crenata microphylla*)
5. Boxleaf holly (*I. crenata convexa*)
6. Espaliered yew (*Taxus media*)
7. Dwarf holly (*I. crenata* Stokes)
8. Azalea Palestrina (white)
9. Mountain laurel (*Kalmia latifolia*)
10. Flowering crabapple Almey
11. Early-flowering heath (*Erica carnea*)
12. Firethorn (*Pyracantha lalandi*)
13. Pachysandra
14. Juniper (*Juniperus sargenti*)

Landscape by Henry M. Feil

(6)

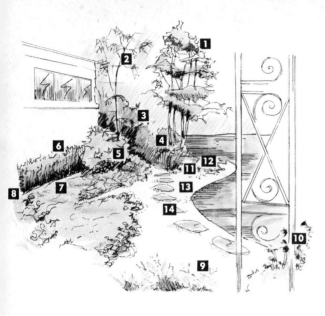

Plants can be arranged decoratively to accent the corner of a house. In the plan shown here a selection of plants was placed carefully to complement the architecture and to form a transition between the house and lawn. Plants corresponding to the numbers are:

1. Gray birch
2. Sourwood
3. Japanese black pine
4. Kurume azalea
5. Glossy privet
6. Hicks yew
7. English ivy
8. Japanese holly
9. Rock cotoneaster
10. Kurume azalea, Snow
11. Coast leucothoe
12. English ivy
13. Crushed spar
14. River stone

Landscape by Mitchell Tanner for Allan Dalsimer, Inc.; Gottscho-Schleisner

the "walls" of the landscape, the home owner can see where baffles or screens would be needed.

These screens need not be at the lot line. A simple hedge or row of shrubs along one edge of the paved area might provide privacy from neighbors on one side, while an informal group of flowering trees or shrubs quite a distance from the terrace and close to the lot line might serve the same role on the other side.

Fences do not have to be continuous enclosures. A simple section of fence, used as a folding screen, could provide the needed privacy.

Privacy—at least some degree of it—is needed in the front yard, too. This is especially true in split-level and ranch-type houses with picture windows. If the house is framed by the usual foundation planting, the family will barely be able to see the plants or enjoy them through the window. Actually, the front yard should be regarded as three-dimensional space. A dooryard garden can serve as an entryway to indoor space.

A few judiciously planted trees and shrubs will make a front yard more interesting for those who pass from the street to the front door. They will also provide something to look out on. In this way the front yard becomes part of the house rather than a part of the public street space.

When organizing the landscape, remember that it is made up of elements besides plants. Paths, fences, house walls, steps, retaining walls, planter boxes and outdoor furniture are all part of it. Even the plants vary widely. They cannot be considered without recognizing their design qualities and functions.

To evaluate the quantities of plant materials available, it is best to think of them in size groups: large shade and evergreen trees; small trees and large shrubs (eight to thirty feet); medium shrubs (six to eight feet); small shrubs (three to six feet); dwarf shrubs; vines and groundcovers. Then plants can be selected according to the job they are to do.

A six-to-eight-foot shrub is recommended for the hedge along the side of the terrace. Anything lower would not provide a screen. For a leafy awning to shade the picture window, a small flowering tree or tall treelike shrub is needed. For a low barrier to subdivide the backyard space and provide a background planting, a row of small shrubs (sheared or unsheared) might be suitable.

In all cases it important to analyze the situation, decide the function and then select the material. A row of shrubs, a solid board fence, a wire fence or a lattice covered with vines, each three feet high, will do essentially the same job in the landscape. Selection will depend on the best design for the property.

Last to be considered are the annuals, perennials and bulbs which provide the sparkle to make the outdoor space more interesting. Even the minimum-maintenance garden can contain daffodils, small bulbs, daylilies, hostas and other easy-to-grow plants. The hobbyist gardener and specialist will probably want a wide variety of flowering plants.

And remember that the landscape may be in view during the winter, so enough evergreens or structural elements should be provided to prevent a bleak winter look.

Open Areas Improve Garden Design

BARBARA M. CAPEN

OPEN grass areas give a sense of space and design to any property, small or large. But too often the openness is lost as trees and shrubs are scattered across the lawn without any relation to each other or to the design. Flower beds, too, seem to be placed with no particular relation to any other planting.

To avoid such spotty effects, even the smallest garden can be planned for space by locating open areas on the ground. Any trees and shrubs that are to be planted within the next few years can be grouped around these open areas. Flower beds can be placed so that they fit into a pattern of planting rather than intrude on the open lawn.

On the street side, the lawn areas should be planned as a setting for the house. If the house faces a busy street, some screen planting

may be needed to deaden the noise. This should be a thick border of shrubbery placed as near the front property line as possible.

This same general arrangement of planting—as much open area as possible between boundaries and the house planting—should be continued on all sides of the house. The open area behind the house is usually developed for the family's outdoor living. It should be as spacious as possible to accommodate lawn games which are increasing in popularity.

Planting along the property lines forms both a screen from the neighbors and a pleasant view for the family. The front edge of the border planting should be arranged so that it does not follow the property lines but traces a series of long shallow curves that will always be pleasing to the eye. One or more shade trees may be placed on the lawn as needed.

Such a simple arrangement is the basis for planting a large property, too, but a more interesting lawn area can be developed if it is partly divided into smaller sections not entirely separated from each other. From the property-line planting, deep curved shrub beds can swing into the lawn, forming smaller areas of varying shapes, each one interesting in itself but still part of the whole. And for variation, each of these may be treated as a separate garden picture.

One small area could be developed as an azalea garden, one as a lilac garden, another as an old-fashioned shrub rose garden. Or, for those whose garden interests are not specialized, an attractive treatment would be a spring garden of flowering shrubs, trees and naturalized bulbs, or an autumn garden where berried trees and shrubs predominate. In an area which is constantly on view, an all-season garden may be planned by selecting shrubs and trees to provide succession of bloom. Groups of floribunda roses may be added along the edges of the shrub beds for bright summer flowers.

The success of either planting scheme depends entirely on grouping the plants in the beds, but this seems to be one of the hardest things for a gardener to do. His natural inclination is to plant each shrub or tree as an individual specimen.

Both trees and shrubs in a plant bed should be arranged in groups of at least three of one kind. In a larger border there may be as many as five to seven in a group. For instance, three small flowering trees may be placed so that each tree is spaced ten to fifteen feet from the

(11)

An open lawn area between the house and birch tree gives dimension to the garden.

Molly Adams

Evergreens and deciduous shrubs form a wall of greenery around a side terrace, while two fruit trees provide shade.

other and preferably in a triangular-shaped group. These need not be all of the same variety; they could be two crabapples and a cherry, two cherries and a redbud, two dogwoods and a hawthorn or any appealing combination.

Evergreens such as white pines or hemlocks may be spaced twenty to twenty-five feet apart in the border, or grouped closer if rapid screening is desired. Large shrubs such as common lilacs, viburnums and forsythias may be spaced six to ten feet apart. The smaller shrubs at the front of the border may be planted closer together—two to four feet apart, depending on their potential spread.

After the planting is completed, the edge of the plant bed should be cut with a spade or lawn edger. All of the sod in the bed should be turned under and the surface soil raked smooth. Doing this serves two purposes. The shrub bed will form an interesting pattern against the lawn and the plants will assume more importance. Also, they will be easier to maintain.

Cutting grass around and between trees and shrubs is difficult and time-consuming. Eliminating this chore and substituting a thick mulch (peat moss, wood chips, buckwheat hulls, decayed compost, etc.) for the sod will benefit both the gardener and the plants. The mulch may be spread over the soil as soon as the planting is completed and the ground soaked thoroughly.

The Natural Landscape

JEAN HERSEY

A CAREFREE garden can be a place of beauty and fine harvestings, with weeding, watering, cultivating and all the other burdensome tasks at a minimum. Such a simplified approach to gardening is a matter of four elements: 1. basic design; 2. wise selection of plants; 3. techniques of growing and 4. a philosophy.

The property should be considered as is—its slope, exposure, soil, and so on. Observe the plants that voluntarily grow there. A deep woods area offers a favorable environment for wild columbine but not for marigolds. Bloodroot and Dutchman's breeches will not grow to perfection in an area exposed to full sun.

Obviously it will be easier to grow plants that are known to thrive under existing conditions than to import soil and to try something foreign to the location. A special kind of beauty and vigor seems to mark the plant or flower that is growing in the naturally right soil and location.

The carefree concept is all-inclusive. For example, does the property feature an old tree stump with its roots half out of the ground? Instead of pulling it out, why not clear around it? In itself an old tree stump is a thing of beauty.

Let the hand of man enhance what nature has already given.

A daisy meadow is a simple substitute for a lawn. It needs mowing but once a year, in August.

Gottscho-Schleisner

Primroses establish themselves in woodland areas quickly to bloom spring after spring.

Gottscho-Schleisner

Make the most of that natural outcropping of rock. Scatter an informal daffodil planting beneath that birch clump by the drive. Such effects will be more appealing, with less effort, than any formal treatment.

One specific way to simplify gardening is to reduce the size of the lawn. On a large property, some of the lawn area could be allowed to grow into a meadow, especially if the land extends some distance from the house. A meadow of black-eyed susans, hawkweed, butterfly weed, wild iris and violets is as appealing as a formal flower bed any day, and a lot less work than either a flower bed or a lawn. Such a "meadow garden" grows by itself. It needs mowing but once a year; the time I consider best for this is late August, after the flowers have reseeded.

Another good work-reduction measure is to consolidate as many beds as possible into one area. There is less edging this way. Vegetables and flowers thrive together, and a mingling of both can be quite attractive.

What are the best plants for keeping the garden simple, productive, beautiful—and yet carefree? Flowering shrubs head the list. Nothing could be lovelier than fragrant lilacs in lavender and white; rich golden kerria; mock orange, with deeply scented white sprays for graceful indoor bouquets; or rugosa roses with gay flowers in June and bright hips (seed pods) in fall.

Forsythia is a delight, especially when its branches can be cut for forcing indoors in January. And the star magnolia is an eye-filling herald of spring with glossy white ribbon petals. A little-known but easily grown flowering shrub is *Daphne burkwoodi* Somerset; its starry pink flowers all but hide the bush through May and June. It is evergreen and grows five feet high and four feet wide.

For further simplification, certain perennials can be naturalized in odd corners of the landscape. In a semi-shaded area in my garden bee balm thrives untended beside a wall. Dianthus flourishes in a sunny meadow. Daylilies fill the troublesome bank. Eupatorium, forget-me-not and iris grow without benefit of special beds or cultivation. Among other "must" perennials, extremely hardy and indestructible, are the fragrant peonies and the hardy hostas or plantain lilies, ideal for a shady corner.

Certain annuals reseed and reappear year after year. Here are some reliable volunteers: alyssum, cornflower, larkspur, petunia, portulaca and nicotiana. Sow these in among other annuals and there never will be need to replant a bed, but merely to add a few different sorts for variety each year.

Bulbs that naturalize should be part of any carefree garden. Scatter the bulbs and plant them where they fall. Among the spring-flowering bulbs which will do well with absolutely no after-planting care are daffodils in all their varied shapes, sizes and colors; crocus in bright golds, blues, purples and white; chionodoxa, blue with dainty white eyes; snowdrops, white and early; the familiar grape hyacinths; the graceful wood hyacinths; and the charming winter aconite, a splash of gold on a collar of green.

Ferns are lovely and easy too grow; most of them require no upkeep at all. Maidenhair fern, with its delicate way of trembling at every zephyr, is one of the finest. The fronds of the New York fern taper at both ends.

The cinnamon fern is extra woolly as its first young curlings emerge from the earth. The Christmas fern is evergreen with each pinna (frond segment) shaped like a Christmas stocking. For a dramatic effect—practically a hedge—grow the tall exciting royal ferns.

The foremost rule for growing plants the easy-upkeep way is to plant correctly at the start. Although this will involve some effort, the result will be worth it. Dig flower or vegetable plots eighteen inches deep and incorporate a wheelbarrow-load of well-rotted manure for each 5x5-foot planting area.

There is a way to have an abundance of vegetables with no weeding, watering, or cultivating. In a fifteen-by-fifteen-foot garden, in one year, I grew 97 heads of lettuce and 207 pounds of other vegetables (tomatoes, broccoli, spinach, onions, carrots, beets and chard). It was all done with a deep hay mulch, close planting and rich soil.

I started with a three-inch mulch when the plants were small, and increased it to six inches as the plants grew higher. The close planting—I call it overlapping—meant that spinach and carrots were sown with a mere six inches between the rows. However, if the spinach seed is sown early and in loamy soil, the plants will be ready to eat by the end of May; this frees the area for the carrots to spread. Similarly, small lettuce seedlings can be set out practically under newly established tomatoes; the lettuce will be harvested long before the tomatoes need room for expansion.

A philosophy which helps keep gardening simple is that gardens are for pleasure, for joy, for beauty. There is a wonderful quality about a garden that is completely peaceful and unhurried. When the gardener finds himself rushing from chore to chore, he should call a halt at once and re-examine things. How can the garden be simplified? What can be naturalized? Which high-upkeep plantings can be eliminated?

It is far better to grow six rosebushes well, with proper but not onerous attention, than to have twenty-six bushes whose care involves a struggle. Three peonies can be a great satisfaction, or half a dozen chrysanthemums. Even one peony and one chrysanthemum, each in a strategic place near the house, can be pure joy in its season of bloom—and no burden in between.

Soil, the Planter's Keystone

JAMES L. CALDWELL

PEOPLE who are interested in growing plants are chiefly concerned with the end product. Many gardeners are of the opinion that fertilizing, watering, controlling diseases and insects and other cultural practices are the answer to obtaining good flowers and vegetables. These factors are important, but unless the plants are growing in good soil, most cultural practices will be in vain.

In order to understand why soil is so important, it is necessary to know just what is meant by the term. Soil often has been defined as "a mixture of weathered particles of rock and decaying organic matter containing moisture and air that covers the earth in a thin layer." Generally, about half of a given volume of soil is made up of solids and the other half consists of open spaces which contain air and water.

The texture of a soil refers specifically to the size of the soil particles. These include sand, the largest; silt, the next largest; and clay, the smallest. Soils heavy with clay absorb large quantities of water and, when dry, tend to crack. These soils are difficult to water since they may hold more moisture than is desirable and, once dry, they are difficult to moisten.

Soils have spaces between the particles of sand, silt or clay; these may be referred to as pore spaces. They may be filled with water or air, depending upon their size. In soils where the particles have grouped together into granules or aggregates, the pore spaces will be small within the granules. Since they are small, they are capable of holding water against the force of gravity. The name given to these spaces is capillary pores.

When water is applied to a soil, some of it will be retained in these small pore spaces and will be available for plants to use. Soils which are high in clay particles will have more capillary pore spaces due to the small size of the particles. Clay soils retain more water than soils with a large quantity of sand particles.

In addition to the small pore spaces that exist between the soil particles of a granule or aggregate, there will be pore spaces between the granules. These spaces are larger and are called non-capillary pore spaces. Water applied to a soil will usually drain through these pore spaces due to the force of gravity, unless the drainage under the soil is poor. Therefore, these pore spaces are generally occupied by air and provide a way for air to move into and out of a soil as well as circulate within the soil.

Although soil moisture is necessary for plant growth, equally important is soil air. This air is present in the non-capillary pores and in those capillary pores from which the water has been absorbed by the plants or evaporated. The oxygen in the soil air is necessary for respiration by roots and soil microorganisms. The oxygen enters the plant as a dissolved gas in the soil solution or directly as a gas through the cell membranes. When a soil is overwatered the plant roots die from lack of oxygen rather than from too much water.

With a better understanding of how soil is made up, the gardener will find it much easier to alter the soil so that it will produce the best plant growth. The under-soil drainage, for example, must be good or the gravitational water will not drain away. The roots of plants growing in improperly drained soil will develop poorly or not at all.

Organic matter is incorporated into soil to bring about better soil aeration and drainage. The physical effect of adding organic matter is to dilute the soil. In the case of a heavy clay soil, organic matter spreads the particles apart, thereby allowing more air circulation. With sandy soils, the organic material will increase the water-holding capacity of the soil.

Since many of the organic materials contain sugar, starch, cellulose and other easily decomposable organic substances, granulation will occur in the soil. What actually happens is that the soil microorganisms digest these materials and, in so doing, secrete gluelike substances which bind the soil particles together. This does not occur when the organic matter is well decomposed as in the case of sphagnum peat moss, since it consists almost entirely of lignin, which resists decomposition. Fresh corn cobs are an example of a material which improves the granulation of soil by virtue of the microorganisms which break down the cobs.

The effect of granulation on a sandy soil is to bring the particles together and form aggregates. This increases the capillary pore spaces within the granule, thereby increasing the water-holding capacity. With clay soils, the particles are brought together and the non-capillary pore spaces are increased, with more air circulation possible.

Soil scientists use the term pH as a means of measuring soil acidity by hydrogen ion concentration. The pH scale reads from 1 to 14. A pH value of 7.0 is considered neutral; any reading below this is acid; above is alkaline.

The main consideration given to pH of a soil is based on the fact that more fertilizer elements are available to plants at a pH of 6.0 to 6.5 (the range usually given for optimum plant growth). Certain plants grow better at lower pH values than this, while other plants may grow at pH levels above this range.

The chemical effect that organic matter has on a soil depends on the material added. Sphagnum peat moss will generally reduce the pH of the soil, which means an increase in acidity. Materials such as straw and manure will raise the pH of the soil, which results in an increase in alkalinity, particularly in the later stages of decomposition of the materials.

Some organic materials have the effect of reducing the amount of fertilizer, particularly of nitrogen, in the soil. Straw and corn cobs will cause a drop in nitrogen. The soil microorganisms decompose these materials quite readily and, in the process, use nitrogen from the soil for the production of amino acids and proteins. As most organic materials break down, there will be any number of fertilizer elements added to the soil.

The biological effects of adding organic matter to the soil have partly been described. These materials generally stimulate the growth and development of microorganisms and greatly increase their numbers. The secretions from these microorganisms cement the soil particles together, which brings about granulation and good soil structure. Most soils, regardless of how poor they are, generally contain a wide variety of invisible plant and animal life, so there is no need to add microorganisms.

Peat moss is rapidly taking the place of manure as a soil additive. Sphagnum peat is considered the best, since it is uniform, slow to decompose and acid in reaction. The coarse grades are generally preferred over the fine. Peat obtained from sedges, reeds and cattails decomposes too rapidly and does not last long enough in the soil to justify its use.

Leafmold is often used since it is readily available. One main objection is that it rots rapidly; this means a large volume of leaves will be needed, and generally little storage space is available around the property. Peanut hulls, where available, make a very good soil additive. They break down slowly and are fibrous. Sawdust or shavings can be incorporated into soil, but precautions must be taken to prevent soil nitrogen starvation due to the action of microorganisms. Several applications of a complete fertilizer will be needed to prevent this difficulty. The material breaks down quite rapidly, so the effect on the soil is short-lived.

Sand is also used in some instances as a soil additive to improve structure. If fine sand is added to certain kinds of clay soils, a pretty fair grade of concrete may result. Coarse sand should be used.

Place a Tree to Shade the House

P. J. McKENNA

ARCHITECTS have for some time been aware of the importance of placing a house so that it gets all the sunshine possible through the greater part of the year. But the landscape profession has lagged a bit in providing and placing trees for shading these homes through

East-west path of sun guides planting for maximum shade.

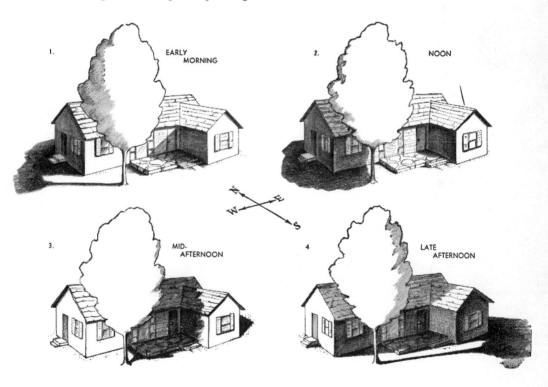

A. BROHMER McKENNA

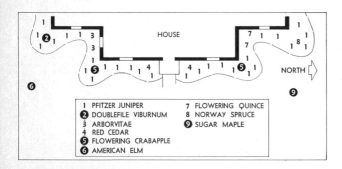

HOUSE

NORTH

1 PFITZER JUNIPER
2 DOUBLEFILE VIBURNUM
3 ARBORVITAE
4 RED CEDAR
5 FLOWERING CRABAPPLE
6 AMERICAN ELM
7 FLOWERING QUINCE
8 NORWAY SPRUCE
9 SUGAR MAPLE

The original landscape design for the home was planned to accentuate the architectural features. In ten years it grew out of scale (below) and concealed the house.

A new planting was designed for the home. This time slow-growing plants were selected to form the basic framework. Circled numbers on the planting plan indicate the original plants that were saved during landscape revision.

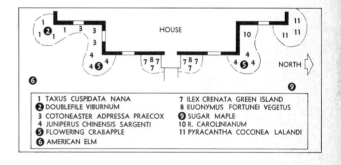

1 TAXUS CUSPIDATA NANA	7 ILEX CRENATA GREEN ISLAND
② DOUBLEFILE VIBURNUM	8 EUONYMUS FORTUNEI VEGETUS
3 COTONEASTER ADPRESSA PRAECOX	⑨ SUGAR MAPLE
4 JUNIPERUS CHINENSIS SARGENTI	10 R. CAROLINIANUM
⑤ FLOWERING CRABAPPLE	11 PYRACANTHA COCCINEA LALANDI
⑥ AMERICAN ELM	

the hot summer months. Moreover, prior to construction of homes and community developments the builder almost invariably roots out all trees irrespective of their value, beauty or placement.

The sapling trees that a builder may set out only point up the barrenness of the place. They will require years to yield any shade. In all such matters, shading the home and grounds is the personal problem of the owner. But he should be warned against the old idea

(23)

Drawing and plans by Milton Baron and Carl S. Gerlach;
photo by Michigan State University

that trees are to be used to frame the house; this notion is obsolete, belonging to the large-home and mansion era when it mattered little what was used. Today's tree must have functional value.

For economy's sake, selection and placement of trees must be done with an eye to maximum effect from a minimum number. But since the house was designed for maximum sunlight, the tree should be selected and placed so that it will not interfere with the light in winter. This rules out evergreens and gives preference to those trees that gradually clothe their branches with leaves in spring as the sun gets warm, and thin them out toward fall until all are gone and the sun comes through the leafless branches.

The most suitable trees for today's homes are found in the medium size class with a maximum height of thirty to forty feet at maturity and a total spread of about the same dimensions. Approximately half of this spread is on either side of the trunk of a properly developed tree. Depending on point of placement, and separated from the house by a distance equal to half the spread, the tree will cast shade on part of the roof and sides either in the morning or afternoon. Through the midday period little shade is cast save directly near the tree itself.

The aspect of the house, whether facing north, south, east, west or points in between, must be determined, as well as the time of day that shade is desirable. The tree is placed according to the east-west path of the sun.

To obtain maximum shade from one tree over a house having its living rooms and terrace facing south, the tree is set at a point east of the terrace, and at an eight- to ten-foot distance from the house. The branches eventually would extend over part of the roof, shading this and the greater part of the house from late forenoon through the noonday period. By 3 P.M. the shade would shift until it would cover the greater portion of the house roof, the south side and all of the terrace and part of the wing. By 6 P.M. the shade will have cleared the terrace, covering the end of the wing. By this time the house itself will cast shade over most of the terrace.

Complete shade coverage of the house would require another tree to the west. But since the shade lengthens as the sun drops west, the tree must be set at a greater distance from the house. A smaller tree at a twenty-foot distance would do. This could be a flowering tree and so serve the double duty of providing color in spring and shade in summer. Generally it works out that trees set to the southwest of the house are given twenty feet. This takes advantage of the lengthening shadows as the sun moves farther west, and checks the slanting beams from shining on the terrace or windows, as they would do if the tree were placed too close to the house.

When buying a shade tree, select one that has its leader intact. If the leader is damaged or has been removed, the tree may produce a flat head; the form will be spoiled unless a new leader can be encouraged. The size to buy depends on the pocketbook, but since shade trees are the most important plants in the landscape scheme, they should be purchased in as large a size as finances will permit. For a tree to give results in a comparatively few years, it should be fifteen to twenty feet high.

Plants for Sunless Sites

ALICE R. IREYS

A SHADY corner or a narrow strip along the north side of the house need not be a problem site. If adequate soil fertility and good drainage are provided, there are many plants that will grow reasonably well.

The landscaping scheme should include plants that will give an effective picture for one season; they might be groundcovers for winter, flowering perennials for spring and summer, bulbs for summer and fall. Ferns are lovely for their lacy appearance, while annuals provide a quick summer show. These plants can be chosen for foliage, texture and color.

Lily of the valley, a low perennial growing from a creeping rootstock, has fragrant white flowers in June. The upright, single lilylike leaf makes an attractive (although rather invasive) groundcover which also can be used under trees.

Evergreen candytuft (*Iberis sempervirens*) has a dense, dark

Daylilies may be grown where filtered sunlight breaks through the trees for part of the day.

Paul F. Frese

green foliage that remains green thoughout the year. When small white flowers completely cover the mat in April and May, a more cheerful sight is hard to find. Candytuft can be used for edging or mass planting.

Violas, low tufted perennials with bright green heart foliage, have flowers of white, blue or violet. The sweet white violet (*Viola blanda*) is one of the earliest to flower. The birdsfoot violet (*V. pedata*) makes a fine groundcover for early bulbs because its fernlike foliage will remain decorative all summer. The violets often bloom again during late August and September.

Bleeding heart, whether it be the large leaf (*Dicentra spectabilis*) or the small (*D. eximia*), is a bright-colored perennial for shade. A charming arrangement is to combine it with *Anchusa myosotidiflora*

(26)

which has gay blue flowers and coarse, dark green foliage. For summer bloom to grace a vacation home, the many varieties of daylilies will stand partial shade and grow profusely. With careful selection, daylilies will provide continuous bloom for three months.

Flowering at the same time as the daylilies are the hostas, funkias or plantain lilies with their round, flat-topped clumps and bright, shiny green foliage. They are excellent for their shade-enduring character as well as their charm in flower arrangements. *Hosta plantaginea* or white daylily has white tubular flowers which appear on vertical stalks in August and September. *H. sieboldiana* has large, gray-green leaves and white flowers.

If a fall picture is desired, then the shady spot should be planted with some of the monkshood (*Aconitum fischeri*). It grows five feet tall and has blue flowers in October. *A. wilsoni* has deeper violet flowers, although both types combine well with the windflowers. Japanese anemone (*Anemone japonica*) blooms from early September until frost. Both the pink Queen Charlotte and the white Whirlwind with daisylike blooms are excellent flowers for cutting.

In one garden a fifteen-foot space between the house and the property line is transformed into a fairyland each summer with tuberous begonias. From early July until frost this spot is brightened by the huge colorful flowers. The large, double camellialike begonias blossom in crimson, orange, pink, white and yellow shades. Their cousins, the smaller-flowered plants, are especially useful in flower arrangements. The variety Mrs. Helen Harns has soft yellow flowers which bloom profusely throughout the summer.

Few people have tried the hardy cyclamen. The evergreen leaves and fluttering pink and white blossoms give a delightfully airy aspect to a shady corner. The soil should be rich and loose with well-rotted manure and limestone chips. *Cyclamen europaeum* is easy to grow and the small crimson blooms appear from late July through August. Another type, *C. neapolitanum*, comes up in mid-September and the charming soft pink flowers are lovely. The leaves start to show just as the flowers are fading and this carpet of green foliage is interesting throughout the winter.

Another little-known shade-loving plant is *Galax aphylla*. The heart-shaped leaves are fine for flower arrangements. Given complete shade and an acid soil, the plants should last for many years. Narrow walks by the house might be brightened with ferns. The hay scented, ostrich, royal and sensitive ferns thrive in moderate shade. For dense shade I recommend the Christmas, cinnamon, bracken or interrupted ferns.

For a bright annual to add color to the north side of the summer cottage, try impatiens; it comes in four different colors. Fuchsia is also effective, as is cleome, the spider flower.

The old lament, "nothing will grow in the shade," is not true because many plants enjoy cool shadows in summer and shelter from the winter winds. With ordinary care these plants will give the home owner many years of flowering pleasure.

Flowers and Shrubs
Brighten Garden Picnics

NANCY R. SMITH

In city and suburb, summer means outdoor living. For many families a daily feature is outdoor dining. Whether the dining setup is a formal terrace or portable grill, attractive plantings add to the fun.

In a paved area, for example, some interstices can be left for plants such as thyme or creeping spicy pinks, which are one of my sunny-spot favorites. The sedums are unusual and varied both in form and in blossom color.

An odd flagstone or a couple of bricks or blocks can be left out of the paving, preferably near the edge of the terrace, so that walking doesn't become a dodge-the-plant affair. These spaces are ideal for verbenas, petunias or sweet alyssum, a trio of trusty annuals for all-summer flowering.

Some degree of privacy is welcome in the outdoor dining room. The planting should be chosen not only to look well and provide a background, but also to contribute color and permit air circulation. Plantings need not be dense. The evergreen shrubs always provide pleasing effects. Yew is a good choice.

Deciduous shrubs such as *Viburnum carlesi* or weigela are good in mixed background plantings. Shade-tolerant nicotiana can provide foreground groups of glistening white trumpets all season. The nicotiana (flowering tobacco) has the added asset of delightful fragrance.

For ease of access, the permanent plantings should be confined to the background and sides. The accent features might include planter boxes set along the paved edge and filled with the gardener's choice of plants. Geraniums, lantanas and the richly scented heliotrope are wonderful in such locations, if they receive a reasonable amount of sunlight.

Annuals are prized for these boxes; a blend of upright and spreading types will enhance any outdoor dining area. Colors can be selected

Daffodils, tulips and azaleas complete the terrace setting.
Gottscho-Schleisner

to complement furniture, too. In the shade, tuberous-rooted begonias provide an exotic and colorful sight. They are available in a wide range of rich and pastel colors.

These and other plants mentioned are suitable also for growing in pots; they can be left in place or brought in for special occasions. Both boxes and pots will need watering daily in dry spells.

Another planter certain to be a conversation piece is a strawberry jar. It can be planted with anything from strawberries (the little Alpine ones are delicious, prolific and productive all season) to herbs or small annuals.

Another alternative is a groundcover, such as *Vinca minor* or pachysandra, to edge the area. These also lend themselves to planting at the base of a tree when the terrace is built around one.

Ferns are decorative when circling the base of a picturesque old tree. For more color in shadier places, annual *Vinca rosea* or impatiens will give a neat display of blossoms in soft rose or white all summer long.

Shade from the midday and afternoon sun is important. If the property lacks mature shade trees, the terrace may be arranged to take advantage of the shady side of the house.

Ants and picnics may go together in the woods, but insects can be controlled in the back yard. Sprays and candles or torch-type lamps instead of electrical lighting will relieve the problem of mosquitoes and flies. (Incandescent bulbs attract insects.) Many communities have insecticide fogging machines to help reduce infestations.

Greenery to Cover the Ground

CLARENCE E. LEWIS

THE proper use of groundcovers often determines whether a landscape will present a balanced and harmonious effect. When carefully selected, groundcovers face down other plantings so that there is not such an abrupt change between shrubs and lawn.

Groundcovers help to prevent soil erosion on steep or gradually sloping banks; they also act as part of the foundation planting where low windows or steps are involved. In addition, these plants fill in small areas not wide enough to accommodate shrubs and they add a touch of green to shady spots where grass cannot grow. The gardener may use groundcovers to define a path or to soften the hard outer lines of a brick or flagstone terrace. A sense of balance can be created by using the same or similar groundcovers in related plantings.

An evergreen groundcover that responds to bank planting is Baltic ivy, a hardy form of English ivy which clings rather closely to the ground. Other varieties of English ivy also do a good job and shade is no problem.

The hardy purple-leaved euonymus (*Euonymus fortunei coloratus*) adapts itself to banks or level areas, but the gardener must not forget to guard the plant against scale. Japanese spurge or pachysandra does not possess the trailing habit of ivy although it will prosper on banks and in deep shade. Another reliable groundcover is the durable and pleasing periwinkle or myrtle (*Vinca minor*).

Although not often thought of as groundcovers, the drooping leucothoe (*Leucothoe catesbaei*) and the coast leucothoe (*L. axillaris*) do an excellent job for low-massed planting. The coast leucothoe, the smaller of the two, may be a little more adaptable. Both are desirable plants in deep shade or sun.

One of the best vines for holding a bank is the semi-evergreen Hall's Japanese honeysuckle. While most useful in holding the soil in check, it is extremely difficult to maintain when planted in combination with other plants. The honeysuckle has a tendency to grow rampantly.

Five-leaved akebia does as well as honeysuckle when used as a groundcover on a bank and it is easier to maintain. Another evergreen that thrives in shade is dwarf Hooker sarcococca, a small, rather expensive shrub.

Found near and on ocean beaches is bearberry, a native evergreen trailing groundcover. It is difficult to propagate and not readily available on the market. Yet the plant will stand strong sunlight and sandy seashore soils. Its red berries add a bright touch to the fall landscape.

The cotoneasters are suited for sunny banks and some are nearly evergreen. Varieties include rock, creeping, bearberry and Pyrenees

Juniper and pachysandra combine to form an interesting leaf pattern.

Landscape by William A. Rutherford; Gottscho-Schleisner

Bishop's weed or goutweed has handsome, variegated foliage.

Landscape by Arthur W. Erfeldt; Jeannette Grossman

Ivy is hardy as far north as New England and is easily trimmed to tailored squares.

Landscape by Lambert Landscape Co.; Gottscho-Schleisner

cotoneaster. Periwinkle grows well with this group in holding a bank or on level ground since the plants are not heavy feeders.

Narrow-leaved evergreens that adapt to full sun, slope or level area, are creeping juniper (*Juniperus horizontalis*) and its varieties as well as Sargent's juniper (*J. sargenti*), Japgarden juniper (*J. procumbens*) and shore juniper (*J. conferta*). These plants need room to spread and should be placed at least three feet apart.

Where adequate sun is available, the semi-evergreen memorial rose (*Rosa wichuriana*) and Max Graf rose are two good choices. They are most striking when used alone rather than in combinations.

For deep shade try yellowroot (*Xanthorhiza simplicissima*). It will grow in some sun, but it is deciduous and not a very attractive plant for winter. Yellowroot grows about eighteen inches high in the shade (taller in sunny spots). A willing sickle keeps this groundcover trimmed to about one foot high.

Many native plants are fine covers in their own setting but are not easily transplanted. They include partridgeberry, a low evergreen with red fruit; bunchberry, a small dogwood with white blossoms and bright red fruit; and wintergreen with its red berries that have such a pleasant odor when crushed.

Occasionally shrubs are suggested for a cover material. One of the best deciduous types for bank planting is the Arnold Dwarf forsythia. It roots readily as it spreads and usually does not grow over two feet high.

Several herbaceous plants are rightly finding their way into the cover category. Those that do remarkably well in rather deep shade are the various epimediums with their soft green appearance. Others are moneywort or creeping jennie (*Lysimachia nummularia*), violets and the bugles (*Ajuga*). The Geneva bugle is no longer a stranger to home owners. The purple-green plant clings quite closely to the ground. The bugle's upright stalks of blue flowers lend charm to the garden.

Other herbaceous plants that can serve as groundcovers are thyme (*Thymus serpyllum*), the wineleaf cinquefoil (*Potentilla tridentata*) and rock cress (*Arabis albida*). Moss pink (*Phlox subulata*) might also be remembered here. These varieties should be placed in full sun or only partial shade. Plants like thyme, wineleaf, rock cress and moss pink are not for extensive plantings since their flowers will be in too sharp contrast with the surroundings.

Planting a Bank

DONALD B. LACEY

SPRING is the best time for planting groundcovers on steep slopes. However, heavy spring rains often wash away groundcover plants before they can become established. Home gardeners can avoid this by adapting the thatching method used by highway engineers.

A thatch of salt hay placed on the bank before planting will shed water just as the thatched cottage roofs do. At the same time a shallow trench dug at the top of the bank will divert water to the sides, where it can be fed into a pipe to the lower level.

Salt hay makes the best thatching material, but straw can be used if there is no objection to some grain coming up on the bank. Several inches of the material should be placed over the bank. A network of strings tied to small stakes will prevent the thatch from blowing off before it has done its job.

When setting the cover plants into the ground, just pull the salt hay to one side. Give each plant a pocket of good soil and leave a little of the hole unfilled to catch water during the summer.

The thatching can be left in place once the bank is planted to serve as a mulch throughout the year. In summer it will keep weeds from germinating and conserve moisture. (The weed-control feature of this mulch alone makes it worth the work of putting it down.) In winter it will prevent plants from being heaved out of the soil by freezing and thawing.

For sunny banks, ivy makes the best groundcover. The Baltic form of English ivy stays greener in winter. Myrtle and pachysandra grow best on shaded banks or those facing north. Space ivy about eighteen inches apart and myrtle and pachysandra about twelve inches apart. Closer planting requires more plants but it provides quicker results. Spring bulbs or fall-blooming colchicums can be added for seasonal color.

In two to three years the bank should be a solid mass of cover. With erosion controlled, the bank becomes an attractive feature of the garden, well worth the extra effort needed to get the planting established.

Vines That Climb

FRANCES HOWARD

THERE are dozens of vines that can be planted to decorate or shade areas of the garden. To plant the right one, the habit of climbing should be considered. Twining vines adjust most easily to wood strips of any thickness. Lath for tendril climbers should be narrow enough for tendrils to reach around it while climbing roses must be tied loosely to their supports.

Color and texture values in adjoining areas should be considered, too. For instance, a small-leaved vine should not be used where most of the near-by plants are large-leaved, and vice versa. Flower colors should blend with those of other plants.

Often it is practical to plant free-flowering annuals, such as morning glory, cardinal climber and nasturtium, together with woody vines to brighten the scene and provide variety. Again, texture and color harmonies should be preserved.

Of the annuals, moonflower and hop give the heaviest and best shade. Scarlet runner bean and balsam pear (*Momordica charantia*), as well as morning glory, cardinal climber and nasturtium, provide striking accents. Annual vines should be planted outdoors after all danger of frost is past. Or they can be started earlier indoors in plant bands for transplanting later. (Most annual vines transplant poorly and should be started in individual humus pots rather than in flats.)

In the woody vine group, there are many selections. Bower

(35)

Wistaria lends its charm to a baffle fence.

Paul E. Genereux

actinidia (*Actinidia arguta*) twines to about twenty-five feet. Its glossy dark green leaves, to five inches long, are carried on red stalks. Small white saucer-shaped flowers are followed by edible fruits. The plant requires a sturdy support and needs protection from strong winds. Overfertilizing causes rank, unkempt growth.

Five-leaf akebia (*Akebia quinata*) twines to twenty feet. The dark green leaves are composed of five leaflets, to two inches long, arranged finger-fashion on purple-tinted petioles. Though delicate in appearance, the plant is strong growing and requires considerable pruning. It prefers sun and a light, well-drained soil, but akebia will grow in a partially shaded site; it tolerates wind.

Porcelain ampelopsis (*Ampelopsis brevipedunculata*) is a tendril climber that grows to twenty feet. It has bright green leaves, to five inches long, grows in either sun or shade and tolerates considerable wind. Monkshood vine (*A. aconitifolia*) has smaller leaves and a more delicate appearance. Heartleaf ampelopsis (*A. cordata*) is perhaps the most durable of the three and has a generally coarser appearance.

Sweet autumn clematis (*Clematis paniculata*) grows to thirty feet in a dense, glossy, dark green foliage mat. The white flowers bloom profusely in panicles from August to October and are followed by attractive, long-lasting plumy seed heads.

C. virginiana is somewhat the same type of plant, but not quite

(36)

so tall or decorative. However, it withstands extremes of climate. Clematis must be planted in an alkaline soil and prefers partial shade in hot areas. It climbs by twisting petioles and needs considerable guidance to prevent tangling growth.

Silver lace vine or fleece flower (*Polygonum auberti*) twines to thirty feet, forming a dense mat of shiny, bright green leaves up to two and one-half inches long. Green-white or pink-tinged flowers, in panicles eight inches long, bloom profusely in summer. Silver lace vine is an extremely vigorous plant and requires little care. Even when the top is killed in the most severe winter temperatures, the roots almost always survive.

Grapevines are exceedingly attractive shade plants with large dramatic foliage and, in some species, edible fruit. They are strong-growing tendril climbers and require very little care. Species should be selected according to climate.

Among the woody vines that are adaptable for accent or specimen use, there is the large-flowered clematis. They are free-blooming, decorative plants that grow about six to eight feet high. *Clematis jackmani*, with velvety violet-purple flowers as wide as six inches, includes blue, rose and red varieties. *C. lawsoniana henryi* has enormous white flowers up to nine inches; the *lanuginosa* varieties produce many interestingly marked flowers. The scarlet clematis (*C. texensis*) has urn-shaped flowers followed by handsome, plumy seed heads. All are outstanding summer-blooming plants. Pink anemone clematis (*C. montana rubens*) is spring flowering, with clusters of lovely rose to pink flowers, two and one-half inches across.

Climbing roses can be obtained in several different types. There are the ramblers, with clusters of flowers up to two inches across, of which the pink-flowering Dorothy Perkins is an example. There are large-flowered climbers like the white Silver Moon and everblooming kinds like Blaze. The yellow-flowered High Noon is an excellent example of a climbing hybrid tea rose.

Chinese wistaria (*Wistaria sinensis*), which grows to about thirty feet, has large, lacy, light green leaves and huge, dense clusters of violet-blue flowers in spring. It requires a rich soil and protection from wind. For best results, pruning to within five buds from the base should be done annually. There is also a white variety.

There are several general rules to observe in growing any vine.

Clematis adds handsome decor to a house wall.

F. S. Lincoln

First, soil must be prepared deeply and well before planting, since the vigorous, deep roots send out long, strong growth which must be nourished. Plants prefer a good loam mixed with manure. Apply a well-balanced commercial fertilizer once in spring and summer, and a mulch of manure in fall.

Water is essential during the growing and blooming period. Occasional overhead watering freshens the foliage of the plants and discourages insect infestation.

Because of their rampant habit, vines should not be planted too closely. Along a pergola, woody vines should be spaced eight feet or more apart at staggered intervals on either side of the support, but not opposite each other.

Early training is necessary to prevent stems from intertwining and to guide the plant in the desired direction. Pruning is important to keep plants tidy and under control. Do not be afraid to cut back hard. The plant will respond with a renewed production of stems and flowering in the subsequent growing season.

An all-purpose insecticide-fungicide spray should be applied to vines twice a year in spring and late fall. Usually this is all the spraying required unless a specific trouble develops.

Winter protection varies with the climate. In cold areas vines should be well watered before the ground freezes. Where winter temperatures fall below zero, soil or a mixture of soil and straw should be mounded around the base of tender plants. Or the roots can be loosened on one side and the plant laid in a trench and covered with soil.

A well-pruned grapevine shades a sunny terrace.

Landscape by Lawrence Halprin; Gottscho-Schleisner

A geometric fence design divides the driveway and lawn.

Jeannette Grossman

Fences Have Many Functions

ALICE UPHAM SMITH

A FENCE can be more than a property enclosure. With proper placement it can make a terrace private, shield a service area or give new prominence to beautiful plantings. Because a fence rarely changes in appearance from season to season, it is a useful garden ornament.

To be effective, a fence does not have to envelop an area. Many times a short length of fence will do wonders to solve a special garden or landscape problem.

Ready-made fences are available in many styles in convenient sections and heights. An eight-to-ten-foot length is adequate to hide a service area, including wood pile, trash cans and compost heap. Two sections placed at an angle will cover a rotating-type clothesline. For hiding such necessary clutter, the fence should be of a close-fitting material such as woven cedar, basket weave in cedar or redwood, or one of the new colorful plastics.

The fence should be placed so that it can fill a double-duty role, if desired. Not only will it hide undesirable features, but a fence will also hold up a climbing rose or make a backdrop for an espaliered shrub or tree.

A small, low piece of fence can make a corner into an outdoor living room. This would give a feeling of privacy and enclosure without shutting out air and the view. An ell between two sides of the house or between the house and garage is a logical place for a small length of fence.

Sometimes a short length in front of the house will set off a neat dooryard garden. Nothing is as pretty as a low fence with a mass of colorful spring bulbs or gay summer annuals in front. Fencing also keeps children and dogs from running through a flower bed.

Another place where a section of fence can be useful is on the line between a house and garage or carport. There it will tie house and garage together. Either a low or high fence will do. If a high one is selected, it may be desirable to have a louvered type to let the breezes through. And by a kitchen door a ten-foot section of high wire fence covered with morning glories creates a sheltered private spot.

A fence should always blend with the architecture of the house in material and color. With the wide range of styles offered by several manufacturers, this is easy to do. The wood can be stained to match or contrast with the siding. If the fence is cedar, it can be allowed to weather to a soft silver gray.

Post-and-rail fences are good with some contemporary houses, and picket fences, usually painted white, go well with colonial styles. Plastic in one or several colors makes a very modern addition. Fence sections come complete with matching posts, gate and hardware, so they are easy for anyone to put up.

Cedar and Douglas fir make lasting, durable fence material. Posts should be treated with creosote for the parts that are buried underground to prevent rot and termite damage. The creosote or other wood preservative must be allowed to soak deeply into the fibers. Let the posts stand in the liquid for twenty-four to forty-eight hours, or give the wood several generous treatments with a paintbrush.

To insure sturdiness, at least a third of the post length should be sunk into the ground. Dig the hole about two or three inches wider than the size of the fencepost. Set in the post, using a carpenter's bubble to keep it straight and true in the hole. Then anchor it with concrete or a filling of tightly packed stones.

There are times when home owners may wish to use their own ingenuity and creative talent in designing a fence. Many interesting features can be incorporated into the fence, such as seating, lamps or perhaps a signpost for the house number.

ABOVE: Louvered fence panels screen the terrace for privacy.

Jeannette Grossman

LEFT: Redwood fencing, faced down with pots of petunias, screens an entranceway.

Landscape by Arthur W. Erfeldt;

Jeannette Grossman

Handsome Hedges

DONALD WYMAN

ALMOST any kind of shrub as well as many trees can be pruned to form a hedge. Some plants make better hedges than others because they are denser in growth and respond to heavier pruning. Others grow more slowly.

This last characteristic should not be overlooked by the gardener. So often the easiest and cheapest hedge to plant is privet; it is also one of the most vigorous. Another rampant one is the hedge rose (*Rosa multiflora*), which can grow as much as six feet in a year. There are few places on the small suburban property where gardeners can accommodate it.

The ideal hedges are the slow growers. Some evergreens grow only a few inches annually and do not require too much attention. Then there are plants which need to be pruned only about once every other year to appear in perfect condition. The busy gardener can save time and trouble by considering these factors. He should also analyze why he wants to plant a hedge and where it should stand.

All hedges should be pruned so that they are wider at the base than at the top to allow plenty of light on the lower branches. Lack of sufficient light at the base causes dieback of the bottom branches, which tends to disfigure old perpendicular hedges. This fault is often impossible to correct in evergreens.

Evergreens are excellent hedges because they are handsome all year. There are several kinds of Japanese yews, some narrow and upright like Hicks or Hiti, others low and wide like *Taxus cuspidata densa*. By choosing several pistillate plants the gardener is assured of colorful fruits in the fall.

Arborvitaes are also used. They do not flourish nearly as well as the yews unless the climate is moist and there are no long, hot, dry

Dwarf euonymus can be clipped to form a dense hedge.

Paul E. Genereux

summer spells. Mugo pine makes a low, dense hedge but it should not be grown in areas exposed to scale.

Canada hemlock is one of the best hedge plants, especially when the gardener is not certain of the eventual hedge height desired. Hemlocks can be kept three feet high. Or if there is room for proper development, the plants can be allowed to grow taller each year.

Japanese holly should be considered, along with yews and hemlock, as one of the finest evergreen hedge plants available.

Tall, deciduous hedge plants well over eye level, include English beech and hedge hornbeam (*Carpinus betulus*). Thorny plants like the Washington hawthorn (which retains its bright red fruits most of the winter) and the cockspur thorn (*Crataegus crusgalli*) are frequently used. Another fine hedge is the native shingle oak (*Quercus imbricaria*). Its long, lustrous laurel-like leaves turn a rich bronze in the fall. They frequently remain on the oak far into the winter.

Deciduous hedge materials of medium height would include the all-purpose Japanese barberry, an excellent plant to use in poor soil or shaded locations. If the barberry will not grow in such a spot, it usually is useless to try to find another plant that will. The Mentor barberry has semi-evergreen leaves and is popular in drought areas of northern Ohio and the Midwest. The flowering abelia (*Abelia grandiflora*) has bright blossoms all summer and is seen from Florida to New York.

Forsythia makes a poor clipped hedge because pruning removes many of the flower buds. But as an informal hedge it is useful in a spacious area. The Cornelian cherry (*Cornus mas*) also is gaining favor.

The true Regel's privet, with its strictly horizontal branching, is another graceful but vigorous grower. Seedlings should not be purchased because they do not have the truly horizontal habit of plants that are grown from cuttings.

Another newcomer is the dwarf form of the burning bush (*Euonymus alatus compactus*), which is naturally dense and mound-like. The bush need be pruned only once every other year and it will still retain its formal appearance.

One-foot high hedges would include the dwarf box (*Buxus sempervirens suffruticosa*), several small barberries such as Crimson Pygmy and *Berberis thunbergi minor* and the arborvitae Little Gem.

Where space is truly limited, a six- or ten-inch-high wire mesh fence can be erected. English ivy can be trained to climb the fence and, with shearing, may be an attractive (but fast-growing) hedge.

Hedge Planting

WALTER SINGER

BEFORE actually proceeding with planting of a hedge, the gardener must know how wide the hedge will be at maturity. He should also check local ordinances if the hedge is to edge a property line. Usually a distance of three feet is sufficient.

Planting begins with the digging of a trench. It should be about twelve to eighteen inches deep and about eighteen inches wide. Size will vary with the plants. The bottom of the trench is loosened and good compost, well-rotted manure and bonemeal added. Bare-root plants should be soaked in a pail of thick muddy water before planting. Balled and burlaped plants should be watered.

It takes two to plant a hedge: one to hold it in place and another

The planting trench for a hedge should be about twelve to eighteen inches deep and about eighteen inches wide. A line stretched across the trench will guide the placement of plants.

Walter Singer

to fill in with soil around the roots. The hedge plant should be set sufficiently deep so that the soil marks (caused by the previous planting depth) are even with the rim of the trench. Tramp the plant in firmly and water thoroughly. A line stretched along the center of the trench will guide the depth and straightness of the planting. Proper distance between plants can be marked by tying strings along the line.

Pointers on Espalier

RUSSELL M. BETTES

ESPALIERED plants (those that are trained against a wall, fence or other upright surface) are becoming increasingly important in modern landscape design. Most suburbanites are familiar with the decorative effects, but the pruning method and tying of these plants pose a problem.

The espaliering must be done properly or it will give a shaggy, unsatisfactory result. To prune properly any plant for an espalier, it is essential to understand the habit of the plant and how it will react after pruning. Two popular espalier plants—roses and firethorns (*pyracantha*)—are treated in entirely different ways. These plants are good examples to guide the handling of many other similar kinds which also may be effectively espaliered.

The firethorn is closely related to other pome fruits such as apple and pear. If grown in the open, the firethorn will send up strong branches that arch downward from their own weight. With support against a wall, and without pruning, a firethorn will eventually reach a height of thirty to thirty-five feet.

To contain it, therefore, in a neat, flat panel, the gardener should first select three or more strong upright stems. These will be allowed to continue to grow as would the main trunks and branches of an apple tree. Unneeded canes or shoots from the base are cut back to the main stem. Side growth, however, should be shortened but allowed to remain; this will encourage more short fruit spurs.

The best results will be obtained by a twice-a-year schedule of pruning. In the winter or early spring, before growth starts, the heavy corrective pruning and the tying or retying should be done. Ruthlessly cut out competing or crossing stems. Prune the side growth back into shape and, lastly, cut back the terminal shoots if the plant has reached the desired height.

For tying branches to a masonry surface there are several types of wall nails of various weights that will hold the lighter branches firmly in place. For heavy stems it may be necessary to use a heavy screw eye inserted into a rawl plug. To this anchor the gardener can tie the branch without danger of the screw springing out. The space to be occupied determines whether the grower should use a fan arrangement of main stems or allow the plant to spray out two or more branches in a horizontal cordon fashion.

By summer or early fall the firethorn will have clothed itself with new growth that not only stands out too far from the wall but also hides the fruit clusters growing on the shortened spurs. The grower should, therefore, trim back the growth (with pruning shears, not hedge shears) close to the fruit or within one or two eyes from the main stem, as the case may be. Again, shorten any terminal growth that has gone beyond the desired area of coverage.

(47)

Climbing roses should be handled in an entirely different manner. The objective is to constantly renew the main canes or stems or to preserve the new one-year-old canes from which the best flowering wood will develop the second year. The newer "repeat blooming" varieties, in particular, need periodic pruning throughout the growing season.

First, therefore, it is best to untie the bush from its supports and lay it on the ground, if possible, during the early spring. This is done to simplify the pruning operation. Start by cutting out pieces or sections of old flowering wood; it is usually dark in color and heavily branched. Avoid disturbing any strong new stems.

Determine how many canes or main stems need to be saved in order to cover the wall or trellis area with at least a one-foot spacing between stems. If there are not enough new, strong, one-year shoots, select the most promising two-year stems and prune back everything else close to these. The remaining stems are then tied back to the supports and the tops trimmed off, if necessary, to bring them below the desired height.

After the first big display of flowers in June, the gardener should

Shiny camellia foliage traces a decorative modified cordon espalier on a painted brick wall.

John Bickel

(48)

Closely cropped euonymus forms a pattern of tidy greenery on the brick wall of a home.

Gottscho-Schleisner

Where it is hardy, variegated ivy can be trained into patterns such as a horizontal cordon.

Mason Weymouth

not neglect these climbers and then wonder why his roses taper off and other gardeners have continuous healthy bloom until frost. Immediately after the blooms fade, cut back the flower stems to within two or three eyes from the main stem. This eliminates the brown, dried flowers and brings the plant into a flat, uniform panel of green. It also forces the plant to start new buds and side growth that, in the repeat-blooming varieties, will flower again. The flower removal process is repeated as needed.

There are a great many other plants, both deciduous and evergreen, that can be effectively espaliered. Among the flowering shrubs, forsythia is probably one of the easiest to handle. It produces good strong stems six feet or more in length. These can be tied onto a garden fence, for instance, to create a soft, space-saving hedge effect. Once the assigned area is well filled with growth, it is advantageous in this type of shrub to thin out the weakest, poorest stems or branches and refurbish the space with new shoots from the base. Corrective pruning and shortening are best done immediately after flowering, to preserve next year's buds.

Garden Lighting

MILTON BARON AND CARL S. GERLACH

PLANNED lighting can transform any garden or landscape into a fascinating setting at night. The surrounding darkness shuts out unwanted things while the lighting accents flowering plants and shrubbery. Landscape lighting is an art that must follow the principles of good design.

There are many reasons for proper illumination after dark. It locates steps and landings, makes drives and walks easily seen and protects the home against prowlers. Night lighting also gives new dimensions to the indoor-outdoor relationship in modern home design.

A planned lighting setup enhances backyard parties, home sports and just plain gardening after dusk.

Good garden lighting is in many respects akin to good stage lighting. In both, the sources of illumination (the fixtures producing the light) are never obvious. Lamps should be screened; the more subtle the light, the better.

Each landscape composition has to be arranged carefully so that, with up lighting or back lighting, existing trees, walls or fences become striking backgrounds. (Up lighting is the term used to describe shielded or torpedolike fixtures arranged to shine on the underside of specimen trees or other plants. Back lighting is the illumination of walls, fences, hedges and so on, so that foreground material is silhouetted.)

Fine structural plants such as flowering crabapples, cherries, dogwood and birches are well suited for under lighting which enforces the line quality of the plant or group, enhances the lovely canopy, or focuses attention on blossom or fruit displays. Garden paths, lawns and vistas can be bathed in soft light by either down or side lighting. This will make the grass look like an emerald carpet. Lighting will entice the eye from one zone of interest to another.

With careful placement, lights can lend a feeling of spaciousness even to the smallest area. This is done by the simple device of de-emphasizing the foreground and emphasizing the background. Clever gradation of light intensity is invaluable in this scheme.

Certain landscape compositions—major scenes, for example—should have permanent illumination. Once the owner decides on an arrangement of lights that will bring out the best of an important scene, he should leave them alone. Such a scene will not be static, for the vagaries of weather and seasons will create many changes.

Usually within any major vista there are many lovely pictures worthy of attention at different periods of the growing season. The mushroom-type down light can show off a group of crocus in late winter or a colony of narcissus or tulips later on, or bring out the studied arrangement of colorful annuals in midsummer. Daily garden interest and night beauty are one and the same thing. Mobile lights offer countless opportunities for varying the night picture. Garden lighting is available for 110-volt and the new 12-volt systems. The latter is considered much safer and somewhat less expensive to install.

Anyone considering landscape lighting would find it advisable to check with local power authorities regarding prevailing ordinances.

On a new home property, the lighting should be incorporated into the original landscape development scheme. The owner should decide first on the strictly functional lighting of steps and so forth, and then go on to the esthetic ideas. While the property plan is still in the works, he should visualize the various effects worthy of inclusion before thinking about the types of fixtures needed.

On the landscape plan, the main wiring routes and waterproof outlets should be marked. On the house wiring plan, provision should be made for switches near doors or windows in the vestibule, living room, den and even the master bedroom.

Circuits should connect to the main fuse panel and pass through the basement wall. To be unobtrusive, all the wiring should leave the house underground. Direct burial cable (the three-wired type with one wire for grounding) is inexpensive. The exact size of cable to be used will depend on the total wattage likely to be on the line at any one time.

For a house already built, the installation of effective outdoor lighting is a bit more complicated. It entails enlargement of existing switch panels or installation of new separate wall switches. Basement walls must be drilled through so that the main circuit wiring can be underground.

In both new and established properties, waterproof outlets are placed around the landscape according to plan. They should be as low to the ground as possible, and concealed by plants, walls and so on. These outlets serve as central sources of power for the lighting fixtures.

The best type of fixture to use is one which has a convenient outlet built into the base; this allows the adding of one lamp to another, with the cord concealed on the ground. Many firms supply outdoor fixtures with about fifteen feet of cord and a waterproof rubber plug. Extension cords can be added where necessary.

For maximum flexibility in the placement of fixtures, use the kind with a spear-type base; these can be set and reset merely by pushing into the earth. This facilitates the experimentation necessary to get the "just right" effect of lighting on a tree or other planting.

The choice of flowering plants for night-lighted scenes is important. Some flower colors, especially whites, pastel tints, cream, yellows and pinks, are reflective and thus give outstanding effects under artificial light. Dark colors have poor reflective quality; deep purples and reds are to be shunned completely.

Trees with light or shiny bark show up well under lights. Paper

Various kinds of electric lamps placed in accordance with the plan shown here can bring out many attractive garden scenes which can be viewed from the window after nightfall.

Sketch and landscape plan by Milton Baron and Carl S. Gerlach

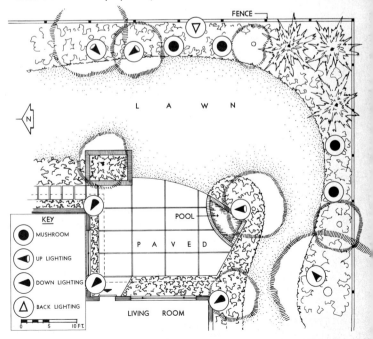

FENCE

L   A   W   N

N

KEY

● MUSHROOM

◀ UP LIGHTING

◀ DOWN LIGHTING

△ BACK LIGHTING

0   5   10 FT.

POOL

P   A   V   E   D

LIVING   ROOM

or gray birch, beech, red maple, shadbush, sycamore, stewartia and flowering cherries are excellent.

Tree foliage, of course, gives different effects with lighting at various periods in the growing season. In spring the new leaves are misty and ephemeral; in summer up lighting in most trees will reflect a cool, pale yellow-green atmosphere (thus red or purple-foliaged kinds are not so pleasant), and in fall yellow and other bright leaf colors are breathtaking when illuminated.

There are a few common but easily avoided errors in night lighting. Among these are:

1. Lights that blind. Lamps should be placed so that observers will not look directly into them. Use fixtures that have hoods or shields. Do not rely on plants to obliterate the source of light; the light will shine right through.

2. Excessively high wattage. It is better to use many small lights rather than a few large ones. Be subtle: use grades of light intensity to increase depth in a scene. Avoid floodlighting; overintense lighting is always garish. At corners of buildings, use flush or recessed down lights rather than fully exposed floodlights.

3. Unneighborly lighting. Be considerate and place the lights so they do not shine in a way that would irritate surrounding home owners. As a rule, beam, spot or floodlights, when indiscriminately directed, give little artistic improvement.

Balanced Pest Control

CYNTHIA WESTCOTT

FASHIONS in garden pest control go in cycles. When chemicals were scarce in Victory Garden days, home gardeners were constantly reminded of the many alternate methods of control. After World War II, when synthetic organic chemicals came on the market in a bewildering flood, gardeners tended to forget the importance of non-chemical measures and went in for spraying almost everything with all-purpose mixtures.

Now we are all concerned with the effect of pesticides on the environment, and chemicals are again used sparingly in an integrated control program.

The first defense against garden pests is exclusion. It means declaring all plant material when returning from vacation trips abroad, and it means careful scrutiny of all plants purchased for the garden. Beware of bargains.

If delphiniums show the slightest hint of puckered leaves or if African violet stems are a bit twisted, leave those plants at the dealer's. Never admit cyclamen mite into the home. If a dormant rose or a euonymus vine has a rough enlargement that may be crown gall, ship it back to the nursery for replacement.

If local gardens still are free from azalea and camellia flower blights and if such shrubs are ordered from areas where these diseases are known, have them sent bare root, all soil washed off, and all flower buds showing color removed. Buy strawberry plants certified free from nematodes and virus diseases, chrysanthemums free from stunt.

Immunization is the ideal control measure for pests already in an area, and plant breeders are constantly producing varieties more or less resistant to rusts, wilts and some other diseases—and even to certain insects. The pests, however, are constantly developing new races to which the new varieties are susceptible.

Seed catalogues list many vegetables resistant to various troubles, and a few ornamentals—wilt-resistant asters, rust-resistant snapdragons and gladiolus—that will not succumb to yellows. Asiatic crabapples are not harmed by cedar-apple rust, and there are albizzia clones resistant to mimosa wilt. Almost no rose varieties are resistant to all the strains of the black spot fungus, but a number are tolerant of the disease, and keep their foliage.

Eradication is an attempt to stamp out a pest before it can spread or to eliminate one already established. Sometimes, as when Japanese beetles appeared in California in 1961, it calls for all-out chemical war, soil treatment and foliage sprays. Sometimes it means getting rid of an alternate host.

Long before farmers knew what a rust was, or that fungi caused disease, laws were enacted (1660 in France, 1726 in Connecticut) requiring the destruction of barberry bushes near grain fields. In 1914 Virginia's cedar-rust law required the destruction of red cedars near apple orchards. And yet home gardeners still plant ornamental crab-apples next to cedars with complete disregard of the consequences. There should be at least 300 yards between the two hosts.

There are less common rusts that are occasionally troublesome. These alternate between pine and aster, pine and sweetfern, southern pine and evergreen oak, fir and fern, and, in the Northwest, spruce and rhododendron.

Pruning out infested plant parts—tent caterpillar egg masses, branches tied together by fall webworms, branches with borer holes or those blackened with fire blight, pine tips infested with shoot moths, cankered rose canes—is partial eradication. The black spot fungus winters in lesions on rose canes. Some years ago United States Department of Agriculture experimenters found that when canes were cut near ground level at spring pruning, the appearance of black spot on new foliage was delayed for some weeks. Such drastic pruning is not recommended. When, however, a severe winter makes it necessary, there is no cause for alarm. The bush will renew itself and disease control by regular spraying will be easier.

Suppression is the final control measure. Pests are kept at a low level by protective spraying and by cultural methods. Location is important. Plants subject to root rots should not be planted in low, poorly drained spots. Roses subject to mildew should be kept out of corners with little air circulation. New tulip bulbs should not be placed in beds where botrytis blight has been a problem. Healthy seedling lilies should be separated from lilies growing from purchased bulbs, which often harbor viruses. Plantings should be mixed to avoid the build-up that comes when disease starts on one plant and spreads to adjacent plants of the same type.

Sanitation is helpful. Red spiders winter on weeds in rose beds and borers in dahlia stalks. This does not mean that all such organic material must be routed to the bonfire. Most pests die when buried in a compost pile or spaded under in the garden.

Fertilizers may encourage disease. Nitrogen applied in spring when plants are growing rapidly may increase fire blight on apple, hawthorn and similar trees. Cow manure heaped against rose canes over winter may encourage cankers. On peony beds it may blight the new shoots.

The propagation method may either increase or suppress a pest. Crown divisions of chrysanthemums infested with leaf nematodes will almost surely carry these to new locations. But if the old plant is allowed to start in spring and tip cuttings are taken when new shoots are a foot or so high, the nematodes often can be left behind.

Chemicals retain a large place in the over-all control program. Their use should be tailored to the plant and the expected pests. For exhibition blooms and perfect foliage, roses require a weekly spray from early spring to hard frost. To save time this may be a combination of one or two fungicides for black spot and mildew; one or two insecticides for beetles, slugs, aphids and leafhoppers; a miticide for red spiders; and, in alternate weeks, a foliar food. Some shrubs and climbing roses are best left unsprayed to provide a haven for lady beetles and other beneficial insects.

At the other extreme, a single spray is sufficient to control canker-worms on oaks and elms and perhaps for only two or three years in each cycle. One potent dormant spray for bark beetles reduces the spread of Dutch elm disease. Methoxychlor, which is less harmful to birds, has been substituted for DDT but it may be even more toxic to fish. Pools should be covered.

One thorough treatment with dimethoate (Cygon), carbaryl (Sevin) or malathion often takes care of lace bugs on rhododendron, but it may take several sprays, starting in late April, to control andromeda lace bugs. One well-timed spray often takes care of boxwood leaf miner; the holly miner may require two. Since broad-spectrum insecticides, such as Sevin, malathion or methoxychlor, may kill the insect parasites or predators that keep mites in check, it is advisable to add a miticide (Kelthane, Tedion or Omite) to such sprays.

In many situations, the all-purpose combination spray is still the best solution. In others, a selective pesticide for a single problem fits best into an integrated control program.

Outwitting Plant Pests

BEATRICE TRUM HUNTER

By USING effective nontoxic methods and materials, gardeners can out-wit plant pests. It will take some imagination and ingenuity.

One approach, companionate planting, encourages you to become a keen observer of plant relationships, since certain plants bestow protection upon others. If you put garlic around the base of your favorite rosebushes, you may find that the roses develop hearty resistance against blackspot, mildew and aphids. Add clumps of parsley around the same rosebushes, and rose beetles may not come into the vicinity.

In a vegetable patch, plant beans near potatoes to deter both Colorado potato beetles as well as Mexican bean beetles. Chives and garlic can be planted with lettuce or peas to protect these crops from aphid damage. In planting cucurbits, add a few radish seeds in each hill; the growing radishes will help ward off striped or spotted cucumber beetles.

Include herbs in flowerbeds or among vegetables. Rosemary, sage, thyme, nasturtium, catnip, mint, hemp and hyssop succeed in driving white cabbage butterflies from the vicinity of growing cabbage. Plant tansy around cabbage plants to protect them from cabbageworms and cutworms. Plant tomatoes near asparagus for asparagus beetle control. Plant soybeans near corn to keep both chinch bugs and Japanese beetles away.

Another technique is the use of certain plants as traps. They may lure damaging insects to feast upon them, rather than upon your more prized neighboring plants. By planting geraniums near rosebushes or grapevines, you may lure Japanese beetles from the vicinity to the geraniums and save the roses and grapes. Or you may succeed in protecting corn from the ravages of Japanese beetles by planting white geranium or odorless marigolds in the vicinity of the corn. Similarly, marigolds planted near cucurbits may trap many cucumber beetles. Nasturtiums grown near beans will lure Mexican bean beetles that are present. Nasturtiums also protect broccoli from aphids and cucurbits from striped cucumber beetles and squash bugs.

To meet an emergency garden situation, be prepared with a few simple sprays that are nontoxic but effective. The simplest is water! Use it on plants not damaged by frequent watering. Wash off young cabbageworms from plants, or dislodge mealybugs from infested plants by using a forcible stream. Red spider mites can be eliminated by persistent syringing of the undersurface of leaves. Use an ordinary sprayer or pressure tank. Use force but little water to avoid drenching the bed or washing away the soil from the plant. Aphids dislodged with water generally fail to return. Alder blight aphids and other aphids, as well as flea beetles, can be removed with a stiff stream of water. This treatment is especially good during a dry season when these insects are apt to be numerous.

If a small plant is infected with aphids, submerge it briefly in water which is 125 degrees. Use the same treatment for rose bugs with the water between 125 and 135 degrees. The plants will not suffer injury.

Salt dissolved in water is another useful spray. A tablespoon of common table salt, dissolved in two gallons of water, will control cabbageworms without harming the plants. Gardeners with greenhouses have found that a spray consisting of an ounce of salt dissolved in a gallon of water controls spider mites.

Use other kitchen ingredients to meet emergency garden situations. Place slices of a raw onion in an electric blender, add an equal amount of water and blend, strain and use the mixture as a spray against aphids and red spiders. Grind pods of hot peppers, mix them with an equal amount of water and a little soap powder to make the material adhere and use it against cabbageworms, ants, spiders, caterpillars and tomato worms. Ground dry hot pepper dusted on tomato plants will protect them from insect attacks. Dry cayenne pepper sprinkled over plants wet with dew repels caterpillars. Use a spray consisting of cayenne pepper mixed with water against caterpillars and flea beetles.

Try combining several kitchen ingredients to make an all-purpose insect spray. Grind together three hot peppers, three large onions, and a whole garlic bulb. Cover the mash with water, place it in a covered container, and allow it to stand overnight. The next day, strain the mixture through a fine sieve or cheesecloth. Add enough water to make a gallon of spray. Use it on roses, azaleas, chrysanthemums, beans and other crops three times daily for a day or two during a heavy insect infestation. If necessary, repeat the spray after a heavy rainfall. The mash itself can be buried among the rosebushes.

If you grow rhubarb, the leaves should never be eaten because they contain large amounts of poisonous oxalic acid. However, these leaves can be used for garden sprays. Boil the leaves in water, strain, cool and spray on roses against greenfly and blackspot. This rhubarb-leaf solution can also be poured into drillings before sowing brassica, wallflowers and other seeds, as a preventive against clubroot.

Tomato leaves, another discard, have insecticidal value in the garden. Macerate the leaves, soak them in water, strain, and use the solution to control aphids on rosebushes, as well as grasshoppers, flies and caterpillars on eggplants.

Aphids that suck the juices from rosebuds as well as from other flower and vegetable plantings can be outwitted with the use of aluminum foil, a readily available material. The foil, reflecting the sky's ultraviolet rays, confuses the aphids and makes them change course. In experimental plots, flying aphids, which often transmit a damaging virus to plants and also lower crop yields, were deflected from crops protected by aluminum foil mulch strips.

Although many ingenious nontoxic methods and materials exist for outwitting plant pests, remember that the main control will be in preventive measures. Build up and maintain fertile soil. Supply it with ample amounts of humus and compost. Allow for good drainage. Choose resistant varieties. Interplant and rotate, when possible, for diversity. All these time-honored practices will help plants to grow in a healthy state and will bestow upon them a high degree of resistance to insect pests and plant diseases.

PART II

TREES
AND SHRUBS

AS THE ARTIST seeks from a palette the colors for his canvas, so the gardener selects from innumerable kinds of trees and shrubs those plants that will make his landscape beautiful. Great changes are taking place in the garden world. No longer are the outsized plants that soon overtake the property selected for homes. Tidy, slow-growing shrubs are winning appeal. Evergreens, for year-round effect, are dominating the landscapes. Trees and shrubs with interesting form and good flower colors are coming to the fore. The mood of the times is dictating this. Low, spreading homes, compact suburban communities and numerous demands on leisure time are creating a need for plants that are decorative yet easy to maintain.

Many of the newer forms of these plants are scarce during the first few years following their introduction and gardeners often have to search for them. Prices, too, may be a bit higher. But as long as gardeners are discriminating in their plant selections, they will find their efforts rewarded in worthwhile dividends—low-upkeep gardens with distinction and individuality the year through.

Plant Hardiness

FRANCIS DE VOS

THE hardiness of a plant is its inherent ability to withstand low temperatures. The average annual minimum temperature of an area, more than any other factor, determines whether a plant will survive.

This rule of thumb applies to Florida and Southern California as much as to the Northern states. Tropical plants may endure cold injury even when the temperature is above freezing, while plants of the tundra may not be damaged until the thermometer reaches 60 degrees below zero. Freezing injury, winter burn, heaving and bark splitting are the most common types of cold damage experienced in gardens.

Injury or death of plant cells that follows exposure to freezing temperatures is not a temperature effect per se, but it is caused by ice formation within (or between) the cells. Ice formation within cells causes irreversible changes in the living matter (protoplasm) of the cells. Most plant losses by freezing are attributed to this type of injury. Ice formation between cells may not be injurious.

Loss of a plant from freezing injury depends on the extent and the kinds of tissue involved. Injury to the roots or the main stem or trunk at or near the ground level may result in loss of all aboveground parts or the entire plant. The killing-back of portions of twigs and branches is the most common type of freezing injury.

The browning of broadleaved evergreens and conifers during winter is commonly called winter burn. Conditions conducive to severe winter burn are frozen soil, low moisture supply in the soil, strong constant winds and bright warm sun. A dry fall coupled with a constantly or intermittently frozen soil sets the stage for winter burn.

If plants are exposed to strong winds or direct sun, or both, their leaves lose water faster than it can be replaced by the roots in frozen or cold soil. Plants in full winter sun are damaged more than those in shade. Water loss is greatly accelerated by high leaf temperatures, which may reach 80 degrees when the air temperature is below 32 degrees.

The alternate thawing and freezing of the top layer of soil frequently heaves young plants out of the soil or breaks the root-soil contacts of recently transplanted plants. Plants so affected dry out and die back to ground level or are killed.

Differential heating and cooling of the bark of some trees and shrubs results in stresses which cause the bark to split and crack. Young azaleas and boxwoods not completely hardened and plants of borderline hardiness are particularly susceptible. Frequently this injury is not noticed until the dying back of branches or of the entire plant during the late spring or summer.

The degree to which a plant can become hardened to low temperatures depends largely on its inherent ability to respond to environmental conditions that tend to increase frost resistance. Some plants are incapable of being hardened by any known treatment.

The seasonal changes that occur in the temperate zone are largely responsible for the annual increase and decrease in a plant's resistance to cold. The decreasing day length and cooler nights of fall result in increased resistance by causing a cessation of growth and bringing about changes in the physical and chemical properties of cells. With the coming of spring, nearly all frost resistance is lost.

The hardening and dehardening processes are gradual and are subject to climatic changes that are seldom of the same magnitude or in the same sequence from year to year. It is, therefore, virtually impossible to say how hardy any particular plant is at any given time.

In the disastrous spring freeze of 1955 in the Southeast, half-century-old azaleas were killed after coming into active growth. In the fall of the same year in the Pacific Northwest a sudden extreme drop in temperature after a mild fall was equally disastrous. In both cases, plants which had survived lower temperatures in midwinter of other years succumbed at higher temperatures when in an incomplete state of hardiness.

The gardener's first line of defense against winter damage should

(65)

be the selection of plants to be grown. In most plant groups, some species and varieties are tougher and hardier than others.

Reputable nurserymen, landscape architects, plant societies, state agricultural schools, botanical gardens and arboretums can assist in making selections. Also, the Plant Hardiness Zone Map, which is available for 15 cents from the Superintendent of Documents, Washington 25, D.C., outlines in ten zones the average annual minimum temperatures throughout the country.

Satisfactory performance is not guaranteed even from a cold-hardy variety. The gardener still must use his judgment. The hardiest plants should be given the most exposed or coldest site on the property, and broadleaved evergreens should be planted where they will have some winter shade and be protected from the wind. The common experience, particularly with borderline-hardy species, is that one-year-old plants are more difficult to bring through the first winter than two- or three-year-old plants.

The time of planting can also influence the results. Plants which are not well established when winter arrives may be heaved from the soil or may not be able to absorb sufficient water to offset the desiccating effects of winter winds. In the colder states, spring planting gives the best results, particularly for broadleaved evergreens.

Good cultural practices are necessary if a plant's inherent hardiness is to be fully realized. Plants of low vigor because of nutritional deficiencies, poor soil drainage, and insect or disease damage are less likely to endure the rigors of winter weather than healthy plants. At the other extreme, plants with vigorous soft growth produced as the result of late-summer applications of nitrogen fertilizer do not have time to mature and harden; thus they are also highly susceptible to cold injury.

Since winter injury, particularly to broadleaved evergreens, is usually more severe under conditions of low soil moisture, plants should be watered even during the winter if drought is severe. Watering is especially important to plants deprived of rainfall because they are growing near the house foundation or under a roof overhang; they frequently are killed by cold temperatures and drying winds aggravated by the dry soil.

Of equal importance to over-wintering of plants is soil drainage. Heaving is more common in waterlogged soils than in well-drained soils. The active and extensive root system developed by a plant in well-drained soil is the best insurance against the drying effects of freezing temperatures and winds.

A three- to four-inch soil mulch of leaves, wood chips, well-decayed sawdust or pine needles is generally considered to be effective in reducing heaving caused by alternate freezing and thawing of the soil surface. A snow mulch is equally effective but cannot be depended on in many areas. Soils beneath mulches do not freeze deeply or at all, thereby keeping soil moisture more available to the plants.

Recent experiments have indicated that bark splitting of azaleas growing in open fields can be prevented by removing the mulch in fall before freezing weather sets in. The reason is that the temperature above a mulch may be as much as five to six degrees lower than over adjacent bare soil because the mulch prevents the radiation of heat from the soil to the surrounding air. Additional experiments are needed to determine whether the procedure is applicable to azaleas and other woody plants growing in home landscapes.

In recent years, plastic-type sprays called anti-desiccants have been introduced to prevent winter burn. Reports indicate that they are effective when applied in late autumn. These sprays, however, should not be considered a substitute for the selection of hardy varieties or the observance of good cultural practices.

Acclimatization is defined as the natural process by which organisms become adapted to a climate at first harmful. In its narrowest sense, it refers only to heritable changes that occur in the course of generations. Horticulturally speaking, the term is used more loosely; it generally refers to any change following transplanting that enables the plant to become established in its new environment. There is no evidence to support the idea that a plant's genetically based hardiness will be increased by exposing the plant to two or three winters in a colder climate.

The principal adjustment that a plant makes during the acclimatization period is developing an extensive root system. This is no small matter, however, since much of the winter injury is directly related to water loss. Thus it is obvious that the selection of cold-hardy species and varieties and the application of good cultural practices are the keys to winter survival and vigor of many kinds of plants in the garden.

Early-flowering Shrubs

CLARENCE E. LEWIS

THE early-flowering shrubs proclaim spring's arrival on the winter landscape. Flowering dates are not rigid but usually the first to bloom after January 1 are the witch hazels.

The common kind (*Hamamelis virginiana*) produces blooms during October and November, but the Chinese and vernal witch hazels (*H. mollis* and *H. vernalis*) may flower as early as February. The Japanese witch hazel (*H. japonica*) usually is about a week or ten days later. All three have a pleasing fragrance, but the vernal is the most pungent.

Flower buds, which appear on short, curved stems, vary in the Chinese, vernal and Japanese witch hazels. The flower buds of the Japanese witch hazel usually are in twos, pointed and brown; the vernal and Chinese types generally are in threes, round, and yellow to light tan. The Chinese witch hazel has extremely hairy flower buds that are about twice the size of the vernal flower buds. Young stems of the vernal are much duller than those of the Chinese or Japanese kinds. Spidery petals of the vernal flowers are more orange than yellow, while the Japanese and Chinese witch hazels have yellow blooms.

The Cornelian cherry (*Cornus mas*) is one of our best early-flowering shrubs, producing blooms in late March some years, but more often in early April. The flower buds differ from those of the flowering dogwood (*C. florida*) in that they are tan and obovately round, while those of the native flowering dogwood are gray and much flatter. The Cornelian cherry's yellow flowers do not have the conspicuous bracts of flowering dogwood. Cuttings of Cornelian cherry can be forced into bloom indoors during the winter.

In early or mid-April the lesser-known winter hazels (*corylopsis*)

Flowering quince blossoms appear early in spring when the weather settles.

J. Horace McFarland

Ribbonlike flowers of Japanese witch hazel appear from early January into March.

J. Horace McFarland

Cornelian cherry, a member of the dogwood family, can be trained to tree form.

J. Horace McFarland

Sunny blossoms of the aromatic spicebush are among the first to appear in spring.

J. Horace McFarland

show light yellow hanging flower racemes. These large shrubs eventually produce clean, blue-green, heart-shaped leaves that appear after the flowers. Winter hazels are available, but not readily obtained from the nursery. The hardiest include the fragrant winter hazel (*C. glabrescens*), the spiked winter hazel (*C. spicata*) and the Chinese winter hazel (*C. sinensis*). The winter flower buds are semiround, red-toned and often have loose flower bud scales. These shrubs are reluctant to grow where temperatures dip to five or ten degrees below zero, but they can be tried in a warm, sheltered site.

Seldom planted, although worthy, is the native spicebush (*Lindera benzoin*). It abounds in moist woodlands. The clusters of small, yellow, buttonlike flowers appear from early to mid-April on curved, spicily fragrant stems. The large leaves turn a clear yellow color in fall.

Not all of the early-flowering shrubs have yellow flowers. Among the broadleaved evergreen kinds, there are the white-flowered American and Japanese andromeda (*Pieris floribunda* and *P. japonica*). They bear clusters of white flowers in early April. If the temperature does not suddenly rise to the 70's, the flowers may persist for three or four weeks.

The smaller shrub (*P. floribunda*) has erect flower clusters, while the larger, colorful Japanese species has more prolific, pendant blooms. The leaves of the latter are much glossier; there often is a bronze-red winter color in the flower clusters and sometimes in the foliage. (Leaves of the American andromeda are green only.) As in all other spring-flowering species, the flower buds were formed the previous summer.

The first forsythia, Korean forsythia, precedes the other species by about a week, appearing in late March or early April. The yellow flowers are not as abundant as those of the varieties Lynwood Gold, Spring Glory or Spectabilis. But the Korean forsythia (*Forsythia ovata*) is more erect and less competitive when used with other shrubs.

Also proclaiming the spring season are early-flowering shrubs such as spring heath, pussy willow, fragrant viburnum, common flowering quince, February daphne, and fragrant honeysuckle. Shrubs that flower in early spring often are affected by severe frosts. Sometimes the low temperatures are destructive enough to ruin both the flowers and the potential fruits.

Many early-flowering shrubs are excellent for espaliering. When trained against a warm south wall, they usually will bloom earlier than when in shrub form. Species that adapt to espaliering include any of the forsythias, fragrant viburnum, the winter hazels, fragrant honeysuckle, fothergilla, flowering quince and witch hazels.

Plants that are thought of as early spring-flowering shrubs need not always remain as shrubs. Some can be trained to a single standard. Examples of this are Cornelian cherry, the Japanese and vernal witch hazels, Persian parrotia, winter hazels, fothergilla and fragrant viburnum.

Trees and Shrubs for Summer Bloom

MAURICE BROOKS

So MANY trees and shrubs bloom in spring that midsummer and autumn may seem like the famine after a feast. Nevertheless, it is possible to maintain a succession of blossoms on woody plants from July until frost.

There are many handsome and dependable species. For example, the butterfly bush (*buddleia*) attracts hordes of colorful butterflies to its flowers. Blossoms range in shade from pure white, through a variety of blues and purples, to crimson. Severe winters may kill the plant to the ground, but new shoots which develop from the roots begin to flower in July. Bloom will continue until heavy frost.

Sourwood (*Oxydendrum arboreum*), another member of the heath family, produces a wealth of clustered, bell-shaped white flowers in late July. The leaves turn brilliant scarlet by early fall. Under forest conditions this plant sometimes grows to tree size; in the open it usually assumes a shrubby growth habit.

(71)

Sourwood has given its name to a Kentucky mountain as well as to a famous American square-dance tune. In addition, sourwood honey is a local specialty in the southern Appalachians.

Hydrangeas include several useful species for summer and fall bloom. Brilliant blue and pink varieties are excellent for sandy, seaside locations. *Hydrangea paniculata grandiflora* is a hardy, spreading shrub. The large heads of white flowers develop in August; the blooms turn pink as cooler weather arrives. At this stage the flowers are good material for dried arrangements.

The handsome oakleaf hydrangea (*H. quercifolia*), a native of the Southern states, has proved hardy to the vicinity of New York and Long Island. When grown farther north, the tops often die down and there is sparse flowering. This hydrangea is low growing with attractive foliage. The heads of snowy white flowers open in July.

A versatile, low-growing shrub is *Abelia grandiflora*, a member of the honeysuckle family. This semi-evergreen plant is closely allied to *linnaea*, the northern twinflower, which was Linnaeus' favorite. Pink blossoms appear on abelia in late June and persist until cold weather.

Shoots may winterkill, but sprouts from the roots will bear flowers the following summer. Abelia grows best in well-drained, acid soils which have been enriched with peat moss or leafmold.

Rose of Sharon or the althaeas are shrubby members of the mallow family. They produce large, showy blossoms. Under favorable conditions althaeas sometimes assume tree forms. The plants begin to bloom in July and they have a long flowering season.

One of America's most historic and romantic plants is franklinia (*Gordonia altamaha*), a small tree discovered more than one hundred years ago along the Altamaha River in Georgia. The tree has never been rediscovered in the wild. Nevertheless, it was preserved in Bartram's Garden near Philadelphia, Pennsylvania, and has been propagated widely.

Franklinia is a fine ornamental tree, opening large creamy white flowers in August. Blossoms remain until freezing weather. It does best in rich, sandy loam. The tree has proved hardy as far north as Boston, Massachusetts.

Blue is an unusual flower color for summer shrubs, but the chaste-tree (*Vitex agnus-castus*) bears blossoms in a variety of blue shades. It is a semi-hardy plant. Root sprouts bear flowers during the first summer of growth, although these may not appear until August or September. The blossoms rival those of buddleia in their attraction of butterflies. The chaste-tree thrives in full sunlight and fertile soil.

On the margin of dependability for northern gardens are two showy favorites of the South—crape myrtle (*Lagerstroemia indica*) and silk tree (*Albizzia julibrissin*). Both of these are exceptionally handsome summer-blooming plants.

Crape myrtle and silk tree generally succeed as far north as southern New Jersey. Both will survive farther north in sheltered coastal areas. Occasionally, severe winters may kill them. The hardier silk tree variety *rosea* thrives northward to the Boston, Massachusetts area.

Guide to the Needled Evergreens

CLARENCE E. LEWIS

*Among the needled evergreens are some of the finest orna-
mentals for landscape use. To pinpoint those plants with
the best decorative qualities and good growing habits,
Clarence E. Lewis has selected six major groups. In each
he mentions those species and varieties of particular value.
Line drawings by Peter K. Nelson show the representative
characteristics of each group.*

Spruce and Fir

THE firs (*Abies*) and spruces (*Picea*) are not considered the best of the narrow-leaved evergreens for the small home grounds because of their ultimate large size. This does not rule them out for larger areas where they are used for screening or as specimens. Home gardeners can choose some of the slow-growing variations. The dwarf forms of spruce can be effectively used in foundation plantings.

Both genera prefer clean air, not the heat and smoke of most cities. They also need room to spread laterally and vertically. Good soil drainage is important for their best appearance. When preparing the soil, incorporate at least one part peat moss to each part of soil.

Pruning can be done to a certain extent to shape a tree, but a branch should be removed so that no stub is left. Another way to keep such evergreens dense is by pinching out the end buds just before growth begins in spring. Pruning can be done at the same time, but it is not an operation for an untrained person.

The white fir (*Abies concolor*) is the most adaptable of the firs for a wide range of growing conditions. It has excellent blue variations that exceed the qualities of some of the blue Colorado spruces.

Firs that have a rich green foliage include Nordmann (*A. nordmanniana*), Veitch (*A. veitchi*) and Nikko fir (*A. homolepis*), which are easily obtainable. The Douglas fir (*pseudotsuga*), not truly a fir, is well suited to ornamental Eastern and Midwestern plantings, and some good blue kinds are available.

Spruces, other than blue forms or Colorado spruce, include the excellent rich green Oriental spruce (*Picea orientalis*), the widely distributed and adaptable Norway spruce (*P. abies*), the narrow-headed Serbian spruce (*P. omorika*) and the white spruce (*P. glauca*) for the northern states.

There are several dwarf forms of white spruce that are extremely dense and do not exceed a height of ten feet, even after many years. Included are Alberta spruce and Black Hills spruce.

The best dwarf forms of spruce are variations of the Norway spruce. They include such odd shapes as a creeping one (*P. abies procumbens*), a pendulous one (*P. abies pendula*), the dense short-needled, broad-looking nest spruce (*P. abies nidiformis*) and the moundlike Gregory spruce (*P. abies gregoryana*), which is handsome.

False Cypress and Thuja

THE false cypress or retinospora (*chamaecyparis*) and arborvitae (*thuja*) are thought of as being similar because so many species of each have scalelike leaves. Both groups have good fibrous root systems, which encourage successful transplanting, and they can be grown in moderate shade to full sun. Moist—not wet—soils offer no serious problem, and good soil drainage plus a liberal amount of organic matter (peat moss) at planting time are recommended.

Eastern hemlock
(*Tsuga canadensis*)

Japanese yew (*Taxus cuspidata*)

Sawara false cypress
(*Chamaecyparis pisifera*)

Common juniper

(*Juniperus communis*)

Colorado spruce (*Picea pungens*)

Japanese black pine

(*Pinus thunbergi*)

Shearing (not pruning) should be done during March and April, before growth starts. Sometimes it may be necessary to repeat this in July or August. A common occurrence in both arborvitae and false cypress is the browning and dying of inner branches and leaves during the summer and early fall. This happens after the outer new branches and leaves have developed, and it is perfectly natural.

For hedges under four feet, Globe, Woodward and Hovey arborvitaes are suitable, as are dwarf Hinoki, compact Hinoki and dwarf plume false cypress. The following make good screens or tall hedges (six to ten feet): Hinoki and plume false cypress, and Ware, wintergreen and Rosenthal arborvitae.

Taller-growing plants that can be kept in bounds are the narrow steel blue Scarab false cypress (*Chamaecyparis lawsoniana allumi*); the rich green foliaged Hinoki false cypress (*C. obtusa*) and variations of it, the fine-textured plume false cypress (*C. pisifera plumosa*), the stringlike thread false cypress (*C. pisifera filifera*) and the broad, dense but tall-growing Ware arborvitae (*Thuja occidentalis wareana*). The last may be listed as Siberian arborvitae and scientifically also as *Thuja occidentalis sibirica* or *robusta*.

Other tall-growing arborvitaes include the narrow, dense but dark green wintergreen arborvitae (*Thuja occidentalis nigra*). Rosenthal is narrow but spirally branched, as in the Douglas arborvitae.

There are several yellow, golden, gray, blue-toned and sulfur-foliaged examples of arborvitae and false cypress, but it is difficult to combine them with other plants. Also available are globe, oval and other shapes which look attractive at the nursery but do not blend well in the landscape.

As a group, the false cypress are not bothered by insects or disease. However, arborvitaes sometimes are subject to attack by red spider.

Hemlock

MANY gardeners think of hemlocks (*Tsuga*) as forest trees of great heights, but they have found a useful and respected place in the landscape of the American home. There are principally four species found in nurseries—the Canadian or eastern hemlock (*Tsuga canadensis*), the Carolina hemlock (*T. caroliniana*), the Japanese hemlock (*T. diversifolia*) and the Siebold hemlock (*T. sieboldi*). They are all different in appearance. The Canadian is the most widely grown and used, while the Siebold hemlock is not available in many nurseries.

The Carolina hemlock has a darker green color than the Canadian and it has a more irregular arrangement of branches and leaves. There is a tendency for the Japanese hemlock to grow as a large shrub with several main stems.

All three popular hemlocks make excellent fine-textured hedges that can be kept to a height of four to ten feet, and more if desired. It is necessary to prune them at least once a year, more often if needed. Timing is late winter or early spring, then again in July.

There are several variations of Canadian hemlock. The weeping hemlock (*T. canadensis pendula*) is best known. It is broad and spreading, with tumbling branches that look from a distance like a green waterfall. It may be, and often is, no taller than six to ten feet, but may have a canopied spread of twelve to twenty feet. It takes many years to reach this size and is well suited for either side of the broad entrance of a large building. Younger plants can be used by a home entrance. There is a slow-growing and spreading form, Curtis Dwarf, that will take six to eight years to reach a height of two feet.

Other variations are a deep green, dense-needled, slow-growing form (*T. canadensis atrovirens*), a globe form, a prostrate one, and even some with golden foliage that is brightest when the new leaves are first formed. Even an extremely small-leaved variety can be found, among others.

Shade is no problem as long as there are no low, overhanging branches, but hemlocks should have at least a half-day's sun if they are to remain dense. They resent the interference of near-by roots.

Excellent soil drainage is necessary, and hemlocks do like a liberal amount of organic matter in the soil. Do not place hemlocks where they will receive the brunt of prevailing winds or they will burn, nor place them in "closeted" areas where air circulation is poor.

Yew

THE yews (*Taxus*) are the most widely used of the narrow-leaved evergreens for home grounds planting because of their many variations of form, rich green foliage and adaptability to shade. They are fine evergreens for hedges, foundation plantings, deep shaded banks, flat areas and many other spots in sun or shade.

The major soil requirement is good drainage. They will not survive without it. The root systems are densely fibrous, which indicates that transplanting is no problem.

The only species of yew found in the East or Midwest that is not recommended for home gardens is the native Canadian yew or ground hemlock (*Taxus canadensis*), which grows in the shade of many Northern woodlands. It burns badly in sun and does not transplant easily.

Yews that do not usually grow more than four feet tall, or that may easily be kept at this height or less, include the spreading English yew (*T. baccata repandens*). It is one of the very best, with a moundlike habit and rich green foliage. Prostrate Anglojap yew (*T. media* Prostrate) has a flat spreading appearance. Other low-growing spreaders include the prostrate Japanese yew (*T. cuspidata* Prostrate), Ward yew (*T. media wardi*), dwarf Japanese yew (*T. cuspidata nana*), cushion Japanese yew (*T. cuspidata densa*) and Hill Anglojap yew (*T. media* Hill).

For compact forms, but often rounded and generally upright branching, there are the Brown, Halloran and Vermeulen yews, all *T. media*. They will grow to a height of six feet or more unless pruned.

Taller (six feet) spreading forms include Sebian yew (*T. media* Sebian), Berryhill yew (*T. media* Berryhill) and compact Japanese yew (*T. cuspidata intermedia*). Broad, vaselike forms that will grow to a height of ten feet include some very fine yews like spreading Japanese yew (*T. cuspidata expansa*), Thayer yew (*T. cuspidata thayerae*) and Hunnewell yew (*T. media* Hunnewell).

The *T. media* species also supplies some other useful variations. Narrow but tall-growing (to ten feet) yews are ably represented by Hicks, Stoveken and Costich yews. For broad upright forms there are Hatfield, Kelsey, Cole and Andorra yews.

Yews that will reach a height of twenty feet, unless restrained, include the upright Japanese yew (*T. cuspidata capitata*), Adams yew (*T. media* Adams) and the Dovaston yew (*T. baccata dovastoni*).

Juniper

THE junipers (*Juniperus*) have a wide range of forms and sizes and are one of the most adaptable evergreens for the cold areas of the Northern states. In most cases junipers prefer sun or partial shade, but not dense shade. The soil should be well drained, but it does not require generous amounts of organic matter.

Almost all of the junipers can be pruned or even sheared if it is necessary to keep them controlled. The best time to prune is in early spring before growth starts—March 1 to April 15—although there is no objection to shearing for Christmas greens. The only objectionable time is when new growth is soft, from about May 1 to June 15.

Their uses are many, and there is a form for almost every home garden need. For slopes or banks in rich or poor soil there are Bar Harbor, Waukeegan, Andorra, Oldfield, Sargent and Japgarden, which are low and spreading. Recommended for windy areas where screening is necessary are Keteleer, Hill Dundee, Silver, Red Cedar and Canaert. Where broad, vaselike forms are needed, with an ultimate height of six to eight feet, there are Pfitzer, blue Pfitzer, Hetzi and Koster.

Low-spreading or creeping forms that do not exceed a height of one to two feet even after fifteen to twenty years are Japgarden, Sargent, Shore, Douglas and Tamarix Savin, which have green foliage. For blue foliage there is a creeping Andorra that turns purple during late summer, fall and winter. For an in-between height, two to four feet, but spreading, the compact or slow-growing forms of Pfitzer and Savin junipers are recommended.

Several kinds have been omitted, such as Irish, Swedish, Spiny Greek and Meyer. Their forms or colors or both are hard to incorporate into the home landscape.

Junipers do not make the best hedges. This is particularly true where there is little sunlight or where roots must compete with those of near-by trees. During the hot, dry summer most of them are attacked by mites, causing a loss of inner foliage that is unattractive. This can be controlled by thorough spraying with a miticide.

Hardiness is no problem with most of the junipers, since they have

(79)

survived temperatures of fifteen or more degrees below zero. Some wind burning may occur, but it is not serious and the plant quickly recovers. The blue fruits are quite attractive, but are more commonly found on the taller-growing forms of Chinese and red cedar junipers.

Pine

PINES, the name some people erroneously use for all narrow-leaved evergreens, include trees primarily, although there are a few smaller species. They can be used for preventing soil erosion, and some also are well suited for screening, providing a tall hedge. Or they can be used as specimen lawn or patio trees.

They are not difficult to transplant, except for such species as pitch (*Pinus rigida*) and scrub (*P. virginiana*) pines, which grow wild in sandy and stony soils. These pines are not often used in landscape planting, however.

As long as there is good drainage, soil type is not important, although pines respond to a good supply of organic matter. Pruning is done by cutting back stems or removing the terminal buds to create density. The proper time is in late winter or early spring, before growth begins.

Browning and dying of inner leaves in the summer and early fall happens annually and is no cause for alarm. This natural process also occurs in many other evergreens.

The most widely used shrub form is the mugo pine (*P. mugo*), of which there are variations. Some have very short needles and are slow growing and dense.

The white pine (*P. strobus*), a native tree, is one of the most adaptable. There is also a narrow-growing form called pyramidal white pine, which is satisfactory, too. The red or Norway pine (*P. resinosa*) is not well suited to the home grounds, nor is the Ponderosa species (*P. ponderosa*). The loose-growing limber pine (*P. flexilis*) resembles the white, but its twisted growth is quite different—and useful.

Where wind is a factor, the Austrian pine (*P. nigra*) has proved to be a good choice. The same can be said for Scotch pine (*P. sylvestris*), particularly the short-needled forms.

Other possible selections could include the slow-growing compact Swiss stone pine (*P. cembra*), the loose-branched and pendulous-leaved Korean pine (*P. koraiensis*), the lesser-known, slow-growing Japanese white pine (*P. parviflora*), which is useful because of its lateral branching, and possibly the short-needled but dense-looking Macedonian pine (*P. peuce*).

Modern Rhododendrons

ALAN W. GOLDMAN

THE enormous rhododendrons of yesteryear, which graced the large estates reminiscent of England's sprawling manors, are being replaced with neater, scaled-down evergreen shrubs. This new class of rhododendrons, with growth measured in inches rather than feet, is far better suited to the smaller suburban plot.

Outstanding among modern rhododendrons is Windbeam, first raised by G. G. Nearing. It is extremely free flowering and bears pure white blossoms. Exhibiting an air of compact grace, the plant is an excellent choice in front of the foundation of a modern one-story or split-level house. Windbeam also may be used as a low, flowering hedge since the slender leaves remain in good condition throughout the fifty weeks of the year that the plant is out of bloom. Of unquestionable hardiness, it is reported to flower regularly on a windswept Connecticut hillside.

From the same breeder comes the group of semi-dwarf rhododendrons called the Guyencourt hybrids. All six varieties are similar in appearance when out of bloom—they have long, narrow, hairy evergreen leaves and a growth habit very similar to the Japanese barberry.

The Guyencourt hybrids are exceptionally good looking when planted in groups, since the individual plants tend to grow in an open fashion unless held back by tip pruning after bloom. Lenape, a very pale yellow, can be set in a group of pure white Montchanin. Brandywine, pale pink in bud, seems to combine well with Chesapeake, Delaware or Hockessin. The last three mentioned open with an apricot tint, then turn white.

For gardeners who seek scarlet flowers in a rhododendron, Kluis Sensation should be an extremely satisfying plant. It looks more like a typical rhododendron than the dwarfs mentioned earlier. The plant is full and bushy with an erect pod of bright scarlet flowers, frilled at the edges. It will tolerate temperatures down to five degrees below zero and will bloom regularly in late May. Lower winter temperatures may damage some of the vivid blossoms.

RIGHT: Among the dwarf rhododendrons , Purple Gem which rarely exceeds two and one-half feet in height.

Landscape by Henry M. Feil; Gottscho-Schleisner

BELOW: Hybrid rhododendrons provide spectacular display in June.

Gottscho-Schleisner

Any listing of rhododendrons should include the Dexter hybrids. These unique hardy plants were developed by the almost legendary C. O. Dexter. Starting in 1926, Mr. Dexter raised almost 20,000 rhododendrons a year from his own crosses. The plants were unusual for two reasons—the flowers were large and decorative and the plants hardy enough to thrive in the extremely cold Northeastern winters. Unfortunately, many counterfeit Dexter hybrids have flooded the Eastern market.

It is best to get the advice of a knowledgeable rhododendron specialist before purchasing a shrub identified as a Dexter. My favorite is Parker's Pink—a soft pink when in bloom and unusually pleasant to look at with its thrifty habit and light foliage.

The Hillier Nursery in Winchester, England, introduced a compact, low-growing hybrid, Arthur J. Ivens, in the spring of 1944. This plant is just beginning to be seen in better nurseries in the East. The leaves are small and roughly heart-shaped, unusual in a hardy rhododendron. This hybrid variety can withstand temperatures as low as fifteen degrees below zero.

Shallow, bell-like blossoms, the color of a strawberry ice-cream soda, open in late April. After the blossoms have fallen, another show of color begins, equally striking to the eye. Arthur J. Ivens puts out new growth of a peculiar red-bronze hue. Actually, anyone fortunate enough to own this semi-dwarf evergreen plant can count on five or six weeks of color in one corner of the garden.

No list of new rhododendrons would be more than half complete without at least a quick reference to the azalea side of the family. The most satisfying azalea to be developed in many years is the low-growing hybrid Gumpo. This evergreen shrub seems to have been designed especially to grow in front of an evergreen planting of rhododendrons or low-growing conifers.

Gumpo never grows over fifteen inches high. Its generous annual growth spreads horizontally rather than vertically. In late June each terminal opens a pair of pure white flat flowers, almost three inches in diameter. Then, for at least another three weeks, there is a sporadic show of snowy white on the more shaded parts of the plant. Although Gumpo was developed by K. Wada of Japan, the azalea shows none of the tortuous growth habits so often associated with Japanese shrubs.

Pruning Rhododendrons

ALAN W. GOLDMAN

THE home owner often is reluctant to prune a rhododendron that has grown out of bounds, because the shrub represents a sizable investment—especially when it has grown to the size where drastic pruning is necessary. Yet when a large rhododendron has outgrown its location, drastic pruning is the answer. April is the best time to prune rhododendrons.

Since the shrub must be cut over completely, the owner should steel himself to the loss of flowers for one year. If only half the plant is cut back, the goal will not be achieved at all. Instead, the cut-over section will remain dormant while the growing energy will be channeled into the uncut part. The result is a plant more out of shape than before pruning.

When pruning a rhododendron, the best place to make the actual cut is just above the dormant growth bud on the old wood. The dormant growth bud is the point where, in previous summers, the shrub put on a late spurt of growth, which is called "growing through." It is a primary cause of legginess.

Under normal conditions the shrub forms a flower bud just above the dormant growth bud. Then, after the flower is spent, the dormant growth bud produces a few side shoots to make the plant thrifty and full in appearance.

However, if high temperatures and heavy rainfall occur in autumn, the flower bud turns into a leaf bud and starts into growth the same year it is formed. The dormant growth bud remains dormant and vertical growth is made by the plant at the expense of lateral growth.

(84)

Cuts should be made at 90 degrees to the twig and never more than one-half inch above a dormant bud. Wounds need not be painted but the tool used for pruning should be sharp to avoid shredding or tearing of the bark. Pruning shears are best for the operation.

Rhododendrons should not be fertilized immediately after extensive pruning since the cut-over shrub has no foliage to take the feeding. Heavy mulching should be avoided, too. After the first growth has appeared, though, a mulch of wood chips, pine needles or oak leaves should be renewed.

Two forms of minor pruning are used in rhododendron care. Deadheading is the removal of spent flower blossoms before they have had a chance to mature into seed pods. One rhododendron authority claims that forming seed pods uses up seven times more energy than forming flower buds.

On a rhododendron that has just finished blooming, new soft growth begins to push out from just below the spent bud. When deadheading, reasonable care should be exercised to avoid removal of new growth along with faded blooms, for this growth forms the future scaffolding of the shrub as well as the next year's flowers. Small shears, a pruning knife or even the gardener's thumbnail will do the job.

Disbudding, the other form of minor pruning, is the removal of flower or leaf buds while they are still tight and undeveloped. It requires a knowledge of rhododendron blooming and growth habits.

On a very young shrub, terminal leaf buds are "taken" in spring to force the plant to develop a rounded shape. (The terminal leaf bud is thinner and pointier than the fat, terminal flower bud.) Exceptionally good late-summer weather may force a more mature shrub to form two, three or even four flower buds at the branch terminals.

All but one of these flower buds should be taken since the plant presents an unattractive appearance if allowed to develop and flower. The blooms will be small and puny. It is far better to force a single flower bud to magnificent bloom at each apex.

From time to time a grafted rhododendron will sucker—that is, it will develop green shoots below the graft. They can be recognized by the difference in the leaf shape of the under-stock and grafted variety. Suckers should be chopped out with a sharp spade. Merely cutting them back will only cause them to return with renewed vigor.

Selected varieties of azaleas and dogwood blend to brighten a Maytime landscape.

Gottscho-Schleisner

Azaleas for May Color

DAVID G. LEACH

FEW shrubs grace gardens with greater distinction than the azaleas. So many new varieties have been introduced that the gardener may have a difficult time making a selection.

Of the two types of azaleas, persistent-leaved (evergreen) and those that lose their leaves (deciduous) in the fall, the persistent-leaved are the more popular wherever the climate allows their cultivation. Many landscape architects feel that they are too widely planted, especially when the suburbs break out each spring in a harsh rash of violent color.

The introduction of the Glenn Dale hybrids by the United States Department of Agriculture twenty years ago promised relief from the standardized blobs of raw color. Most landscapers thought that the older sorts would be replaced by the government-sponsored introductions with their range of much clearer, softer and more subtle shades. But the stream of Glenn Dale novelties became a flood of almost 500 different hybrids, many of them not hardy in the North. The effort of isolating those that were both hardy and good defeated their popularity in colder climates.

In the course of the last several years some varieties have emerged from the long roster of Glenn Dale hybrids as the hardiest in this large group. Northern gardeners who seek finer color and larger flowers in persistent-leaved azaleas will welcome these newer sorts:

Sebastian, with rose hose-in-hose flowers, blooms in early April; Trouper, nopal red, mid-April; and Aphrodite, free-blooming pale rose-pink, late April. Also blooming in late April are Daphnis, Tyrian pink; Illusion, deep rose-pink, blotched, low grower; and Rosette, four-inch-wide light purple double flowers. Glacier, with three-inch-wide white flowers, and Treasure, with pale pink buds opening to white flowers, four and one-half inches across, are of phenomenal quality. In late April the shrubs form great snowbanks of massed blossoms.

Continuing the succession of bloom are these fine Glenn Dale hybrids: Nerissa, brilliant deep rose-pink, yellow overlay, early May; Gaiety, pale rose-pink, blotched rose-red, early May; Anthem, rose-pink, mid-May; Delos, floriferous double rose-pink, mid-May; and Manhattan, amaranth pink, darker blotch, late May.

It is hard to define the exact hardiness limit of these Glenn Dale azaleas. They are hardier in well-drained sandy soil than in heavy soil. Most specialists consider them to be satisfactory in southern Pennsylvania, southern New Jersey, on Long Island and along the coast well into New England. The azaleas are hardier when planted with a northern exposure, sheltered toward the south, than in an open situation. Older specimens are hardier than small young plants.

The Gable hybrids are an entirely different race of persistent-leaved azaleas, emphatically hardier than any of the Glenn Dales. Here again an extensive list confronts the uninitiated, but in recent years five clones have come to be almost universally regarded as both superior and hardy: Springtime, a lively pink, probably the hardiest Gable hybrid; Louise Gable, smooth salmon-pink, semi-double; Stewartstonian, clear bright red; Rose Greeley, white; and Big Joe, lilac.

For the ultimate in hardiness, there are the azaleas developed by nurseryman Orlando Pride in the severe climate of Butler, Pennsylvania. They are not quite the equal of the Gable hybrids in quality and color range, but they can be successfully grown in regions designated as Hardiness Zone 5, a remarkable northward leap in the cultivation of persistent-leaved azaleas.

The new Pride hybrids are only sparingly available as named clones, but seedlings in pink shades are more freely sold. They bring to all but the very coldest parts of the Northeast the eye-catching drama of azalea color in springtime.

The Exbury and Knap Hill hybrids from England are still the best of the deciduous azaleas. Only the deciduous azaleas have a flower color range that includes yellow, and only they can provide the marvelous pastel range of subtle shades, the electric scarlets devoid of any trace of blue, immense flowers in coral and shrimp

Yodogawa azalea blooms with the daffodils.

Gottscho-Schleisner

pink. Moreover, the blooms often are fragrant and may be ruffled and fluted as well. The English imports have elevated these attractions to an entirely new standard of excellence.

Fanciers delight in the new English hybrids for their great improvement over the coarse, short-lived Mollis hybrids that have dominated nursery lists for generations. But here again the offerings are overly large in number.

The following new English introductions rate a resounding vote of approval: Old Gold, unique deep yellow shade, flushed orange; Orange Ade, soft orange; Satan, clear, vivid scarlet; Persil, white; Toucan, cream, fading white, very large; Cecile, enormous pale pink blooms flushed deep pink; and Sunset Boulevard, luminous clear pink. Also excellent are Honeysuckle, cream, faintly brushed pink; Strawberry Ice, a distinctive shade of salmon-pink; and Princess Royal, ivory, flushed pink with yellow blotch.

In the orange-to-red color range, the latest hybrids on the market, the Ilam strain from New Zealand, are the finest for American gardening conditions because of their heavier flower substance. They are more durable in the atmospheric aridity of our Eastern springs.

The blossoms of the Ilam hybrids are even larger than those of the British azaleas. Many of them are fluted and ruffled, and most of them are fragrant. Some bloom as late as the middle of June. This author's selections, Canterbury and Maori, both orange, are available, as is an early-blooming red, Spring Salvo. A selection made in New Zealand, Red Letter, is outstanding. A New Jersey nurseryman has introduced the author's Copper Cloud, Orange Ball, Sunrise and Supreme, all orange, and the latter two frilled. There are no exotic and unusual color blends among the Ilam hybrids, but in their sharply limited range they are the best deciduous azalea cultivars yet produced.

Most of the Exbury and Knap Hill azaleas appear to be winter-hardy almost anywhere in the Northeastern United States. It will take a few years to determine which are best suited in flower substance and in vigor to our hot Eastern springs and summers. In the meantime, the above list provides startling innovations in flower color and form for gardeners interested in the good, the new and the different.

Camellias Up North

RICHARD THOMSON

It is a curious fact that when the average gardener considers climatic zones he tends to think in a north-south direction only. His is a mental picture of east-to-west areas of equal low temperatures with hardiness zone lines running horizontally from coast to coast and with decreases in temperature as one moves in a northerly direction.

This is an incorrect simplification, for massive topographic features and closeness to great bodies of water make tremendous differences in an east-west direction. Here on the Atlantic Coast, which is warmed by the oceanic breezes, many "southern" plants would not thrive a few hundred miles inland, but they will grow on the coast without undue difficulty.

Certainly the most spectacular of these "southern" ornamentals is *Camellia japonica*. Anyone who has visited the great southern gardens has come away green with envy at the sight of these great plants covered with early spring bloom. Even without flowers, the plants are magnificent. The deep green glossy foliage and the symmetrical plant habit benefit any garden. The blooms in all colors save yellow and blue rival the rose. All in all, *Camellia japonica* is one of the most magnificent flowering shrubs available in the United States.

Outside of the Deep South, the area of success for camellias passes somewhat west of Washington, D.C., swings northeast along the coast in an ever-narrowing band, cuts just west of Philadelphia and New York, and feathers out into the Atlantic south of Boston, including most of Cape Cod. In this narrow but extensive strip, many ornamentals which we normally consider suitable for growing from Norfolk south may be grown with success nine winters out of ten.

Those of us who are of an experimental frame of mind have tried many varieties of camellia in the coastal zone referred to with variable success. After many years of trial, certain varieties have proved to be

Selected hardy varieties of camellias will endure moderate northern winters if they are provided with a sheltered site or a windbreak.   *Gottscho-Schleisner*

good in areas where minimum temperatures rarely fall below zero degrees.

The relative hardiness of camellias varies greatly from variety to variety. In the Deep South, some camellias begin to bloom in the early fall, others in midwinter, and some in early spring. Generally, the peak bloom period of a variety will not last longer than three to four weeks, but with a selection of early, mid-season and late bloomers, the southern gardener may prolong his camellia season through most of the winter.

We northerners are not so lucky, for those varieties which are early and mid-season in the South will mature bloom buds too soon for severe winters. So gardeners in the North must choose varieties which are late-season in the South. These varieties will bloom about the same time as tulips and daffodils.

The buds withstand our winters without damage nine times out of ten. That tenth winter will probably damage most of the buds and bloom will be sparse, but such a percentage in our favor makes the chance well worthwhile. In any case, the plants will suffer only minimal damage even in an extraordinarily cold spell.

As with any of the broadleaved evergreens, camellia planting and siting are of paramount importance. The plants should be placed where they receive relatively little winter sun. This can be accomplished with a north or northwest exposure. Plant reasonably close to any lime-free house foundation. This provides additional protection against sudden warming by winter sunshine on cold days.

The same rule governs the siting of any of the less hardy hybrid rhododendrons, and camellias assort well with them. I have had success in planting camellias under open shade provided by hemlocks and pines. These trees not only give the sort of winter sun protection needed, but they also provide a natural acid soil situation from falling· and decaying needles.

Camellias need the same soil that all other broadleaved evergreens require. I have seen more attempts with camellias in this area fail because of faulty planting than from any other cause.

Usually camellia plants are purchased either in cans or as balled-and-burlapped specimens. The planting hole must be prepared more shallow than the root ball so that the root ball will be about one-sixth above the ground level and will not settle any deeper after planting.

The hole should be twice the diameter of the ball, and the soil mixed half and half with peat moss or similar acid fibrous material. After planting and copious watering, the exposed top of the ball should be covered with several inches of the half-and-half mix. Then the entire area is mulched with peat.

Watering after planting is essential and must be regularly attended to. In my opinion, early spring is the best time to plant new camellias, but others have been successful with late summer planting. After several months the area should be lightly fertilized with any of the prepared acid-plant or azalea-rhododendron mixtures.

I have grown almost forty *Camellia japonica* varieties over a period of about twenty years. My suggestions as to varieties include only those which have proved out over a period of at least fifteen years. They have survived temperatures of at least –5 degrees without important damage. None of the double formal blooms are included, for they seem to be somewhat less bud-hardy than the others. Also, none of the *Camellia sasanqua* varieties are included, for they seem generally less cold-resistant than the suggested *japonicas*. Here are my recommendations:

White—Leucantha

Pink—Bernice Boddy (hardiest of all), Marjorie Magnificent, Doctor Tinsley

Light Red—Chandler Elegans, Lady Vansittart, Monarch

Variegated—Ville de Nantes, T. K. Variegated

Hollies for the Northeast

WILLIAM F. KOSAR

EVERGREEN hollies are valuable plants for landscaping. If they are selected carefully as to hardiness and growth characteristics, Northeastern gardeners can appreciate their decorative effects. Many kinds are available which have variation in texture, growth habit and ultimate size. Glossy foliage and fruits are additional attractions.

An interesting texture pattern of evergreen foliage is formed by contrasting Japanese holly, pyracantha and azaleas. Pachysandra forms a leafy border.

Landscape by William A. Rutherford; Gottscho-Schleisner

Most hollies are partial to acid soil, preferring a pH range of 5.5 to 6. A well-drained sandy loam to which plenty of organic matter has been added is conducive to growth. The roots prefer an undisturbed, cool, moist environment which can be provided by a mulch of German peat moss, oak leaves, wood chips, or similar acid-producing material. Hollies, like other broadleaved evergreens, should not be planted in exposed, windy locations.

The cold-hardiness of hollies varies with species and even with individuals of a single species. When winter injury occurs, it may be evident in various parts of the plants (leaves, twigs, stems, roots or flower buds).

Whenever a holly plant's late summer growth has not hardened sufficiently, leaf or twig damage results. During a severe winter the ground may be frozen deeply enough to prevent absorption of water. If this should occur in combination with winds, desiccation and loss of the entire plant often results.

Some species of holly produce their flowers on the previous season's growth; therefore, the flower buds are exposed to the rigors of winter. In some cases, no berries are produced as a result of cold injury of the flower buds. Other causes of poor fruiting may be injury to early-flowering species by either late-spring frosts or inactivity of pollinating insects during cold weather.

In selecting a cultivated variety to produce a specific landscape effect, the gardener should choose one adapted to the soil and climate of his area. Native species are the safest to use, but often they lack the desired landscape quality. Many cultivars of the native American holly (*Ilex opaca*) have been selected from Northern nursery sources.

American holly is classified as a tree, so this precludes its use in foundation plantings. Where room permits, its use as a clipped hedge, specimen or background planting is feasible. The red-berried female hollies also are a source of Christmas greens.

Other holly species useful in landscapes have been introduced into this country. English holly (*I. aquifolium*) includes some cultivars which are proving satisfactory in the Northeast. These include a few of the original European introductions and several of seedling origin in this country. The hardy types were selected from seedlings grown in Pennsylvania, New York and Massachusetts.

Spiny American holly and smooth-leaved Japanese holly show contrast.

Molly Adams

More recently some of the Pacific Northwest holly selections are being tested. English holly is generally grown as a large shrub or small tree. The foliage and fruit are more attractive than those of the native American holly, although its landscape use is similar.

An introduction from eastern China, the Chinese holly (*I. cornuta*) is noted for compact growth, lustrous leaves and red berries. It is a large shrub and considered tender for the Northeast, but it has been grown successfully in sheltered locations in Boston and on Long Island. The species has sharp spines, but among its variants is an entire-leaved selection, Burford, which is a valuable plant south of Philadelphia. Peculiarly, Burford is considered slightly hardier than the species as a whole.

The most important species for landscaping is Japanese holly (*I. crenata*). It is good for general use in foundation plantings, for hedges and as a background for a perennial planting.

This holly will eventually grow into a large shrub, but it can be pruned to smaller proportions. It is small-leaved, spineless and black-fruited. Japanese holly is an inherently compact grower. It thrives equally well in sun or shade and has few insect pests or diseases. There are many variations in leaf pattern, plant habit, rate of growth and hardiness.

Many excellent dwarfs such as Green Island, Heller, Kingsville and Kingsville Green Cushion are available. An upright, small-leaved, hardy form is known as Microphylla. Another hardy form with shiny, convex leaves and a mound-shaped habit of growth is named Convexa.

I. crenata convexa is used as a substitute for boxwood in the New England states. With proper selection of cultivars and judicious pruning, the Japanese holly may be used with good effects in many situations where a broadleaved evergreen is desired.

In addition to the four major evergreen species (*I. opaca, I. aquifolium, I. cornuta,* and *I. crenata*) there are other species or hybrids of more recent origin which are available, but not plentifully.

The hardiest of the evergreen hollies is a native black-berried, stoloniferous holly called Inkberry (*I. glabra*). The leaves are small and are without spines.

A slow-growing compact form named Compact Inkberry may be the hardiest. This should be a good plant to use as a small hedge or within a foundation planting.

Before buying a hardy type of holly, it is wise to consult a local nurseryman who grows his own stock and is familiar with the requirements of the various kinds. It also is recommended that arboretums, botanic gardens and parks that are within the gardener's own climatic zone be consulted about the hardiness of a holly species.

Plants to Attract the Birds

BARBARA B. PAINE

THERE are many hardy, appealing plants that will invite birds to the garden with bright berries and nesting sites.

Top honors go to the Japanese flowering crabapple (*Malus floribunda*). All small-fruited crabapples provide excellent bird fare

(97)

and they have the additional merits of being decorative for at least two seasons. Also high on the list are the carmine crabapple (*M. atrosanguinea*) and Adam's crabapple (*M. zumi adamsi*).

Other good small trees are the Washington hawthorn (*Crataegus phaenopyrum*), European mountain ash (*Sorbus aucuparia*) and flowering dogwood (*Cornus florida*), each chosen from a genus well known for its popularity with birds. The Washington thorn is especially attractive to winter finches like pine grosbeaks and purple finches, and the mountain ash draws cedar waxwings, catbirds and

Birds can be attracted to a property if they have the shelter of near-by trees for a lookout and the fruits of berried shrubs for winter feed. A windowsill feeder, located where the birds can see it easily, will also attract them during the cold months.

Landscape by Alice Dustan Koller; Molly Adams

robins. Fruits of the various dogwoods are eaten by at least eighty-six kinds of birds.

It has been said that if a gardener could choose only one tree to make his land attractive to birds, he would certainly plant a mulberry. The Russian mulberry (*Morus alba tatarica*) is especially worth while, except for the nuisance of fallen fruits.

Among the shrub selections, old reliable Japanese barberry (*Berberis thunbergi*) is ideal. It offers food when it is needed most—during the winter and early spring—and good cover all year round.

Three viburnums are suggested—arrowwood (*Viburnum dentatum*), nannyberry (*V. lentago*) and American cranberry bush (*V. trilobum*). All can stand considerable shade, and between them they probably attract several dozen kinds of birds. Arrowwood is thought to be the favorite of the birds, but the brilliant red fruits of the American cranberry bush make it the most decorative.

Since shrub dogwoods are as popular with both birds and gardeners as their larger-sized relatives, two species are included: Siberian dogwood (*Cornus alba*) and gray dogwood (*C. racemosa paniculata*). So, too, with the honeysuckles. Of the many varieties available that attract birds, the red tatarian honeysuckle (*Lonicera tatarica sibirica*) is first choice. A new dwarf species (*L. ruprechtiana* H. V. Clavey Dwarf) looks promising for small home sites.

One unusual suggestion is golden St. Johnswort (*Hypericum frondosum*). It has delightful yellow flowers in the spring and seeds which attract juncos and tree and other sparrows during the winter. Another is northern bayberry (*Myrica pennsylvanica*), which grows as well inland as on the seashore.

Evergreens are important for winter interest and wildlife cover. Over fifty kinds of birds eat the fruits of the red cedar (*Juniperus virginiana*) and many nest in its dense, sheltering foliage. The seeds of the Canada hemlock (*Tsuga canadensis*) are eaten by chickadees, nuthatches, juncos, several sparrows and the winter finches like pine siskins and the grosbeaks.

While special plants undoubtedly attract birds, there is no guarantee that they will do so in a particular garden. For instance, no matter how densely planted with dogwoods and honeysuckles, city gardens are not popular with birds except in the migrating seasons.

A Home Nursery

F. F. ROCKWELL

THE new home owner with a limited budget for landscaping often puts off to the last the purchases that should be made first. If a home nursery were started even before the family actually moved to the new property, money could be saved and a supply of sturdy plants assured.

Even those with little gardening experience can have a plant nursery. No more gardening know-how is required to plant and care for a few young evergreens, trees and shrubs than to grow most annual flowers and vegetables. In fact, with few exceptions, it is easier to grow trees than flowers.

As to the space required, a very small nursery plot—ten feet wide by fifteen or twenty feet long—will accommodate a surprising number of small evergreens and trees. There will even be space for a collection of perennials for propagating, such as iris, daylilies, phlox and chrysanthemums.

Evergreens are a good example of what may be achieved with a home nursery. They may be bought as seedlings or transplants. Seedlings are usually two to four years old and cost five to ten cents each for common species such as Scotch pine, white pine and most spruces. Hemlocks are slightly higher. At these prices, the minimum order from commercial nurseries is usually fifty of a kind, which is more than the average home owner would have use for unless the plants are for hedges. But usually a neighbor or two will be glad to share the order.

Transplants are older than seedlings and have been transplanted once in the nursery. Transplants cost about twice as much as seedlings.

In three to five years these little trees will grow into sizable specimens. They require no care except weeding and watering.

Shrubs, of course, are much less expensive than trees. Nevertheless a shrub border of any size is expensive. Small-sized plants of most shrub species, after one or two years in the home nursery, will be ready to provide an immediate effect when shifted to the garden.

The small area set aside for the home nursery should have good, well-drained soil which has been thoroughly prepared (dug at least one foot deep). Work a generous amount of manure into the soil. Lacking that, turn under a three-inch layer of peat moss, plus balanced fertilizer.

The nursery site should get at least half a day of sun. Equally important is an ample and convenient supply of water, for vigorous growth cannot be expected under drought conditions. Mulching is advisable for most plants. Great care should be exercised with labels, too, for plant names are easily forgotten in a year or two.

One thing more: Buy plants from a reliable dealer. Often they may be procured from a local nursery, although a wider selection of species and varieties may be available from the mail-order firms that specialize in seedlings and transplants (and rooted cuttings) at wholesale.

Trees with Character

DAVID H. ENGEL

WIDE expanses of glass in modern houses bring more of the garden into view. It is important, then, that trees and shrubs have interesting character, especially during winter when many plants are leafless. Specimen plants of unusual form are sometimes called living sculpture.

The idea that plants are living sculpture is not new. The exquisite boxwood topiary of formal English and French gardens are sculptural forms, although they do not relate to the natural appearance of the plant. Topiary is considered as a block of living material to be sheared in whatever shape fancy dictates.

Specimen trees and shrubs are permitted to grow in their natural forms. They are valued as specimens, however, for their flowers or foliage or for the shade they provide. But in the Orient, where beauty of line is emphasized more than mass, a plant is valued for its bare structure and the lines of its branches.

In some plants the sculptural quality of the structure is natural and "built-in," so that only light pruning is needed to maintain the lines. Typical examples are Harry Lauder's walking stick (*Corylus avellana contorta*), Hankow corkscrew willow (*Salix matsudana tortuosa*), silk tree (*Albizzia*), umbrella pine (*Pinus*), Japanese maple, nandina and beach plum. Other plants, with lines hidden by masses of foliage and wood, require severe pruning and a perceptive eye that can see through excess underbrush.

Sometimes nature, in the form of wind, drought, lightning, snow, hail, arrested disease, rugged terrain or old age, does the drastic shaping. The result may be a bent pine on a seacoast or rocky mountainside, a straggling line of gnarled old black willows along a stream bed or a worn-out apple tree in an overgrown orchard. Their beauty is in their structure, a structure which symbolizes the strength they have developed to survive.

Unfortunately such natural sculptured forms are rarely found ready-made in a garden. The gardener, therefore, must either collect them from the wild or buy nursery plants that have possibilities of development. Before the final effect is achieved, the pruning shears will have to be used to reveal the plant's true character. Throughout the life of the plant the gardener-as-artist must guide growth to preserve an ideal proportion and scale of parts.

In selecting a plant for living sculpture, it is better to choose one that is slow growing and that already has an interesting basic structure. Taste must guide selection, too. It is not merely a question of finding a plant with the most erratic or grotesque habit or complex system of branching. Look for a plant that already has achieved an interesting or finished sculptured form through the forces of nature, or one that can be pruned to show simple strength, rhythmic flow of lines, asymmetrical balance or delicate tracery.

In addition to trees already mentioned, others that are adaptable to selective pruning are pines, dogwoods, flowering crabapples and

A gnarled, windswept pine is a handsome focal point for the foundation planting of a ranch-style home. *John Bickel*

hawthorns. Shrub possibilities include some euonymus varieties, Japanese holly (*Ilex crenata*), mountain laurel, huckleberry, Japanese andromeda (*Pieris*), Ibota privet (*Ligustrum ibota*), firethorn (*Pyracantha*) and Siebold viburnum.

Size must be considered first in placing the plant in the garden. What is its scale in relationship to adjacent buildings, walls, fences and plants? Color and texture of the background must also be taken into account so that the plant is displayed to best effect. Trees and shrubs with dark-colored bark and foliage should have a background of light-colored material, and vice versa. In the same way, plants of complex or intricate branching should have a plain background.

Sometimes a better effect can be achieved by grouping trees or shrubs of the same species if they appear too weak or insignificant standing alone. Or a plant may form a composition with a rock arrangement or piece of sculpture. The final criterion is that the plant be so much a part of the over-all garden composition that it looks as though it had been there from the very beginning.

A Few Unusual Narrow-leaved Trees

CLARENCE E. LEWIS

THERE are many unusual narrow-leaved evergreens that can add distinction to the home property. Although some of these plants may not be generally available in nurseries, they are worth a bit of searching.

The true cedars deserve greater use in landscaping. Three species are especially recommended—the Atlas cedar (*Cedrus atlantica*), historic cedar of Lebanon (*C. libani*), and the deodar cedar (*C. deo-*

dara). The Atlas cedar is the hardiest and most easily obtainable of the three.

The blue variety of Atlas cedar (*C. atlantica glauca*), has excellent silver blue, needlelike leaves. It will reach a height of twenty-five feet in about thirty-five years.

The green-needled Atlas cedar and cedar of Lebanon are similar in appearance. They are both branched laterally and make interesting focal points for almost any lawn. Deodar cedar has a looser but very attractive habit, with longer gray needles than the other two cedar species. However, it is not completely hardy in Northern climates unless partially protected from prevailing winds. It, too, has a blue-leaved variety that is hardier than the species.

Cedars can be successfully transplanted, although they become increasingly more difficult to move as they grow larger. Good soil drainage is a must for best growth. True cedars are not inexpensive, but they will give the gardener the satisfaction of having top-quality plant material.

An unusual evergreen from Japan that has been in cultivation for about 100 years is the Japanese cryptomeria. This narrow columnar tree attains a height of forty feet around New York City but it may grow to a 100 or more feet in Japan. The foliage resembles that of the big redwood (*Sequoia gigantea*) of California. From a distance the branches and branchlets present a clumplike appearance which is different from that of any other narrow-leaved evergreen.

The red-brown bark of Japanese cryptomeria is somewhat shreddy, adding to the unusual appearance of this somewhat droopy, whip-branched tree. When young it has good density, but with maturity a partial openness develops, although it is not objectionable. A slightly hardier and more clumpy variety is the Lobb cryptomeria. A slow-growing dwarf form is listed as *Cryptomeria japonica nana*.

A narrow-leaved evergreen that in no way resembles any other is the umbrella pine (*Sciadopitys verticillata*). The long, dark green fleshy leaves radiate out at the tips of branches like the stays of an umbrella. This narrow pyramidal tree is seldom taller than twenty-five feet in this country, but will reach 100 feet or more in its native Japan. The umbrella pine has no serious insect or disease problems. In the winter, when planted in shade, the tree's long straplike needles become almost black-green.

An interesting true pine is the bristle-cone pine (*Pinus aristata*), which is slow growing with curved, whiplike branches. It can be grown in a planter or tub. Other pines worth investigating are the lateral-branched, blue form of the Japanese white pine (*Pinus parviflora glauca*), which is suitable for a terrace. The blue-green loose-needled Himalayan pine (*P. griffithi*) has lateral but graceful branching. The lace-bark pine (*P. burgeana*) also is showy. Its mottled bark develops green and tan tones, becoming almost white as the tree matures.

The Spanish fir (*Abies pinsapo*) has radial needles that look as though they were filled with water. Its blue variety also is attractive. These trees are recommended for larger properties rather than for the average home grounds. A spruce that has extremely sharp-pointed, long radial needles is the tiger-tail spruce (*Picea polita*).

The cone-bearing trees that have no leaves during the winter are the dawn redwood (*Metasequoia glyptostroboides*) and the golden larch (*Pseudolarix amabilis*). Dawn redwood was known only as a fossil for many years, but in the mid-forties it was discovered in the northeastern Hupeh Province of China. It is now sold by several nurseries. The tree is quite hardy; the foliage resembles that of our Southern bald cypress.

A large horizontally branched tree, the golden larch has beautiful leaves that turn yellow in early fall. The new leaves that appear in spring are a fresh rich green.

Small Trees with Flowers

ROBERT B. CLARK

SMALL flowering trees are ideally suited to the average-sized suburban property. If they are placed properly and selected wisely, they can provide bright accents of seasonal bloom during late winter, spring, summer and even early fall.

A few warm days in March will bring out the yellow flower clusters of the Cornelian cherry (*Cornus mas*). If the weather remains cool, the flowers last for about a month, a display that is more subtle than the bright, sometimes garish forsythia.

The Cornelian cherry's shrublike tendency can be overcome if the young plant is trained to one or two stems. Then it will develop into a tree form and grow twelve to fifteen feet tall.

The foliage of this dogwood species is neat, smooth-margined and dark glossy green. In July, short-stemmed cherrylike red fruits appear among the leaves but they are eaten quickly by birds. The red autumn foliage drops in October to reveal budded stems.

Another early-flowering, small tree is the Kobus magnolia from Japan. White-petaled, faintly scented flowers cover the gray, leafless branches in mid to late April. Hardy, this magnolia is at its best in an open spot. In a protected place the tree may bloom too early and the flowers would be browned by late frosts. The pink-flowered saucer magnolia (*M. soulangeana*) is later blooming.

For a shower of deep pink bloom when the grass is new, few small trees can equal the weeping Higan cherry (*Prunus subhirtella pendula*). The blossoms may be featured against the somber backdrop of spruce, pine or hemlock. This graceful tree will grow wherever peaches succeed. There is a double-flowering form which remains in bloom longer than the common type. Often rather washed-out pink forms are offered for sale and the gardener would do well to visit a reliable nursery when the trees are in bloom before ordering his own plants.

Amanogawa, which means "Milky Way," is a narrow columnar form of the oriental flowering cherry. The blooms are double, pale bluish. The smooth, red-toned bark and unfolding red leaves make an enchanting setting for them. Since this cherry has emphatic vertical lines, it can accentuate a grouping or be used instead of Lombardy poplars where space is limited.

A springtime snowstorm is suggested by the crabapples. There are many kinds, usually spreading in habit. They are of medium to low stature (fifteen to thirty feet tall), and white or pink in bloom. Commonest in the Eastern states is the Japanese flowering crab (*Malus floribunda*). New selections now are available including Katherine, a double white, and Dorothea, a double pink.

The loose, hanging clusters of the fringe tree appear during the warm summer months.

Gottscho-Schleisner

America's contribution to springtime beauty is the flowering dogwood (*Cornus florida*). The notched white showy bracts are abundant on the wide spreading branches. They last for about two weeks in early May, before the leaves appear. These trees rarely reach twenty feet in height.

The Japanese species (*C. kousa*) extends the dogwood blooming season well into June. The square-pointed flowers appear after the leaves have unfolded, creating a startling effect of summer snow above the bright green leaves.

Fragrant, feathery white clusters of flowers are featured in late May and early June by the white fringe tree (*Chionanthus virginicus*). The male blooms are showier. Like holly, the fringe tree requires pollination by the flowers of another tree in order to produce the olivelike berries which are deep blue, but not very showy. The foliage of the fringe tree is handsome but coarse, so the tree is best placed by itself.

With its ranks of fringed white petals that recall the shoulder

Japanese flowering dogwood is a dramatic tree which blooms in summer when the leaves are full.

Paul E. Genereux

ornaments of Civil War soldiers, the epaulette tree (*Pterostyrax hispida*) can be a conversation piece in any sheltered garden spot during late May. The fresh green foliage expands just as the pendant flower clusters appear. In July the fuzzy fruits develop.

Another attractive May-blooming member of the storax (styrax) family is the white-clustered silverbell tree (*Halesia carolina*). The branchlets of both trees bear shreddy bark.

Summer-blooming trees are few in number but three are notable: stewartia, sourwood and the Chinese scholar tree. The first two are native to the Southern Appalachian Mountains.

The mountain stewartia (*S. ovata*) bears cup-shaped white flowers a few at a time during July. Inside the glistening petals of each flower is a fringe of orange stamens. Glossy green leaves make a handsome setting for the blooms. The variety *S. ovata grandiflora*, called the showy stewartia, has larger flowers with purple stamens. An oriental species, *S. koreana*, has brown bark that flakes off to reveal green and pink inner bark. Stewartias often have several trunks. Since

(109)

stewartias come from Southern climates, they respond to a sheltered situation in Northern gardens.

A hardier Southerner is the sourwood or sorrel tree (*Oxydendrum arboreum*). It has peachlike foliage and lily-of-the-valleylike flowers. Flaring strings of white bell-like blooms appear at the tips of branches in midsummer. A display lasts for several weeks while the flowers change into straw-colored fruits that remain showy during the fall foliage season. Sourwood's autumn leaves rival those of sour gum or pepperidge in earliness and glory of color.

Summer heat and drought seem easier to take if there is a Chinese scholar tree (*Sophora japonica*) on the property. This medium-sized tree provides welcome shade and refreshing color with its shiny green foliage and clusters of pale yellow flowers. A member of the pea family, it thrives in hot dry situations. The scholar tree is the largest species of hardy flowering trees and one of the last to bloom.

Twelve Nearly Perfect Trees

RAYMOND P. KORBOBO

WHAT makes a tree perfect for the home property? Ideally, it should have a graceful appearance at all seasons, fine foliage, attractive flowers, good fall color, interesting bark, a strong branching habit, deep roots, resistance to ice and wind damage, and a wide tolerance of soils. In addition, the perfect tree should be free of insects and disease and withstand dry spells, severe winters and the rigors of transplanting.

Obviously, the gardener's dream tree does not exist. But there are an even dozen that, in my opinion, come extremely close to perfection.

The Chinese scholar tree (*Sophora japonica*) is a truly beautiful tree. It has more width than height and its branching habit resembles that of the elm. Foliage is refined, with many leaflets per leaf, and

A planting pocket left in the broad terrace paving provides space for a pin oak to shade the outdoor living area.

Landscape by William A. Rutherford; Gottscho-Schleisner

flowers appear in August. It is strong and practically free of insects and disease.

The pin oak (*Quercus palustris*) is a true veteran. In its favor are refined foliage, availability, ease of transplanting, rapid growth, good fall color, strong branching habit and tough wood. Pin oak is one of the best choices for wet soil. The scarlet oak (*Q. coccinea*) has identical virtues, plus another advantage: pruning is less of a chore.

Professional arborists can find a lively topic in the relative hardiness of the willow oak, an unusual, refined species. A safe hardiness limit would be an imaginary line from New York City through Easton, Pennsylvania. North of this line there is spotty evidence

(111)

that the tree is not reliably hardy. The growth pattern of the willow oak resembles that of the pin oak, while its foliage resembles that of the willow. The tree, at any age, is something to admire.

The ginkgo or maidenhair tree (*Ginkgo biloba*) is the perfect shade tree—with one exception. It refuses to become handsome in anything less than eighteen or twenty years. The form and fan-shaped foliage of this living fossil are unique. It is completely free of insects and disease. Gardeners should buy male plants only. The female forms are ugly ducklings, for their ripened fruits have an offensive odor that makes them unwelcome.

Sweet gum (*Liquidambar styraciflua*) is another fine shade tree that will do well in a wet location. The five-lobed leaves are star-shaped. In the fall their rich purples and reds are unmatched. Many plants tend to form a twin trunk, which is sometimes a needed break from the monotony of all perfectly straight trunks. If the sweet gum has a serious demerit, it would be seed burrs in the lawn. However, they create no problem if the lawn is raked clean in early spring.

Honey locust (*Gleditsia triacanthos inermis* Shademaster) is, except for the *Sophora*, perhaps the most graceful tree there is. Filtered shade is its strongest feature. At the present time, all of the honey locusts pose a possible insect control problem. Some are sus-

These three shade trees are suitable for small properties.

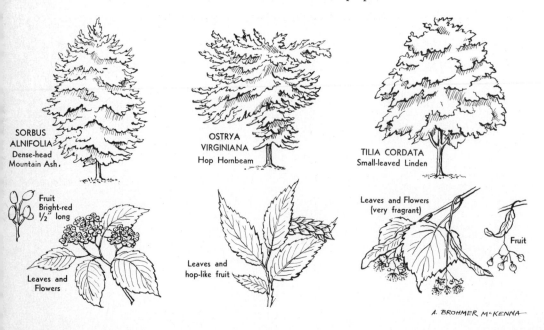

SORBUS ALNIFOLIA
Dense-head Mountain Ash.

Fruit Bright-red 1/2" long

Leaves and Flowers

OSTRYA VIRGINIANA
Hop Hornbeam

Leaves and hop-like fruit

TILIA CORDATA
Small-leaved Linden

Leaves and Flowers (very fragrant)

Fruit

A. BROHMER M^cKENNA

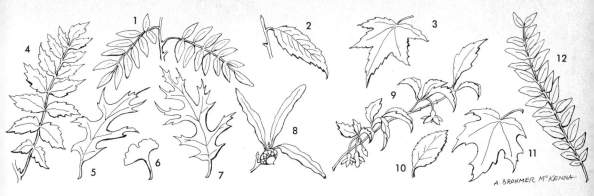

1. Chinese scholar tree; 2. American hornbeam; 3. Sweet gum; 4. Golden rain tree; 5. Pin oak; 6. Ginkgo; 7. Scarlet oak; 8. Willow oak; 9. Japanese silverbell; 10. Flowering crabapple; 11. Sugar maple; 12. Honey locust.

ceptible; some are not. In spite of this failing, I still feel it belongs among the best.

The maples almost missed this list. The troubles that accompany these trees could make a full-length article. However, the beautiful bark and breathtaking fall color of the sugar maple (*Acer saccharum*) forces me to include it.

Certain smaller trees belong on the dozen-best list. Some day Japanese silverbell (*Styrax japonica*) will rival the magnolias, crabapples and cherries in popularity. In early June the tree is almost covered with delicate, white, pendulous, bell-shaped flowers with clear yellow centers. It is fast growing, tolerant, strong and even does well in partial shade.

The golden rain tree (*Koelreuteria paniculata*) is a medium-sized tree with beautiful clusters of golden-yellow flowers in midsummer. Seed pods add interest for many more weeks. In the same height category are the flowering crabapples. The varieties are too numerous to mention—they are best inspected at first hand when trees are in bloom.

Rounding out the list is the American hornbeam (*Carpinus caroliniana*). Many people feel that if a small tree does not have conspicuous flowers, it is worthless. Here is a native of this area so tough and interesting that it needs no bright flowers to captivate gardeners. The American hornbeam, among small trees, comes as close to the ideal tree as *Sophora* does in the large tree group.

Nut Trees to Grow in the Suburbs

MAURICE BROOKS

NUT-BEARING trees, either native or introduced, are handsome accents for the home property. Some species are among the largest and most beautiful of the shade trees. Furthermore, the harvesting of nuts can be a lively autumn pastime for the family.

Deservedly the most popular of native Eastern nut trees is the black walnut (*Juglans nigra*). Its botanical range extends from Maine to Texas, although the tree reaches its best growth in the rich alluvial soils of the Ohio and Mississippi valleys. In the Northeast *J. nigra* will succeed in almost any fertile soil that is deep enough for its extensive taproot.

Black walnut is splendid as a lawn shade tree, if it has plenty of room to spread its crown. For reasons little understood, black walnut seems to inhibit the growth of certain other plants. For example, rhododendrons, azaleas or other members of the heath family should not be planted within the spread of black walnut roots. Under some conditions apple trees die if they are too closely associated with walnuts.

Many horticultural black walnut varieties now are being propagated. Of these, perhaps the best is Thomas. Over a long period of time it has proved to have more desirable characteristics over a wider geographical range and in more varied soils than any other variety. Thomas grows rapidly and vigorously. It begins bearing at an early age. The nuts are of superior flavor and have good cracking qualities. Stambaugh and Ohio are other superior varieties.

White walnut or butternut (*J. cinerea*) is another native tree of great value. It reaches its best growth somewhat farther north than does black walnut. Ordinarily, butternut does not reach the size of black walnut. *J. cinerea* produces particularly rich and flavorful nuts.

(114)

The shells are rather thick, and the kernels are difficult to remove. Established varieties include Sherwood and Buckley.

Introduced walnut species for Northeastern planting include Persian or English walnut (*J. regia*) and heartnut (*J. sieboldiana cordiformis*). Persian walnut succeeds as far north as southern New England, while heartnut thrives northward to southern Canada.

Persian walnuts are best planted on an experimental basis in the East. They prefer limestone soils and should be given sheltered locations. Heartnuts are much hardier; their flavor compares with butternuts.

Close relatives of the walnuts are the native hickories. The most popular species is the pecan (*Carya illinoensis*). The best Northern hickories are the shagbarks (*C. ovata*) and the shellbarks (*C. laciniosa*). Both species produce nuts of fine quality, although kernels are difficult to extract. Among the superior named varieties are Stratford, Glover and Fairbanks.

Pecans grow into attractive small trees as far north as Long Island, although they do not always produce crops. Major and Greenriver are good varieties for Northern plantings. Promising hybrids between pecans and Northern hickories, called "hicans," now are available.

The best available substitute for the vanished American chestnut is the blight-resistant Chinese chestnut (*Castanea mollissima*). This species is treelike southward, but often is shrubby north of the Middle Atlantic states. It produces nuts of good flavor and is an early bearer. Young trees require constant moisture during the growing season.

The American filbert or hazel (*Corylus americana*) is a hardy shrub that bears flavorful nuts. Crops are borne irregularly, however, and nuts are smaller than those of the European filbert (*C. avellana*). Many varieties of this introduced species have been tried in the Northeast, usually with indifferent success. Most filberts bloom too early for cold springs.

A superior American filbert, the Rush variety, has been used extensively to hybridize with European filberts. The most promising results of this hybridization is the Bixby variety, usually a reliable bearer of good nuts. Filberts are self-sterile and must be planted with other varieties if they are to produce crops.

Most nut-bearing trees have very long taproots and must, therefore, be planted in deep, well-drained soils. Abundant organic matter is a prerequisite for success. Since trees in good situations grow quite large, they must not be crowded.

Gardeners who plan to use a few nut trees in their home plantings should obtain named varieties from specialty nurseries. First costs will be higher, but results are almost certain to be better.

PART III

MAINLY FOR FLOWERS

PEOPLE EVERYWHERE respond to nature's most magnificent displays—the flowers—with their arrays of brightly colored petals in infinite designs. Few are the landscaped grounds that do not have some semblance of a flower bed. More likely than not, there are decorative arrangements of seasonal blooms everywhere that there is proper space.

The secret of the beautiful flower garden is discretion. Herbaceous plants should be selected with consideration of their cultural needs as well as their design. Flowers should complement other greenery. Those blooms that have seasonal appeal, like the early-flowering bulbs, should be put where they show to advantage.

Color is important to consider, too. Subtle variations in reds, blues and yellows occur within flower types and these should be matched with care or selected to contrast. Soil is another factor to be taken into account. Some plants like lilies prefer ideal soil conditions, while nasturtiums thrive anywhere with carefree abandon. Many flowers such as phlox are good companions, whereas regal roses are exclusive; they prefer a place in the sun all their own.

Plan Perennial Plantings with a Color Theme

BARBARA M. CAPEN

PLANNING a border of perennials takes time, but it is indispensable if the gardener wishes to avoid a hodge-podge of flowering periods and blossom colors. A good way to start is to read catalogue descriptions (especially the fine print) and to make notes on old favorite perennials as well as new varieties. From such notes the gardener can make a plant list that will be the start of a rough plan.

For a sound foundation, the list is started with the six perennials that are succession of bloom in a nutshell—iris, peonies, delphinium, platycodon, phlox and asters. Then each can be supplemented with

Black-eyed susans and phlox bloom freely along a rustic split-rail fence.

Gottscho-Schleisner

more perennials that have similar bloom periods. The "companions" of the basic six might be:

>   IRIS—pyrethrum, flax, columbine and wild Canadian phlox.
>   PEONIES—lupines, coralbells, peachleaved bellflower, early day-
>   lilies, rockrose and perennial foxglove.
>   DELPHINIUM—phlox Miss Lingard, Japanese iris, lythrum
>   and daylilies.
>   PLATYCODON—daylilies, Shasta daisies, Stoke's aster and
>   astilbe.
>   PHLOX—veronica (V. *longifolia subsessilis*), aster Wonder of
>   Staffa, helenium, heliopsis and globe thistle.
>   ASTER—early chrysanthemums and eupatorium (perennial
>   ageratum).

After the list has progressed this far it is time to think about the color scheme. For the average gardener the most satisfactory results will be obtained with a plan in which a single color dominates. In other words, it could be primarily a yellow border, a pink one (but with the salmon and rose shades well separated), a red border, a blue or even a white one. However, none of these plans needs to be dull. Flowers of contrasting and blending colors may be combined with the dominating color.

When the dominant color has been decided upon, the expanded plant list is corrected to include only the perennials that conform to the color scheme. For instance, if the border "theme" is to be pink, there should be no yellow, orange or scarlet flowers on the list. The plan should include only perennials in shades of pink, blue, lavender, purple or white (although a small amount of very pale yellow might be added for a bit of extra accent). Thus a typical list of basic plants and companions for a pink border might look like this:

>   IRIS (pink, purple)—pink pyrethrum, blue flax, pink, white and
>   blue columbine and lavender Canadian phlox.
>   PEONIES (pink, white, red)—pink, blue and white lupines,
>   rose coralbells, blue and white peachleaved bellflowers and
>   cream perennial foxglove.
>   DELPHINIUM (all shades)—white phlox Miss Lingard, white
>   and purple Japanese iris and pink lythrum.
>   PLATYCODON (blue, white)—white Shasta daisies, blue
>   Stoke's aster and pink and rose astilbe.

PHLOX (pink, white, crimson)—purple veronica, lavender aster
Wonder of Staffa and lavender globe thistle.

ASTER (pink, purple)—lavender perennial agerátum and pink
and white early chrysanthemums.

The named varieties of some of these perennials are then
selected and added to this pink border list. For instance, the pink
iris might be Harriet Thoreau or Chantilly if tall ones are needed at
the back of the border, or pink Ruffles if a lower one is needed nearer
the front of the border. For the purple variety, try Sable; it is a handsome dark iris. Storm King is a good medium purple.

There are many named varieties of peonies, so the choice is wide.
Myrtle Gentry and Therese are both good double pink kinds. For a
little variation a single peony could be added to the border; Mischief
is a handsome light pink.

Among the named varieties of Japanese iris, two superior whites
are Betty Holmes and White Giant. Pyramid and Purple Giant are
good purples. With Shasta daisies it is better to start with the single
varieties such as The Speaker and Edgebrook Giant.

Good astilbe varieties are Peachblossom, a light pink, and Gloria
Superba, a rose pink. There are many pink phlox, but my vote goes to
Daily Sketch, Lillian and Mies Copyn for this border. World Peace
is a tall phlox with large white trusses.

The chrysanthemums selected for this pink-theme border should
be the earliest blooming kinds. Thus their flowers will start to appear
while some of the other perennials are still blooming.

When the variety list is complete a rough plan of the bed or
border is worked out to determine how many plants will be needed.
With an ordinary ruler the plan can be laid out on paper. A border
six feet wide is most satisfactory.

First a space about one foot (use a scale of one inch equals one
foot) is marked off for edging plants at the front of the sketch. The
six key plants on the list are penciled in at varying intervals throughout the plot. Tall plants go toward the back (tall means height of
bloom not of foliage). Medium-height plants are arranged through
the middle of the plan. The low growing specimens go just behind
the edging. The spaces between plants are filled in with the other
perennials on the list.

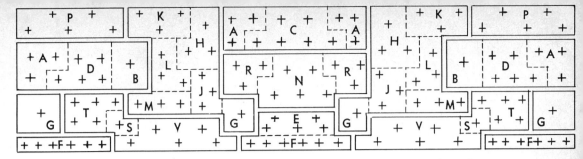

The plan is for a border 6 × 25 feet. Gardeners may choose either of two color schemes which will provide three continuous bloom periods.

Plan by Barbara M. Capen

KEY TO PERENNIAL BORDER

PINK

A. Peony, Seashell and Indiana Night
B. Oriental poppy, Purity
C. Lupine, white
D. Anchusa, Dropmore
E. Painted Daisy, E. M. Robinson
F. Coralbells
G. Peony, Seashell and Walter Faxon
H. Delphinium Belladonna hybrids
J. Phlox, Miss Lingard

K. Lythrum, Morden's Pink
L. Japanese iris, Betty Holmes
M. Peachleaved bellflower
N. Phlox, Daily Sketch
P. Lavender bee balm
R. Fragrant white plantain lily
S. Aster, Wonder of Staffa
T. Phlox, Lillian
V. Chrysanthemum, Powderpuff

YELLOW

A. Iris, Moonlight Madonna and
   Golden Majesty
B. White gasplant
C. Lupine, blue
D. Blue flax
E. Hybrid columbine
F. Coralbells
G. Peony, Kelways's Glorious and
   Primevere
H. *Campanula lactiflora coerulea*
J. Daylily, Modesty

K. Blue balloonflower
L. Japanese iris, Pyramid
M. Evening primrose, Young's
   variety
N. Phlox, World Peace
P. Globethistle
R. Helenium Riverton Beauty
S. Japanese speedwell
T. Phlox, Mia Ruys
V. Chrysanthemum, Golden Mound

Peonies are planted singly and should be allowed a space of eighteen to twenty-four inches in diameter in which to grow. All the other plants on this list should be planted in groups of at least three, some as many as five. They are spaced twelve to eighteen inches apart.

After the paper plan has been completed, it is time to consider which plants may be purchased and planted in the spring and which are best left until fall. Some plants may be raised from seed. Peonies and iris should be planted in the fall. The spaces that have been allotted to them on the plan can be filled in with annuals or summer-flowering bulbs for the first summer. Pyrethrum, flax, columbine,

(123)

lupines, bellflowers, foxgloves, delphiniums and Shasta daisies may be sown in late spring.

Old-fashioned Flowers

KENNETH MEYER

THE old-fashioned flowers that graced grandmother's garden have more than sentimental value. These plants of bygone days are extremely hardy and provide quality blooms. It would seem, therefore, that among the hybrids and newly introduced varieties some space could be left in the garden for a few of the old favorites—the stand-bys which have proved so satisfactory for many generations.

Bleeding heart has universal appeal. Every spring when the huge clumps are in bloom in my Maryland garden, visitors stop to enjoy them. The tall-growing *Dicentra spectabilis* and the lower growing *D. eximia* are both splendid for a sunny, sheltered spot. They thrive in deep rich soil. The clumps increase in size every year and can be counted on for a fine display each spring.

A pleasing effect can be had by planting Virginia bluebells (*Mertensia virginica*) among clumps of bleeding heart. They bloom about the same time, and the delicate blue flowers of the *Mertensia* are charming with the rosy pink pendants of bleeding hearts.

Sweet shrub prefers a moist location, although it can adapt to seemingly adverse conditions. The foliage and growth habit are not especially attractive, however, and so an out-of-the-way spot is preferred. Another species (*Calycanthus fertilis*) has much larger flowers, but they are not as fragrant as those of *C. floridus*, and are considerably lighter in color.

Another old favorite is lily of the valley. Its modest loveliness and simple grace have been enjoyed for centuries. In one of the earliest gardening books printed in English in 1568 the author refers to it as "a flower marvelous sweet, flourishing in the springtime, and growing properly in the woods."

(124)

Lily of the valley is useful for planting near a terrace or outdoor living room, since its exquisite fragrance is never cloying and may be enjoyed at close range. A particularly good location is on the north side of a house where there sometimes is a narrow border along a walk. Lily of the valley and ferns fill such a space admirably. A woodland plant by nature, it is quite at home growing among ferns. Such a planting can be left undisturbed for several years, except for an annual dressing of fine leafmold and a very light application of old and well-decayed manure.

Lilacs and mockoranges were taken for granted in most old gardens, and are still favorites. I have grown many hybrid lilacs and all the newer mockoranges. While some are superb, I have yet to find greater satisfaction than is to be had from the old-fashioned kinds. The flowers are not as spectacular, but they are usually more fragrant. They also have a simplicity and delicacy sometimes lacking in the newer varieties. Many varieties still may be found at nurseries specializing in these plants.

A well-grown and properly pruned specimen of old-fashioned white lilac in full bloom is something to remember. Its haunting fragrance quickens the memory and will often recall favorite scenes of bygone days.

Almost every garden of yesteryear had its clumps of early peonies. The fine old variety (*Paeonia officinalis rubra*) usually blooms well ahead of Memorial Day, even in Northern latitudes. The flowers are not as large as many of the present-day exhibition varieties, but they are long lasting and have a quiet beauty. The blossoms appear early, when vivid red is still a scarce color in the garden. A white form (*P. officinalis alba*) blooms about the same time and is useful for contrast.

Once established, peonies live for years and require very little attention. Work in a trowelful of bonemeal around each clump in early spring, and keep the soil loose so that spring rains can be absorbed readily.

Mignonette, with its dainty unassuming little flowers, usually was tucked away in a sunny corner of even the most modest plot. When growth is weak and of poor color, a generous application of lime will mend matters speedily. When cut back after the first burst of bloom, mignonette will bear a second crop of flowers. It will bloom satisfactorily until the end of summer. A good soaking in dry weather also is helpful.

Sweet william flowers when bloom is not too plentiful, and is excellent for cutting. It adds vivid color at a time when the garden has passed its peak. If grown from seed, the plants should be started in a coldframe or seed bed in late summer for bloom the following year.

All these plants, and many others, are rich in interest. There are tuberoses with their perfume on warm summer evenings, the simplicity of heartsease and sweet violets, the stimulating aroma of southernwood (*Artemisia abrotanum*), the spicy pinks and the bed of herbs with its apple-scented mint and fragrant sprays of sweet lavender.

Monochromatic Borders

ALICE R. IREYS

THERE are many unusual possibilities in arranging plantings with flowers of the same color. Perhaps white could be selected to brighten the terrace in the evening. Blue could give a cool effect to all or part of the perennial border and plantings of annuals.

A corner of a perennial border might be selected to give a constant succession of white flowers. In spring, candytuft (*Iberis sempervirens*) is followed by white coralbells (*Heuchera*) and late white tulips. Their place is leased for the summer by phlox Miss Lingard, regal lilies and white balloonflowers. The foliage of these plants blends well together and stands out against a tall yew hedge as background.

The phlox can be planted in a large clump of five or seven plants, with the lilies interplanted. The balloonflowers are placed in groups of four or five plants on each side. As the summer flowers fade, potted chrysanthemums of selected white varieties may be set in. Thus a small section of the perennial border can be attractively planted with white flowers.

LEFT: Petunias provide masses of blooms all summer long.   *Gottscho-Schleisner*

RIGHT: Soft-textured ageratum traces a path.

Gottscho-Schleisner

Equally delightful would be white-flowered annuals in a small garden just beneath a bedroom window or outside the dining room. There are many white flowers that are very fragrant.

The lovely edging plant sweet alyssum may be sown in place and will germinate in two weeks. Behind this, for medium height, use clusters of white petunias and masses of white geraniums. The stately spires of stock with its spicy fragrance, and the white, fragrant nicotiana will fill the evening air with a wonderful perfume.

For another possibility, a small garden area on a roof or adjacent to a terrace can be made attractive with foliage plants. Tuberous begonias have fine foliage and flowers.

Caladiums, the white, fancy-leaved variety, will also remain decorative all summer. The bulbs can be planted in pots and sunk into the ground or used in ceramic containers at the edge of a terrace. White-leaved coleus remains bushy if pinched back.

Blue flowers always have an air of coolness. In the perennial border the choice for early spring blues includes polemonium, *Phlox divaricata*, columbine and any number of the lovely new German iris. If a good summer effect is paramount, use the bluebells (*Campanulas*) in quantity. The low Carpathian bluebells make an excellent edging and the taller varieties of Canterbury bells can create a very effective picture in the center of the perennial bed.

There is nothing quite so stunning as well-grown delphiniums. While in many places it will be necessary to replant them each year, they are well worth the effort. *Echinops* or globe thistle is the third member of this blue group. It has large prickly leaves and the blue thistlelike balls will bloom for many weeks. For the fall, to carry out the scheme, plant monkshood and blue asters.

For the annual bed, use ageratum as an edging, behind which the spires of blue salvia will give a misty gray appearance. The common cornflower or bachelor's button makes a quick filler planting. For fragrance, use heliotrope and lavender, a perennial that gives emphasis to blue-flowered annuals.

For the terrace planting I would suggest plumbago as a ground-cover. Its bright blue flowers appear from July to frost. The funkia, *Hosta glauca*, is an excellent foliage plant to use either in sun or shade. Both leaves and flowers are attractive. Also valuable for a bold, one-color terrace treatment are blue-flowered hydrangeas.

Aromatic Shrubs, Herbs and Flowers

BARBARA M. CAPEN

A SWEET fragrance wafted on a summer breeze is so delightful, it is surprising how few gardeners plan for it for their own garden. They may enjoy the perfume of honeysuckle in a weedy woodlot or lilies of the valley naturalized on an old estate, but they forget that the extra dimension of scent can be added to any small terrace or porch garden.

Herbs might well form the nucleus of any aromatic planting. Both foliage and flowers can provide fragrance. With some plants fragrance is picked up by a passing breeze; with others leaves must be crushed first.

A bed three to four feet wide and ten to fifteen feet long is large enough for a summer full of fragrance. At the back of the bed two or three plants of southernwood (*Artemisia abrotanum*), two to three feet high and wide, will form a mass of finely cut, spicy gray-green foliage. Also at the back of the bed the beebalms—*Monarda didyma* with dark red flowers and M. *fistulosa* with lavender flowers—will provide both color and fragrant foliage.

In the middle of the bed several plants of English lavender (*Lavandula vera*) will form mounds of interesting gray foliage as well as the familiar lavender flowers. After flowers have faded, the foliage echoes their scent. Also in the middle of the bed a few plants of lemon balm (*Melissa officinalis*) will add a lemon-oil scent. Flowers are white and insignificant but the foliage is pleasant when crushed.

Either of the spicy santolinas, the gray *Santolina chamaecyparissus* or the green S. *virens*, makes an interesting edging. Both of these small plants, like lavender, are small evergreen shrubs. In severe winters the santolinas die back to the ground and grow back from the roots in summer. Along with the santolinas the common thyme (*Thymus vulgaris*) makes a foot-high edging of fine, dark green foliage. Though its fragrance, too, is airborne, it is far stronger when leaves are crushed.

In addition to these hardy herbs there are some less well-known tender ones which can be treated like annuals in colder climates, or they can be potted before frost and taken into the house for the winter. One of the most delightful is the pineapple sage (*Salvia rutilans*), which is not hardy north of Virginia. It grows into a tall shrub during the summer and late in the season produces delicate, red flowers about the same shade as the common red salvia. The rose-scented sage (S. *dorisi*) is even taller and coarser but it, too, has a delightful fragrance. Anyone who brushes against the plant with hand or clothes will be surprised at the strong perfume in the air.

There are several fragrant-leaved geraniums that are worth planting. The rose geranium is probably the best known. Several lemon-scented kinds are available, one with a large, finely cut leaf called

Skeletonleaf, and Prince Rupert, with small leaves. Another pleasant addition to the group is the velvety peppermint geranium.

All of these with the exception of Prince Rupert grow to be tall and spreading plants. They are perhaps best placed as underplanting for medium-sized shrubs rather than in a bed with more delicate-growing herbs. Usually geraniums are left in pots and pushed into the soil. Before setting out the plant, place gravel in the bottom of the hole to prevent a long root from attaching itself to the earth.

Lemon verbena is another popular fragrant herb. Since it grows tall and shrubby, it could go at the back of the bed near the beebalms. Rosemary, planted just in back of the edging, is not generally hardy. It may survive two or three winters in a protected place if the weather is mild but, if possible, it should be lifted and taken into the house for the winter. Where it is hardy it will produce light blue flowers early in summer, but it is worth growing for the pungent leaves alone.

The old-fashioned four-o'clock, with its faint lemon fragrance, is a terrace favorite. It tolerates semi-shade while another old-time flower, mignonette, does better in hot sun. The delicious sweetness of violets is unforgettable and gardeners use them for their intrinsic beauty as well.

A few regal and auratum lilies planted at the back of the bed and tuberoses near the front will provide additional fragrance during the summer. If *Daphne odora* is hardy, it is worth growing for the heavy perfume of the flowers in early spring. *D. cneorum*, which is hardier though sometimes temperamental, is also worth growing for its spring perfume. The fragrant viburnums, *Viburnum carlesi* and *V. burkwoodi*, could be planted in the corner of the bed for the fragrance of their flowers in May.

In a slightly moist place the swamp azalea will thrive and surprise everyone with its unusual cinnamon-scented flowers in July. *Clethra alnifolia*, the summersweet, also likes some moisture in the soil but it will grow under drier conditions than the azalea. Summersweet produces fragrant flowers in late July and early August.

The fragrant-foliaged shrubs are few compared to the perennials, but there are two worth growing. The young foliage of the sweetbrier rose (*Rosa eglanteria*) is as fragrant as any rose. The chaste tree (*Vitex agnus-castus*) has aromatic gray-green foliage. It produces spikes of lavender flowers in August that have the same fragrance as the foliage.

(130)

PLANTING MONTHS FOR BULBS

SEPTEMBER
- ACIDANTHERA
- ALLIUM
- BRODIAEA
- CHIONODOXA
- CROCUS
- ERANTHIS
- EREMURUS
- ERYTHRONIUM
- FRITILLARIA
- GALANTFLUS
- HYACINTH
- IXIOLIRION
- LEUCOJUM
- LYCORIS
- MUSCARI
- NARCISSUS
- ORNITHOGALUM
- OXALIS
- PUSCHKINIA
- SCILLA

OCTOBER
- BLACKBERRY LILY
- BULBOUS IRIS
- CAMASSIA
- CROCUS
- IXIA
- LILY
- TULIP

NOVEMBER
- LILY
- SPANISH IRIS
- TULIP

APRIL
- ANEMONE CORONARIA
- RANUNCULUS

MAY
- CALADIUM
- CALLA LILY
- DAHLIA
- GALTONIA
- GLADIOLUS
- ISMENE
- TIGRIDIA
- TUBEROSE
- TUBEROUS-ROOTED BEGONIA
- ZEPHYRANTHES

JULY
- GLADIOLUS

AUGUST
- AUTUMN CROCUS
- COLCHICUM
- LILIUM CANDIDUM
- STERNBERGIA

A Bulb Primer

ELDA HARING

HARDY bulbs are those that are planted in the fall to root and bloom in spring. Many multiply and persist for several years.

In the fall, garden centers feature hardy bulbs. Counters display photographs showing the variety and color. Mail-order catalogues also feature bulbs and describe their color, size of flower, height and cultural suggestions. Bargain bulbs prepackaged in mixed colors and offered at very low prices are seldom worth the money since only a small number of these bulbs will bloom the first year.

Generally, the large-flowered bulbs like daffodils and tulips are best used in flower beds or perennial borders. Daffodils also lend themselves to naturalizing in lightly wooded areas where wildflowers abound. Tulips, not so long-lived as daffodils, deserve a featured spot. Place them along walks, in solid beds or in small blocks throughout the perennial bed. Plant the fragrant, formal hyacinths in beds, along walks or in prim rows in front of foundation plantings.

Small bulbs—crocus, grape hyacinths, snowdrops and scillas—should be planted in small groups in rock gardens, in little nooks and crannies or under deciduous trees and shrubs. They are delightful around natural rock outcroppings. Most spring-blooming bulbs can be planted in full sun or in partial shade under deciduous trees. Even rather poor soils will produce good flowers, but top-quality bulbs warrant careful soil preparation.

The inexperienced gardener would do well to start with some of the well-established hardy bulb varieties. They are reasonably priced and available for early, mid-season or late-spring bloom.

Among the daffodils are early blooming King Alfred, Unsurpassable or Golden Harvest; for mid-season there are Mrs. R. O. Backhouse, the double Twink and John Evelyn. Good late-season daffodils are some of the *tazetta* or Poeticus types such as Geranium, Cheerfulness and Laurens Koster. Excellent rock garden species include the Hoop Petticoat (bulbocodium) and the *triandrus* hybrids. Thalia is a lovely species for late bloom.

My favorite tulips for early bloom are the *fosteriana* hybrids, of which Red Emperor is the best known. Other charming early tulips for use in the rock garden, under trees or in the shrub bed are the *kaufmanniana* or waterlily tulip, Fusilier and *Tulipa tarda*. In mid-season there are the double earlies and the *greigi* hybrids.

The peak of the tulip display in May features the Darwins and Darwin hybrids. Their flowers are large and held on long stems, with a color range through the whole spectrum. I would recommend deep purple Queen of the Night; white Zwanenburg; Flying Dutchman, a good rose-red; Princess Elizabeth, rosy-pink; Gudoshnik, creamy-peach; and Sunkist yellow. To climax the season, plant a few lily-flowered and late double tulips (also called peony-flowered) and the unusual Parrot tulips.

(132)

TOP LEFT: When planting tulips in rows, a ruler and string lines are helpful to keep bulbs even.   *Herman Gantner*

TOP RIGHT: Metal hoops are handy to keep clusters of tulip bulbs in place when setting out patterns.   *J. Horace McFarland*

BELOW: Tulip bulbs are planted in late October or early November for Maytime blossoms.   *Herman Gantner*

Hyacinths bloom early. Choose good-sized bulbs in whatever color suits the garden scheme. L'Innocence is a gorgeous white, Jan Bos is deep rosy-red, City of Haarlem is a pale yellow and Delft Blue is delicate.

Among the small bulbs, the first to bloom are winter aconite, a light yellow flower; *Iris reticulata*, with deep blue flowers; and the white snowdrops. Crocus, *Chionodoxa* and scillas also bloom early, followed by grape hyacinths and *Scilla campanulata*.

I like to fork the soil deeply and add peat moss or compost to the depth of two to three inches. Next I add bone meal at the rate of five pounds to 100 square feet and blend it thoroughly. When planting pockets of tulips or daffodils in perennial beds, dig an irregular hole adequate in size to accommodate the number of bulbs. Break up the soil in the bottom of the hole and sift in a handful of bone meal. Place bulbs with pointed end up. Most directions suggest planting tulips and daffodils six to eight inches deep. However, if they are to be overplanted with annuals, plant them at least ten inches deep. Space bulbs four to six inches apart in the hole and replace the soil, gently tamping to firm it.

To keep established bulbs growing well over a period of years, apply dry cow manure at the rate of five pounds per 100 square feet with a dusting of bone meal in late autumn. Some may prefer to apply a 5-10-5 commercial fertilizer at the same rate. Dried blood, high in nitrogen, is an excellent fertilizer for tulips and the small bulbs. Fertilizer can be applied again in early spring as the tips of the bulb foliage come through the soil. This application not only feeds the bulbs but also serves as a deer and rabbit repellent.

Mulching bulbs, while not essential, is good cultural practice. On new plantings do not mulch until hard freezes, because the purpose of the mulch is to keep the ground frozen. A year-round mulch inhibits weeds, conserves moisture and keeps foliage and flowers clean. Some good mulches to use are pine needles, buckwheat hulls or well-rotted sawdust. Personally, I favor pine or fir bark nuggets.

Although daffodils, tulips and hyacinths may be planted any time from September to December, the preferred time in the northern tier is about October 15. The small bulbs such as *Chionodoxa* and grape hyacinth deteriorate quickly and need a longer growing season for producing roots. These should be planted without delay, preferably in September, as soon as they are available.

When narcissus are naturalized in the lawn,
they provide spring cheer for many years.
Gottscho-Schleisner

Narcissus Are Cheerful

R. R. THOMASSON

Few garden flowers are more versatile than narcissus. They add touches of early color at the edges of borders and paths or in naturalistic settings. Some of the smaller varieties are ideal for the rockery. In the cutting garden, certain kinds of narcissus will furnish magnificent blooms for cheerful spring bouquets.

Narcissus are most spectacular in a mass planting, although many gardeners do not have a large enough area for a naturalized planting. But there usually is room for a few clumps grouped at the edge of the border. For this it is better to have one variety in one location. Some of the more desirable named varieties and species of narcissus can be purchased for $2 or $3 a dozen.

Recent introductions include Indian Summer, golden yellow with orange-scarlet cup; Chungking, rich golden yellow perianth with red cup; and Chinese White, broad, smooth, circular white perianth with suggestions of green in the small cup. I also grow Mahmoud, white with red crown, and Pepper, which has a deep yellow perianth and orange-red cup.

For a spectacular effect some people like to combine Red Emperor tulips with Unsurpassable daffodils. I prefer a more subdued pattern, such as a few clumps of Mount Hood daffodils in front of Spring Glory or Lynwood Gold forsythia. Clumps of daffodils also can be used with flowering crabapple and cherry trees. For an early effect the cyclamineus hybrid February Gold can be set out at the base of a clump of white birch.

Cheerfulness—either white or yellow—Beryl, Tenuior or one of

Assorted narcissus varieties can be naturalized along woodland paths.

Gottscho-Schleisner

the jonquil groups are appealing in combination with periwinkle. Try them also at the side of garden steps or along a brick or old stone wall.

Narcissus bulbs can be grouped at the base of a bird bath with iris for later effect. If the color of the bird bath is mossy green or tan, the white-flowered types are best. If the bird bath is gray or white, more colorful varieties such as Aranjuez or Scarlet Elegance will provide contrast.

For the cutting garden the possibilities are unlimited. Good white daffodils include Mount Hood, Beersheba and Roxane. Good yellow-flowered daffodils and other narcissus are Winter Gold, Fortune, Rembrandt, Carlton, John Evelyn, Gertie Millar and Dick Wellband. Of the numerous small-flowered narcissus, I like Cheerfulness, Trevithian, Thalia, Leprechaun, Cherie, Goldilocks, Topaz, Pencrebar and Golden Perfection. Fine *Narcissus tazetta* varieties include Geranium, Cragford and St. Agnes.

For bouquets in May be sure to plant the old Poeticus narcissus Pheasant's Eye, Laurens Koster, N. *tazetta* and N. *biflorus*. Other good late named varieties are Cheerfulness, Columbine, Dactyl, Cantabile, Cushendell, Frigid, Isola, Chinese White and Reprieve.

When considering narcissus for cut flowers, bear in mind that the jonquils have a delightful fragrance. One of the most popular varieties is Trevithian. It has about everything that one can ask for, including long stems. Other good jonquils are Golden Goblet, Golden Perfection and Goldilocks.

There are many small-flowered narcissus that are charming in the rock garden. The old white trumpet species N. *moschatus* is excellent. Other suitable species include N. *jonquila*, N. *odorus* and N. *tenuior*. The gardener also can choose some in the *triandrus* group, such as Thalia, Silver Chimes and Dawn.

Some varieties can be forced in pots to bloom indoors during winter. Good sorts are King Alfred, Golden Harvest, Magnificence, Rembrandt, Carlton, February Gold, March Sunshine, Orange Queen and Laurens Koster.

For the apartment dweller there are sorts that can be grown in pebbles and water. Of these Paperwhite, Grand Soleil d'Or and Cragford are the most popular. Never use chemically treated water. A few lumps of charcoal help to keep the water sweet.

Species Tulips

ALYS SUTCLIFFE

GARDENERS who want to add special brightness to their spring gardens should make ample provision for the species tulips. They are planted as soon as possible in early fall.

The species tulips are natives of West and Central Asia, Europe and North Africa. They are reliably hardy but, like other tulips, the bulbs of many of the larger species break up after flowering and tend to disappear.

Many of these tulips need a thorough baking in warm dry soil during their dormant period in summer. This is not always possible, particularly if the bulbs are near plants that need watering in summer. The little tulip bulbs can be dug up after flowering and put in the sun for several days, then stored until planting time in fall. This method would be impractical with large plantings but well worth while with special treasures. On the other hand, a few dollars spent each year on new bulbs will ensure success.

Species tulips flower earlier in spring than their larger relatives; this is one reason for their popularity. A small clump of the crocus tulip (*Tulipa pulchella*) or the yellow-flowered *T. biflora* blooming in a sheltered corner in March is enough to assure the most despondent gardener that spring is on the way.

All species tulips will grow better if planted in sunny places in well-drained gravelly soil. With a boulder or low-growing evergreen as a background, even two or three blooms of a species tulip will make a complete picture.

The small varieties make a wonderful addition to the already long list of small bulbs and iris which are the backbone of a rock garden. The taller ones are handsome along the edge of the perennial border.

A planting depth of two inches is recommended for the smaller bulbs, and three to four inches for the larger ones. Gardeners who seek a wide selection of species tulips should visit (or request catalogues from) the firms which specialize in unusual bulbs.

A brief description of some of the many excellent species tulips available follows. The approximate flowering periods listed are for the New York metropolitan area. Farther south the bulbs can be expected to bloom earlier; farther north, later.

T. biflora, blooming in March, is pale to deep yellow, with from one to five flowers on five-inch stems. *T. pulchella* produces six-inch-high stems with rosy purple blooms in March. The April-flowering *T. chrysantha* bears yellow and cherry-colored blooms on six-inch stems. *T. clusiana's* eight-inch-tall stems display soft rose and white blossoms in April. This stately little species is known as the lady tulip. The flowers come up for several years and are long lasting.

T. eichleri has larger flowers than most of the species. The scarlet and yellow blooms, on ten-inch stems, are April accents. *T. fosteriana* can be found growing wild on the mountain slopes of the Asiatic desert. The large, vivid scarlet blooms can, in brilliancy of color, compare with the best of the cultivated hybrids of the tulip world. There are a few hybrids of this species. The best known is Red Emperor, which flowers in April.

T. greigi is another vivid scarlet of which there are about ten hybrid varieties. *T. kaufmanniana*, known as the waterlily tulip, is a gay low-growing species which flowers early and comes up year after year. It needs little care and is wonderful in the large rock garden.

Toward the end of April and into May, three more species tulips appear. They are among the smallest and gayest of the group *T. patens* is three inches tall with yellow and bronze fragrant blooms. *T. linifolia* is four inches tall with scarlet flowers. *T. tarda (dasystemon)* is four inches tall with yellow and white blooms. The last, although not so brilliant in color as some, is one of my favorites. It is growing in the gravelly soil of the rock garden, where it seeds itself and comes up and flowers all over the place year after year.

The Little Bulbs

MOLLY PRICE

THE little bulbs that bloom earliest of all provide striking spring displays when planted in large clumps in early fall.

Gardeners, who a few years ago grew only the large-flowered crocus, now plant hundreds of the species. These intrepid miniatures bloom in the snow and blooms still are showy when their more familiar cousins flower in April.

Because they are so small, it is better to plant these winter-flowering crocus in some sort of raised position such as a sunny bank, along the steps or among rocks, with a groundcover of creeping veronica or small sedums. They make entrancing pictures when naturalized under south-facing deciduous shrubs, or in front of broadleaved evergreens. For maximum effect, they should be spaced two to four inches apart and planted three inches deep. Fifty to a hundred bulbs each of two or three kinds planted in drifts will create a more pleasing effect than a mixture, which is almost certain to look spotty.

Because new corms form on top of old ones and eventually push the plants out of the ground, replanting every few years is desirable. This is easy to do when the narrow leaves begin to yellow and fade in early summer.

Chipmunks enjoy the corms as much as I enjoy the blossoms, so I keep planting to try out different species. Favorite kinds are *Crocus chrysanthus* and its varieties in yellow, cream and white-and-gold combinations; *C. sieberi*, lavender with a yellow throat—a lavish flower; Cloth of Silver (*C. versicolor*), white, feathered outside with violet; and Blue Pearl, a really tiny pearly blue variety of *C. chrysanthus*.

The little netted iris, *Iris reticulata*, is another garden joy in early

Bulbs of the early scilla multiply and spread quickly.

J. Horace McFarland

Spring-flowering crocus signals spring's bloom parade to start.

J. Horace McFarland

Diminutive grape hyacinths are among the first bulbs to bloom.

spring. If the bulbs are planted in a sheltered, sunny spot, they will bloom in early March. The named varieties come in shades of blue, violet and purple. Cantab is a light blue variety; L. S. Dijt, a red-violet. The related *I. danfordiae* is yellow.

Also blooming before the snows have gone are the familiar common snowdrops (*Galanthus nivalis*), with drooping green-marked white flowers. The double *G. nivalis flore-pleno* is pretty, but less distinctive. *G. elwesi* from Asia Minor is a handsome larger-flowered species twelve inches tall. Snowdrops show up best when planted in small clumps in sheltered nooks.

Though not quite living up to its name glory-of-the-snow, the charming chionodoxas should be in every garden. The small flowers in loose racemes of *Chionodoxa luciliae*, the best-known species, are a white-centered soft blue. They look especially well when planted together with the brilliantly blue Siberian squill. There is a white form, too, and the large forms, Gigantea and Grandiflora, have showy flowers nearly two inches across. All the chionodoxas will thrive in any good soil, but they need an ample supply of moisture and plenty of light.

Close planting is the secret of using most of the small bulbs effectively. Succession planting—species crocus, Siberian squill and grape hyacinth, for instance—gives a fine extended show. Such combinations, which must be planted unusually close, need frequent renewal. The effect is brilliant, however, and many gardeners will consider it well worth the extra work.

All the scillas are exceptionally desirable in the spring garden. Different kinds vary in time of flowering, from mid-March to late May. The Siberian squill, *Scilla sibirica*, is the bluest; *S. bifolia* the earliest and tiniest. Its racemes of deep gentian blue flowers are lovely when grouped with the white of snowdrops. *S. sibirica*, variety Spring Beauty, is a truly dazzling blue. Six bulbs planted as many years ago have formed a blue carpet and contributed bulbs to start new colonies in other parts of the garden.

S. pratensis produces a raceme of tiny blue flowers in late May. The two important May-flowering squills are known as wood hyacinths or bluebells. Both come in blue, white and lavender-pink, and both are perfect for naturalizing in open woods or for grouping in the shady informal garden. *S. nonscripta* is about a foot tall with stalks of airy bells; *S. hispanica* is taller and larger flowered. Among the many named varieties of the latter is Excelsior, an excellent, strong-growing blue.

S. tubergeniana, prized for its early flowering, is very like the later blooming little bulb *Puschkinia scilloides libanotica*. Both produce informal clusters of blue-white flowers striped blue. The latter blooms with daffodils and hyacinths.

The fragrant grape hyacinths produce spikes of tiny bell-shaped flowers, multiply freely and colonize. *Muscari armeniacum* is an excellent blue species, blooming with late daffodils and tulips.

The fine white *M. botryoides album* combines charmingly with the earlier little species tulips, *M. latifolium*, which has, usually, only one broad leaf, produces dainty bi-toned flower spikes—sterile flowers pale blue, fertile ones dark blue. *M. tubergenianum* is similarly designed but produces a larger, more brilliantly colored flower spike. This is a superb flower which always attracts a good deal of attention in the garden.

Even the unusual feathered hyacinth, *Muscari comosum plumosum*, is beginning to be listed in popular catalogues. This is a showy, pretty violet-plumed plant, effective with tall bearded iris.

Not many bulbs thrive in moist, shaded ground, but *Camassia esculenta* will do well in such a problem spot, producing numerous blue starry flowers on a two-foot spike in May. The golden garlic, *Allium moly*, will grow in the same situation, though it does prefer the open border or rock garden. It is low growing, with many attractive umbels of light yellow flowers in late May.

The tiny hoop petticoat daffodil, *Narcissus bulbocodium*, and the cream-white angel's tears, *N. triandrus albus*, bloom at the same time and like the same lean, gritty soil. The blue flowers of *Pulmonaria angustifolia* make a bright foil for these little bulbs, which are so small and delicate, they would be lost in the middle of a border. I plant them together at the rocky edge of a raised bed. Rocks behind them are effective, too, for shelter and background.

Other delightful small bulbs are the hardy anemones—*Anemone blanda* and *A. fulgens* St. Bavo—the fritillarias, especially *Fritillaria meleagris*, the erythroniums and the spring star-flower, *Brodiaea uniflora*. All are fun to try, and rewarding.

Perennial Companions for Bulbs

NANCY R. SMITH

COMBINATIONS of perennials and bulbs provide some of spring's gayest garden pictures. Early-flowering perennials that are to bloom with bulbs should be set out in the fall. They need time to establish good root systems before freezing weather arrives.

A favorite perennial companion for the early little bulbs is blue phlox (*Phlox divaricata*). It is a native woodland plant, but lends itself with charm to cultivated settings. From the end of April into June, it forms a foot-high mass of lavender-blue bloom.

Ideally, and for best effect, blue phlox should be planted in colonies rather than in a straight row across the front of a border. A patch of a dozen plants, although it may take a season to become established, will increase in depth and beauty each year.

Colonies of blue phlox in front of shrub plantings are an unforgettable sight, particularly if yellow or pink tulips are planted, too. Against evergreens, this perennial combined with white tulips is stunning. Another possibility is a medley of blue phlox with pink, white and blue scillas (in clumps of at least a dozen bulbs). *P. divaricata* is also effective with tulips in dark shades of red or purple. The blossoms of the tulips will take on an almost velvetlike quality.

A small grove of trees can harbor phlox, grape hyacinths or scillas and daffodils, from the earliest to the latest-blooming kinds. Ferns, too, might be induced to thrive. A bird bath could be added to make the area a delight all through the growing season.

Very different from the phlox is the daisy-flowered doronicum or leopard's bane. This charming golden flower appears in April and May. Plants should be set a foot apart. Along with phlox, the doronicum will prosper in sun or light shade. The blossoms are carried on eighteen-inch stems.

Another combination I have used for years on a sunny bank is mountain pink (*Phlox subulata*) with blue grape hyacinths coming up through it. When the light pink and white phlox begin to look ragged, I work handfuls of enriched soil through the clumps. Trimming is also in order after flowering, but I take care not to cut off the foliage of the grape hyacinths (the leaves must be allowed to ripen if there is to be bloom the following spring).

An ideal underplanting for vividly colored tulips is the snowy rock cress (*Arabis alpina*). Available in single or double flowered form, it makes a six-inch-high carpet in April and May.

If the bulb plantings are new, the arabis is set out right over the spot after the tulips have been planted. It can also be added in fall over established plantings of bulbs. The tulips have no difficulty in coming up through the perennials.

Summer-flowering Bulbs

MARTHA PRATT HAISLIP

THE summer-flowering bulbs can be used singly or in mixed plantings for dramatic color accents. They are particularly valuable for camouflaging spring bulbs and out-of-bloom perennials.

These bulbs are set out as soon as the ground is warm. In Northern areas the tender species are dug up and stored over winter for replanting the following spring.

Among the best-liked of the tender summer bulbs are the gladiolus. They flower with minimum requirements in almost any climate. Gladiolus produce magnificent bloom from July until frost if bulbs are set out at two-week intervals from May to midsummer. Six-inch-deep planting is recommended.

Gladiolus flower forms range from miniatures (wonderful in flower arrangements), doubles, dragons and exotics, to novelties and innumerable standard and giant types that grow from three to six feet tall. They offer every color (and color combination) except blue.

The combination of spiked bloom and swordlike foliage is decorative with such massive perennials as peonies, summer phlox, gas plant and gypsophila. Especially effective are white gladiolus with purple phlox, or purple gladiolus with white phlox or gypsophila, pale yellow gladiolus against a background of Heavenly Blue morning glory, and clear pink, salmon and lavender gladiolus with pink phlox or blue belladonna delphinium.

Another bold and highly ornamental summer bulb is agapanthus, the blue lily of the Nile. It produces luxuriant straplike foliage from which rise tall stems topped by large clusters of blue lilylike flowers. The plant provides a handsome accent at the terminus of pathways, in tubs on the terrace or by steps.

A personal favorite is summer hyacinth (*Galtonia candicans*). From August until frost the four-foot stems carry creamy white bells, lovely against an evergreen background or with perennials. The bulbs need to be planted four to five inches deep in rich soil and full sun; watering during dry spells is vital.

Equally valuable is the tuberose. Both the single and double sorts are easy to grow, beautiful and exceedingly fragrant. All they need is the hottest, sunniest spot in the border and good soil.

Another of my cherished summer bulbs is *Hymenocallis calathina*, the Peruvian daffodil or basketflower (sometimes listed as ismene). The wide foliage is attractive all summer. The enormous, sparkling white flowers with fringed petals and long stamens are one of the delights of the border. With blue veronica, with any color of phlox, or used as a white accent—and as a cut flower—hymenocallis is a delight. Culture is the same as for the tuberose.

The modern, varied forms of tuberous-rooted begonias are magnificent in size and color. No other plant can replace them for flowering in shady places. Among the diverse flower forms are double carnation, double picotee, camellia, rosebud, ballerina and crested. Producing smaller flowers, and more of them, are the multifloras. Fire Dragon is a worthwhile new variety. I also like the pink-flowered hardy begonia, *Begonia evansiana*.

Dahlias are a must for the summer border. Not only is their abundant foliage attractive, but the bloom is colorful and long lasting.

Strong stems support lycoris.

J. Horace McFarland

Gladiolus show stately spikes.

J. Horace McFarland

Pots of begonias and fairy lily
line the steps.

Gottscho-Schleisner

While the decorative types are individually magnificent, the pompons,
miniatures and singles add more color and require less care. They produce quantities of bloom without disbudding. Dahlia tubers should
be planted about five inches deep in good, well-drained soil, in full
sun, with occasional cultivation and plenty of water in dry weather.

The new giant-flowered and dwarf cannas have generally replaced
the harsh-toned older sorts. Colors are soft and sparkling in salmon,
rose, yellow and blends. Individual bloom is enormous and borne in
large, bouquetlike trusses. The new Grand Opera cannas are exquisite;
colors include cherry red, Chinese coral, porcelain rose, primrose yel-

(147)

low and shell pink. Bulbs are planted about two feet apart and four inches deep, in full sun. They need water during dry spells and a moderate amount of fertilizer.

Excellent for border use are the fancy-leaved caladiums. They grow equally well in full sun or light shade. Their leaves are as decorative as flowers. White, pink, red-ribbed and blotched-leaved forms are superb. Caladiums prefer a fairly rich and moist (but not wet) soil. Plant bulbs nine inches deep and apart.

Calla lilies, of velvety texture and exotic appearance, are appropriate in modern home landscaping. The yellow calla (*Zantedeschia elliottiana*) is a magnificent species with an abundance of flowers. It often persists for years outdoors in temperate climates. The pink-flowered *Z. rehmanni* is small but exquisite. Calla bulbs planted in May will provide August and September bloom. Plant bulbs a foot apart and four inches deep.

The gloriosa lily is a challenge but worth the effort. This unique climbing lily will reach three feet or more in height, if grown in full sun and good soil. The wavy, reflexed segments and long stamens of the bright orange, purple-edged yellow or crimson and gold flowers are curious. The tuber should be planted on its side with the eye (growth bud) pointing upward.

No collection of summer-flowering bulbs is complete without a few of the little bulbs such as anemones, tigridias, tritonia and ranunculus. The St. Brigid strain of anemones (often seen in spring in florists' windows) display May and June color from early spring planting. Tigridia or shell flower flaunts triangular rose, orange and crimson-spotted bloom. The buttercuplike ranunculus has closely folded red, pink, white or yellow petals. Tritonia bears slender spikes of bright red, orange or yellow flowers.

Unusual and well worth growing are such summer-flowering bulbs as zephyranthes (fairy lilies), which often pop into rose-pink, white or golden yellow bloom after a rain; *Milla biflora* (Mexican star), with waxy, fragrant white flowers on four-foot stalks; exotic pineapple lily (*Eucomis comosa*), with green-flushed ivory blooms; and *Bessera elegans* (lady's eardrops), with delicate pendant bells of coral, orange and white.

Annuals in a Border

MILTON BARON AND CARL S. GERLACH

ANNUALS are some of the most satisfying of all types of garden flowers. They have a long blooming season which surpasses biennials and perennials. With some care during dry periods and consistent removal of faded flowers, annuals will provide three months of bloom or more.

Within the last few years, there have been many new varieties and greatly improved strains of annuals available. By altering the chromosome count, plant breeders have developed types with greater vigor, more luxuriant foliage, disease resistance, larger flowers and countless new colors. Now there are double as well as single-flowered forms of many favorite annuals.

In the suggested plans, annuals have been selected for their abundance of bloom. The newer improved varieties have been recommended because they are much superior. The planting plans have been made in three color schemes: a yellow-white color combination, a pink-white color combination and a multicolored combination using annuals that might easily be grown from seed sown outdoors. The last list is recommended for those with summer cottages, as the plants require very little care.

The simplest method of starting an annual garden is to obtain sturdy, well-grown plants from a reliable local source. The plants should be showing some color. They should be well budded with an occasional open flower.

In the case of late-blooming kinds, like zinnias and asters, plants should be bushy and compact with deep green color. They should be grown with sufficient space for seedlings to be shaped properly.

If many plants are needed, buy flats or half-flats, using a kitchen knife to cut between the plants to get a cube of soil without disturb-

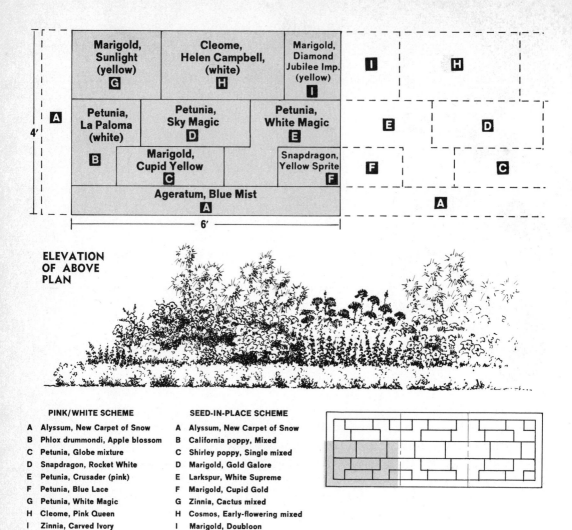

PLAN

Marigold, Sunlight (yellow) **G**	Cleome, Helen Campbell, (white) **H**	Marigold, Diamond Jubilee Imp. (yellow) **I**

Petunia, La Paloma (white) **B**

Petunia, Sky Magic **D**

Petunia, White Magic **E**

Marigold, Cupid Yellow **C**

Snapdragon, Yellow Sprite **F**

Ageratum, Blue Mist **A**

A 4' 6'

I **H** **E** **D** **F** **C** **A**

ELEVATION OF ABOVE PLAN

PINK/WHITE SCHEME

A Alyssum, New Carpet of Snow
B Phlox drummondi, Apple blossom
C Petunia, Globe mixture
D Snapdragon, Rocket White
E Petunia, Crusader (pink)
F Petunia, Blue Lace
G Petunia, White Magic
H Cleome, Pink Queen
I Zinnia, Carved Ivory

SEED-IN-PLACE SCHEME

A Alyssum, New Carpet of Snow
B California poppy, Mixed
C Shirley poppy, Single mixed
D Marigold, Gold Galore
E Larkspur, White Supreme
F Marigold, Cupid Gold
G Zinnia, Cactus mixed
H Cosmos, Early-flowering mixed
I Marigold, Doubloon

The annual border plan may be repeated or used in sections to suit the size of the planting area. The basic plan (shaded) is for a yellow-white scheme. The alternate bloom schemes include a multi-colored border which is seeded directly outdoors. The borders look best when set against a backdrop fence or hedge.

For a free-standing border which will be viewed from all sides, the plan is overlapped. Only one section with taller plants is used in the center while the edging of low border plants is put around the bed.

Plan by Carl S. Gerlach and Milton Baron

ing roots. Set plants in the soil to almost the first leaves and firm them in well. Aluminum, fiber and plastic plant trays are popular. They are available in half-dozen or forty-plant trays. Another handy way to buy plants is to select those that are growing in peat moss or fiber composition pots. Pot and plant are placed right in the planting hole and the roots of the seedling grow through the fiber into the soil.

Garden centers are swamped with customers in spring. Plant buyers should not wait until the last minute to make their selections, especially for specific varieties and plants. Sometimes garden centers will obtain special order plants if they are requested early or they will recommend suitable substitutes. New color forms are continually being introduced to the trade. It might be advisable to check annually for current and improved varieties.

The spacing of annuals really is no problem. Those which are seeded in place must be thinned to give ample growing room. The extras are transplanted elsewhere. Edgers, such as alyssum, ageratum, iberis and verbena, need six inches between plants.

Low-growing annuals such as dwarf marigolds and zinnias require eight inches. Petunias and similar plants need ten inches between plants. Tall marigolds, cosmos and cleome should have eighteen inches of room for best performance.

Certain annuals are difficult if not almost impossible to transplant. These should be seeded where they are to grow. Poppy, nasturtium, love-in-a-mist, lupine, rose moss and sweet pea belong in this category. Although a few of the annuals will grow in some shade, most of the colorful flowering types demand good sunlight. Choose a sunny site where there is good circulation of air.

After transplanting, the annuals are shaded from direct sun for the first day to prevent wilting. Or, better than that, do the transplanting on a cloudy day.

Water seedlings with starter solution of water-soluble fertilizer. Directions for dosage are given on the packages. The only further culture needed for annuals is an occasional cultivation to kill the weeds, watering if rains are lacking and removal of dead flowers to prevent the plants from going to seed. Once the plants are flowering well, careful cutting for indoor use is beneficial. If done judiciously it will not spoil the display effect.

In addition to the border plans there are many other ways that annuals can be used around the home. They are easy to cultivate in rows in a cutting garden. Window boxes and movable planters are perfect for annuals to provide high spots of color. In addition, annuals are excellent temporary plants to set among new plantings of perennials, shrubs and evergreens. They fill in the gaps until other plant material matures.

A Commuter's Bloom Schedule

SARAH E. PULLAR

Commuter-gardeners who spend their days at an office can plan their gardens to accommodate their schedules. Flowers can be planted for bloom during early morning or evening hours.

Early morning presents flowers at their best—sprightly and fresh from the cool of night, stems stiff and refreshed, colors at their purest. This is the time to cut bouquets. Red roses will not have taken on a bluish tinge, nor will strong sunlight have faded yellow ones to white. Poppies picked in the morning can be caught in the act of opening, as the green sepals suddenly break apart.

Phlox is irresistible to pick, too, with its fragrant, handsome stalks that are so abundant in late summer. White plantain lily (*Hosta plantaginea*) has waxlike flowers which open at dawn. Its sweet scent makes it doubly pleasing.

The business man may enjoy wearing a freshly cut boutonniere from his own garden. There are several long-lasting flowers suited to this purpose that are easy to grow. The French marigold is perhaps the best of marigolds for this purpose because of its size.

Similar but more varied in color are different kinds of zinnias— the Lilliputians, for example. Then, too, there is the obvious favorite —bachelor's button. Gathered early in the morning, flowers are partially hardened off and should last well through the day or even for a second day.

Further pleasure can be gained from a morning garden by locating it in view of the breakfast table or near the terrace. Double petunias and the newer giant double ones might form the backbone of this garden. These have a very slight fragrance.

Another early attraction is the morning glory. If seeds are soaked in warm water before planting, they germinate more quickly. Varieties are available in red and white, as well as blue. All are large, with fine darker ridges that create a starry effect.

The late afternoon-evening garden should surely include spider plant (cleome) and flowering tobacco (nicotiana). While they may look faded and woebegone during the day, they open to their fullest beauty in the cool of evening.

Cleome is quite striking. It is a tall and bushy plant, sometimes used as a barrier hedge in an annual garden. It flowers profusely and becomes covered with showy pink or white flower clusters.

The fragrance of cleome is strong but sweet at a distance. Flowering tobacco has a spicy fragrance which scents the air about it.

Moonflower resembles morning glory, but its timing is just opposite. The blossoms open at night. Flowers bloom when they do because they have received the exact amount of required daylight hours and darkness, and in just the right proportion. The plant is an excellent climber, and so is useful on trellises or against walls.

Two rather novel flowers for evening gardens are angel's-trumpet (datura) and gas plant (dictamnus). Both are available in white and are luxuriously fragrant.

Angel's-trumpet is a rather tall annual that produces large, trumpet-shaped flowers of glistening white. Gas plant, a perennial, has showy blossoms, too.

An added attraction of planting evening flowers is that nearly all of them are sweet-smelling and therefore attractive to moths and other insects. Late in the afternoon bees and flies still come.

Then, as twilight descends, the clear-winged humming moths appear along with other smaller insects. All these help to pollinate the flowers which may have been tightly closed during the sunny hours of the day.

White flowers should be planted liberally, if only to catch the moonlight in a summer garden. Excellent choices include sweet rocket (hesperis), Madonna lily, stock, petunia, phlox and sweet alyssum. When the daylight beauty of the garden has disappeared, the commuter-gardener can enjoy his favorite blossoms in company with some of the graceful moths and the twinkling fireflies.

Flowers for Drying

ESTHER C. GRAYSON

WHEN planting annuals for summer color, the wise arranger reserves a row or two in the cutting garden for those flowers which can be dried. May is planting time for these annuals, and they all need a sunny spot. If the flowers are cut and dried as they come into bloom, a rich store of material will be ready for winter arrangements.

Annuals for drying can be roughly divided into four categories: the old favorites which, like strawflowers, have been used for generations as materials for dried bouquets; the more delicate blossoms which can be dried by modern methods in such a way as to preserve both color and form; the foliage plants which contribute so much to floral compositions; and, finally, the plants which produce interesting seed pods.

In the first group are strawflowers (*Helichrysum bracteatum*), with white and yellow or orange blossoms, and winged everlasting (*Ammobium alatum*), with white and yellow flowers, woolly foliage and winged branches. The latter is a hardy annual that thrives in sandy soil.

There are several popular *Helipterum* species. Among these are *H. humboldtianum*, with yellow-green disk flowers and gray-white leaves; *H. manglesi* or Swan River everlasting, with small blooms surrounded by conspicuous white or pink bracts, and *H. roseum*, with larger flowers also rimmed by large bracts.

Xeranthemum annum or immortelle has papery flower heads in white, pink, rose, lavender or purple, and gray-white foliage. The limoniums (statice or sea-lavender) produce panicles of airy flowers in yellow, blue, lavender or white on slender but sturdy branched stems. The sea lavenders prefer sandy loam.

All of these, except the everlastings, are easily dried by setting the cut stems upright in a jar or box in a warm, dark and dry shed, attic or closet. Bells of Ireland, baby's-breath, calendula, celosia, datura, polygonum and sunflower may be dried in the same way.

On the other hand, everlastings, centaurea, catananche, globe amaranth, hollyhock, marigold and scabiosa are hung upside down on a line. Tie them carefully in small bunches, using soft string. Allow ample space for air circulation between the bunches.

Among the annuals dried for color and form are Canterbury bells, cornflower, dianthus, foxglove, larkspur, lupine, snapdragon and zinnia. The blooms should be buried carefully for two to three weeks in a mixture of two-thirds white cornmeal and one-third borax. This will preserve both the color and form of the blooms.

The spike-type blooms are laid down and covered, stems and all. Single blossoms are cut off with one-inch stems. After drying, false stems are attached to the flowers.

The leaves of canna and caladium are most useful in dried arrangements. They are preserved by standing the cut stems three to five inches deep in a mixture of one-third glycerine and two-thirds water until it has been absorbed to the leaf tips.

With this glycerine dip, the leaves can be kept indefinitely, for they are pliable and not paper-dry. This glycerine mixture also is useful for preserving branches of deciduous trees and broadleaved evergreens with leaves attached.

Coleus, snow-on-the-mountain, artemisia and ornamental grasses are valuable for drying. The first two are dried by the borax method, the last two by standing them erect in a large-mouthed jar until ready for use.

Many plants have interesting seed pods. To mention a few, there are okra, *Cobaea scandens*, poppy, datura, proboscis (unicorn plant), leeks, chives and onions. They are dried by the upright method.

Lunaria, or honesty, is an old favorite. Once established, it seeds itself almost too freely in the garden. The outer coverings must be stripped from the flat, oval seed receptacles to reveal the satiny, mother-of-pearl-like inner covering of the seeds. Branches of this interesting biennial—it is also called silver dollar and Peter's penny—are as popular today as they were in grandmother's time.

Roses to Grow for Cutting

IRENE ROUSCH

SELECTING rosebushes that will produce an abundance of flowers for cutting presents no problem to the rose arranger. Many beautiful, easy-to-grow varieties—blends, bicolors and new colors—are available.

There are plants with large, medium or small blooms. In fact, so many good roses are on the market today it is impractical to include them all. I have listed the following varieties because their color, form and substance (keeping quality) make them especially fine for arranging. Fragrance is now being added to many new varieties.

Among the hybrid teas are Chrysler Imperial, fragrant red; Mr. Lincoln, large red; Charlotte Armstrong, light red with silver-tipped petals; Swarthmore, large-flowered medium red. White roses are Sincera, perfect form; Garden Party, large-petaled with a tinge of pink; John F. Kennedy, beautiful as a bud. Summer Sunshine, Apollo and Arlene Frances are yellow roses to consider. There are so many fine pink and pink-blend roses that I almost hesitate to select any, but those I would want are Pink Peace, large, many-petaled and fragrant; Tiffany, exquisite as a bud or open bloom; Confidence, delicate yellow coloring; Chicago Peace, an interesting blend of pink, red and yellow; First Prize, a new rose, long-lasting and beautiful in all stages; Portrait, another long-lasting rose. Sterling Silver and Lady X are two lavender roses used by arrangers.

Excellent floribundas for cutting include Circus, orange-red; Red Gold, colored as its name; Orangeade and Orange Sensation, both a blend of orange and red; Vogue and Fashion, both good pink blends; Gene Boerner, lovely clusters of perfect pink blooms; Europeana, a fine dark red; Frensham and Lili Marlene, dark red. Ivory Fashion is a large-flowered white, and Angel Face, an interesting mauve.

Grandifloras have proved to be favorites and should be included

LEFT: A free-blooming climbing rose puts the finishing touch on an old-fashioned gate arbor.

Gottscho-Schleisner

RIGHT: Cheery climbing roses bloom intermittently all summer long.

Gottscho-Schleisner

in a garden for arrangers. This class includes Queen Elizabeth, a really deep pink; Pink Parfait, a small flower, but lovely; Mt. Shasta, white; Duet, a pink blend; Apricot Nectar, a peach-pink; Granada, a blend of many colors; El Capitan, Scarlet Knight and John Armstrong, all dark red and beautiful; and Montezuma, an orange that is quite interesting.

The gardener who wants a rose garden for cutting should follow the same procedure for buying and planting as the gardener who is planning an exhibition planting or creating a landscape design. The informal rose garden can be beautiful with the colors generally mixed —the reds, pinks, blends, whites and yellows all making a pleasing picture.

Of course the newer "hot" varieties—reds and oranges—will clash violently if planted next to the more stable reds. Spartan, Montezuma, Hawaii and Tanya fall into this group of vivid orange or orange blend; these varieties should be planted carefully with soft-colored roses.

Buy a minimum of three plants of a variety to insure sufficient color in the garden after blooms are cut for arranging. First-year plants should be allowed to develop as much as possible. The arranger, therefore, should plan on small bouquets with short-stemmed roses the first year. Of course, many long-stemmed beauties can be cut for years from a fully grown bush.

Cut roses should be hardened before arranging to make them last longer. Stems should be cut with a sharp knife or shears, placed in warm water and kept in a cool spot or refrigerator for several hours. When arranging the roses, cut about a quarter of an inch from the bottom of the stems. Glass and silver are lovely types of containers for rose arrangements, as are those of copper, brass, wood and pottery. In fact, an arrangement often is more attractive when there is an interesting contrast between rose texture and the container.

Miniature Roses

MARY C. SECKMAN

MINIATURE roses are exquisite replicas of full-sized roses on a small scale. They truly must be seen to be believed, for it is difficult to imagine a rose so small that several blooms can be accommodated in a thimble.

Belying their daintiness, miniature roses are rugged plants. They are as hardy as the best of the larger varieties. They have tiny rose leaves and bear a generous number of flowers all summer. The blossoms, less than an inch across, open from buds that are scarcely larger than a grain of wheat. Up to sixty petals may be counted in the double miniature rose blooms. Plant and lacy foliage are in perfect proportion.

These diminutive roses make attractive edgings for pools, walks and borders—where there is no danger of their being shaded by other plants. They may be grown in rock gardens, miniature and children's gardens. They are particularly suitable for outlining beds of the full-sized roses. It is important, however, that the little plants are not robbed of nourishment and moisture by the larger plants.

Strawberry jars make interesting containers. As many as ten or twelve small rosebushes can be planted in each jar for a colorful display.

While many flowers are as old as history, these roses, so far as is known, really are "something new under the sun." No mention of them has been found in early garden books or rose catalogues. Data on miniature roses go back to the English clipper ships that sailed the

RIGHT: Miniature roses, completely winter hardy, are ideal for planting beside steps or in pockets of rock outcroppings.   *Gottscho-Schleisner*

BELOW: Nearly a dozen miniature roses can be planted in a large-sized strawberry jar.   *Star Roses*

China Seas. Along with cargoes of silks and spices, they carried tiny roses from Asia, the *Rosa indica minima*. In the early part of the nineteenth century Englishmen named the plants fairy roses or *Rosa lawrencea* in honor of Mary Lawrence, an English artist famed for her rose paintings.

More than a generation ago a tiny rose belonging to the same group (*R. indica*) was discovered high in the Alps in Switzerland by Colonel Roulet. He found plants blooming in home window boxes. M. Correvon, a Swiss rock garden expert and friend of Colonel Roulet, named it *Rosa rouletti* and introduced it into commerce. It is still listed today and highly regarded.

A sport of *rouletti*, Oakington Ruby, was announced in 1933 by C. R. Bloom of Oakington, Cambridge, England. This was the first of the newer small roses to be catalogued commercially. However, the first true miniature from seed was Tom Thumb, a self-seedling of *rouletti* developed by Jan de Vink of Holland. Tom Thumb is rich crimson with a touch of white at the base of the petals. Sometime later the same breeder introduced the now popular Pixie and Midget.

More recent introductions include Cinderella, Bo-Peep, Red Imp and Sweet Fairy. There are larger-flowered miniatures, less compact and symmetrical, as well as miniature tree roses now available.

These tiny roses have become so popular that they are now more widely distributed and may be found in plant marts and garden centers as well as in nurseries. Potted and in bloom, they are delightful as valentine gifts, Mother's Day presents or special favors for children's parties.

Perhaps the most unusual use for miniature roses is as house plants for winter flowering. A special technique has been developed by which the plants are given a dormant period outdoors in the cold so that they can be brought into bloom indoors in wintertime. Blooms can be expected in seven to eight weeks.

The roses are potted according to directions, then set on outsized trays of pebbles and water. The water level is kept just below the level of the pot. Sunlight is necessary for successful flowering. The ideal location for these miniature roses is a southern window which receives three or four hours of sunlight a day.

Plants are watered regularly, although the soil should not be soggy. Fertilize the roses during the growing season but not at planting time.

One of the most fascinating uses for fairy roses is as cut flowers for miniature arrangements. Containers have been designed, smaller than the size of a thimble, to hold these tiny blooms. (A little pitcher from a child's miniature tea set might hold a dozen flowers.) These arrangements can be used effectively with place cards at the dinner table.

Roses of Yesteryear

RICHARD D. THOMSON

OLD-FASHIONED roses can add new dimension to the flower garden. But to appreciate them fully, the contemporary rose grower must learn to see them through the eyes of the period in which they were introduced. Rose styles of yesteryear are quite different from those of today. Most of the plants are shrubby, and blossoms appear nearer spring than summer.

Among the loveliest of the *gallica* roses is Cramoisie des Alpes (Alain Blanchard), an open bush carrying myriads of semi-double crimson blooms brushed with black. Cardinal de Richelieu shows small rounded balls of the deepest velvet-purple. *Gallica versicolor* produces a bush that grows to four feet laden with semi-double flowers of blush white, heavily striped and speckled with crimson-red. Camaieux is another of the striped varieties, but the plant is small. Blooms are striped with purple. Fanny Bias roses have large pompons of exquisite flesh pink shading.

The damasks are somewhat larger plants and the flowers more pendant. All of them are intensely fragrant with the true old "Attar of Roses" scent. Celsiana, an old, old variety is one of my favorites. The silky, light pink blooms are warm and inviting. Madame Hady is one of the great roses of all time. The plant grows to five feet in my garden and the flat, cupped blooms are of pure and sparkling

Bourbon rose La Reine Victoria is very fragrant and free blooming.

Will Tillotson's Roses

white. They come in small clusters. While the bloom period is short, the effect is magnificent.

Rosa *alba* is another group which deserves representation in gardens of today. These are the true flowering shrubs. They have a noble stature which compels admiration. Maiden's Blush is also available in nurseries. The plant grows to seven feet and is resistant to any and all diseases. The rough blue-green foliage is decorative throughout the summer. This rose is without competition as a garden shrub.

Among the *centifolias* (the cabbage roses) are such delights as

Rose des Peintres, rich rose-pink in a double, tumbled mass of petals and Vierge de Cléry, a snow-white bloom, with grand fragrance. The greatest productions of the *centifolias*, however, were the moss roses. In this group the bud is enveloped in soft, green growth. Among the many varieties are Cristata. The sepals are covered with tiny whisk brooms of green. The bloom itself is beautiful, of tender rose shade.

The original moss rose is known botanically as *Rosa centifolia muscosa*. It is far better known to gardeners as the Old Pink Moss. This is perhaps the loveliest of the pure types. Pink blooms are enveloped in a copious mass of luscious green sepals. The open flower is extremely fragrant. There is also a white sport, the Old White Moss.

Hybrid classes of roses appeared after 1800. Essentially they were a typical array of crosses between Chinas, teas and the old European roses. When they closely resembled the China side of the parentage, they were called Chinas or bourbons; when they leaned more toward the old rose side, they were called hybrid perpetuals or hybrid Chinas.

Many of these hybrids are available today. The greatest bourbon available is without a doubt Souvenir de Malmaison. Blooms are flesh pink to white, and the plant deserves consideration as a member of any current hybrid tea planting. Another old-timer which would combine with modern floribundas is Hermosa. Blooms are small, cupped-shaped and grow in clusters.

There are several good hybrid perpetuals. Baroness Rothschild, Mrs. John Laing and Marchioness of Londonderry are in flesh to dark pink tones. In reds Henry Nevard, Triomphe de L'Exposition and Gloire de Chedanne-Guinoisseau should give great color and fragrance.

Hybrid perpetuals are treated like big hybrid tea plants. When they have finished the spring bloom, laterals are cut back to two eyes. If kept well watered and fed, the hybrid perpetuals will give plenty of summer and fall blooms.

Among the hybrid Chinas are many great roses, such as Variegata di Bologna, which has the striping of the old *gallicas*. If there is room to let it grow and sprawl, this rose will be the talk of the neighborhood. Last of all there are the old Chinas themselves. Few are left, but the old Pink China should be a part of every rose selection. A grand, quite hardy shrub to five feet, it is never without clusters of dainty, semi-double blooms the entire season.

Almanac for Roses

RUTH ALDA ROSS

Roses are ordinary shrubs that happen to have the most extraordinary flowers. Many types, such as shrub roses, will bloom beautifully with occasional attention. The more spectacular types demand regular care—pruning, feeding, watering and spraying. A routine for roses, timed approximately for gardens in the New York City area, is given below.

April

1. Remove winter protection gradually as ground thaws.

2. Plant rosebushes as soon as ground can be worked, preferably before April 15.

3. "Prune roses when forsythia blooms," . . . when rose leaf buds swell but before growth begins. Remove any winterkill.

Hybrid teas: prune lightly for plentiful flowers, moderately for fewer but handsomer blooms, severely for exhibition blooms.

Floribundas: prune moderately.

Hybrid perpetuals: cut back all stems to two feet; leave only four to five stems.

Tree roses: prune crown hard as soon as winter wrappings are removed.

Climbing, rambler and old-fashioned roses: reserve major pruning until after bloom.

4. Give established hybrid teas first of three annual feedings, floribundas first of two, climbers and shrubs annual dose.

5. Late in month, begin weeding by *shallow* cultivation. Alternate method: mulch.

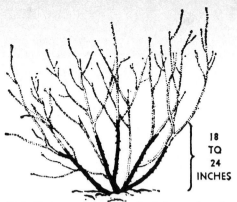

Hybrid tea rose canes to be left on the plant are shown solid black. Dotted canes are pruned.

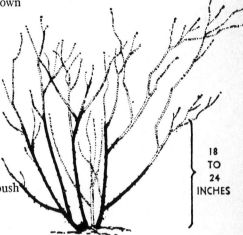

Five to seven floribunda canes are left on the rosebush to encourage abundant flowering.

May

1. Begin weekly or ten-day-interval spraying, to continue through October; use three-purpose spray.

 2. If roses must be planted now, choose potted bushes in full leaf or bud.

 3. If aphids become a nuisance, spray with nicotine sulfate.

June

1. Second feeding.

 2. Optional: rose beds can be edged now.

 3. Hot weather calls for a mulch if it was not put down earlier; do this after weeding and a good rain.

 4. When weekly rainfall is less than an inch, water to a depth of two-to-three inches; avoid wetting foliage.

Rosebushes may be planted either in late fall or early spring. They should be unwrapped and soaked for several hours in a bucket of water, prior to planting.

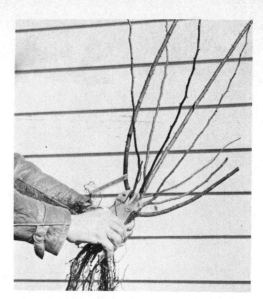

ABOVE: Weakened canes or those that overlap should be cut out.

ABOVE: The planting hole should be dug to a depth of eighteen inches, and the soil should be improved by adding peat moss or decayed compost. A mound of soil in the center of the hole will support the rosebush so that the knob or graft union is just at soil level.

ABOVE: When the hole is partially filled with soil, the ground should be tamped firmly to settle the roots.

ABOVE: Water is then applied generously, and the hole will be filled in when the water drains away.

LEFT: When the hole is filled a mound of extra soil from another part of the garden will be heaped over the crown. This protects the rosebush until new leaves push out and it is recommended for either spring- or fall-planted rosebushes.

Vanderwerth from Monkmeyer

(167)

5. If Japanese beetles are numerous, spray or hand pick.

6. Cut blooms on new rosebushes sparingly and with very short stems. Cut off spent blooms.

7. Disbud hybrid teas for exhibition blooms.

July

1. Third feeding of hybrid teas early in the month.

2. Sprays applied at midday or during a drought may damage foliage temporarily.

3. Prune old-fashioned ramblers immediately after bloom; remove at ground level all canes that have bloomed; tie new canes to a support. Thin out old growth on climbers, leaving ample new growth for next year's bloom.

4. Gather rosebud petals for potpourri on a sunny afternoon.

September

1. Do not neglect weekly spraying, especially if defoliation was heavy in summer.

2. Nicotine sulfate may be needed for aphids.

November

1. Write for rose catalogues; order bushes.

2. Plant rosebushes.

3. Rake up fallen leaves between plants for anti-black spot sanitation.

4. About the third week or before frost is expected, hill hybrid teas with a six-to-eight-inch mound of soil. Some floribundas, hybrid perpetuals and polyanthas and a few tender climbers may need protection, too.

5. Dig tree roses after the first late freeze, lay them on the ground, cover with soil. Alternate method: protect and wrap crown with waterproof paper.

Potpourri Preserves the Scents of Summer

RUTH ALDA ROSS

POTPOURRI—a mixture of dried flower petals kept in a jar for scent—captures the loveliness of summer in the garden. Petals of flowers are dried and blended with other fragrant ingredients to enhance their odor. Then a vegetable fixative is added to the mixture to preserve the scent for years.

To make a dry potpourri or scent jar, few materials are needed. The prime requirement is one rosebush in bloom, some other flowers and herbs—enough to make at least a quart of dried petals. As to how much of each kind should be used, a good rule is "follow your nose." Many potpourri makers feel that the only blossoms which really retain their fragrance are those of roses and lavender; the rest are just for fun or color.

Additional equipment includes an ordinary window screen, spices from the kitchen, orris root or other fixative from the drugstore and perhaps some essential oils. A large container with snug-fitting cover is handy for mixing and storing. Some pretty jars should be collected for the finished product.

The actual preparation of potpourri is leisurely. Petals need several days to dry, depending on humidity, and about six weeks to mellow after they are mixed. If bloom is scarce or if time does not permit, mixing can be postponed until enough dried petals are accumulated. They can be stored in an air-tight container.

The first step is to cut flowers in full bud or just as they are about to open. Blooms should be gathered on a sunny afternoon after

(169)

dew has disappeared. Harvest is then brought indoors out of wind and sun, which evaporates the fragrance oils. Petals should be pulled off gently and spread thinly (to prevent mildew) on a flat window screen. For better air circulation, the screen can be propped up on bricks.

Petals are stirred daily until as crisp as cornflakes; then they are ready to be blended. To a quart of dried petals add one tablespoon of fixative, either orris root, storax, crushed roots of calamus or gum benzoin. This will prevent evaporation of oils and make fragrance last. Any drugstore with a good prescription department should stock one of these fixatives; cost is about $1 for two ounces (about five tablespoonfuls) of each.

Kitchen spices are added next: one tablespoon of a mixture of allspice, cinnamon, cloves, nutmeg and mace. Ready-ground spices are satisfactory, but whole spices crushed in a mortar will give a fresher product. If available, a vanilla bean can be included, too, and/or bits of lemon or orange rind that have been allowed to dry for a day. Another variation is to add a dash of crushed anise seed.

At this point, a discreet drop or two of a fragrant oil may be added. Among the possibilities are patchouli, rose geranium, eucalyptus, rosemary, vetiver, lemon verbena and peppermint. Druggists charge about 25 cents for an eight-ounce bottle of each, except for rose geranium, which is about 75 cents.

After these ingredients are mixed thoroughly, place the snug cover on the container and store for about six weeks. Stir the potpourri with a wooden spoon occasionally or just give the container a vigorous shake. The finished potpourri can be spooned into fancy jars, either the special rose jars sold for the purpose or little apothecary jars from the five-and-ten-cent store.

If glass containers are used, dried petals of non-scented flowers and those that do not retain their scent might be added for color. Especially true to their original tints are blue cornflowers, delphiniums and larkspur and red beebalm. Since white roses dry to an unappealing brown, it is better to add petals of white flowers like Shasta daisy. For a finishing touch, a pressed pansy can be glued, face out, to the inside of the jar. Egg white makes an efficient but imperceptible glue for this purpose.

PART IV

LAWNS

T HE FIRST MERIT BADGE that any gardener worth the name likes to earn is that of lawnsman. A handsome greensward provides a beautiful setting for his home. And the neighborhood bestows upon him that high gardening honor—the order of the green thumb.

Perhaps no other phase of tending plants occupies so much of the home owner's attention as the green grass that grows all around. From early spring when the first wisps of grass appear until a November breeze pushes the last leaf to the ground, the lawn work goes on. To help him be the lawnsman that he is, our tiller must keep in fighting trim a power mower, trimmers, weedkillers, grubproofers and fertilizers.

Too much emphasis on effort can make lawnsmanship an ordeal. The secret lies in a simple but consistent upkeep program. Once the particular lawn needs are recognized, the gardener's job is merely one of following through.

Those who are starting a lawn from a bulldozed mud patch in front of their new home would be wise to heed the advice of the experts in putting down a proper seed bed. For all turfmen agree that a lawn is only as good as its foundation and construction material—high-quality seed.

The Best of the Grass Types

J. M. DUICH

MANY common lawn problems can be avoided with the proper selection of grasses. For many Northeast situations new ryegrasses and blends offer the best assurance of continued success.

Annual and perennial ryegrass—long known for quick germination and endless mowing—are being rapidly replaced with truly "turf-type" perennial ryegrasses. Manhattan, Pennfine and NK-200 are the most desirable new varieties now offered.

Turftype ryegrasses sprout and establish quickly, but without the rapid vertical growth rate of the common annual and perennial ryegrasses. They are fine-textured, leafy, mow well, and present an attractive appearance. These characteristics make the turftypes valuable for home use.

New lawns, particularly bluegrass, can be established with considerably less time and problems by incorporating approximately 20 percent of the improved ryegrasses in a mixture. Large amounts may be used under less favorable conditions. In many instances, it will be difficult to distinguish between bluegrass and turftype ryegrass. Under growth and management conditions favorable for bluegrasses, the ryegrass will be crowded out in a smooth transition. Otherwise it may persist for many years and provide an adequate turf cover.

Turftype ryegrasses are also very useful for overseeding lawns deteriorated by heavy wear, diseases, insects and improper establishment. The technique is greatly simplified by the use of a mechanical rake or dethatcher, available from garden rental centers. Steps consist of several machine passes to loosen surface debris, the application of seed and one or two additional passes to cover seed. Loose surface material should then be removed, followed by irrigation if available. Fertilizer should be withheld until the new grass is mowed several times. Results can be most gratifying when utilized in conjunction with sound lawn management practices.

Mixtures of Kentucky bluegrass and creeping red fescue have been the long-time standard of Northeast lawns. Following the introduction of Merion bluegrass in 1952, there has been considerable single use of Merion and other bluegrass varieties. As frequently noted, improved bluegrass varieties have produced dense lawns of an excellent quality and uniformity. These features have been made possible through a plant reproduction process which yields seeds that are genetically identical to the mother plant.

Since no one bluegrass variety is resistant to all diseases, many lawns are succumbing to various blights. In particular, stripe smut and Fusarium roseum (the frog-eye disease) have devastated many single bluegrass lawns. They cannot even be practically controlled with fungicides. Severe local outbreaks of these and other diseases or insects have been disenchanting to many owners of once-beautiful bluegrass lawns. These problems can be alleviated with the use of bluegrass "blends."

Top-quality blends are composed of superior bluegrass varieties. Recent additions to the improved seed list are Pennstar, Fylking, Nugget, Baron, Windsor, Adelphi and Sodco. University and private company breeders are working diligently on further improvements. Many will undoubtedly use these varieties alone based on individual advertising claims. It cannot be overemphasized that they can be best utilized in combinations.

Improved varietal status is based on the ability to produce a dense turf under close mowing, general adaptability, resistance to several major diseases and a pleasing color and texture. However, each may react somewhat differently to climate, soils and management practices. Pennstar and Fylking, for example, are highly resistant to striped smut.

Again, a good case for blends.

Other named bluegrass varieties such as Newport, Delta, Kenblue, South Dakota Certified, Park, Cougar, Campus, Geary and Palouse will produce a lower-quality lawn in the Northeast. Due to poor general adaptability, they require the highest possible height of cut. Sod growers may have varieties and blends which are not available to the public as seed, such as A-20.

Red fescues are useful components in Kentucky bluegrass mix-

(175)

Grass seed mixtures with a good balance of red fescue will prosper where shade trees spread over the lawn.

Gottscho-Schleisner

tures for general lawn use. Their adaptability to shade and poorer soil conditions offers a further buffering quality to lawns. Pennlawn, Jamestown, C-26 and Highlight fescues are the preferred varieties. Red fescue-bluegrass mixtures are generally used in a two-to-one ratio by weight due to the large seed size of the fescue. Bluegrass-fescue mixtures are compatible and may persist as such or shift to the species favored by growing conditions.

Many poor lawns are the direct result of inferior seed purchases. Foremost among these is the excessive use of annual and perennial ryegrass, either alone or in mixtures.

Similar to the ryegrass problem is the overuse of redtop. This rapid-sprouting and growing grass contains approximately six million seeds per pound. Mixtures containing 5 to 30 percent result in near-total redtop stands due to subjugation of other components. A rapid decline of common ryegrasses and redtop, often as soon as the first winter, leaves lawns open to gross weed invasion.

Unfortunately the most common variety of tall fescue sold is Kentucky-31 or K-31 fescue. Unknowledgeable consumers may easily mistake portions of the name with Kentucky bluegrass or red fescue, the most desired of turf species. Perhaps this is the intent of certain seed suppliers. Because of the absence of selective chemical control and perennial growth, tall fescue is rapidly becoming the number one weed problem in this region.

Ironically, tall fescue is a most useful species for many conditions where Kentucky bluegrass and red fescue will not prevail. Under poor and droughty soil conditions, heavy use or at the seashore, it will provide turf cover otherwise impossible. For these uses it should be seeded alone at approximately six to eight pounds per thousand square feet.

Seed Shopping

JOHN F. CORNMAN

THE buyer of grass seed is protected by law against fraud and deception on the part of the seedsman. The seedsman welcomes legal control as a protection against unfounded claims. To take advantage of this legal protection the purchaser needs to pay close attention to the analysis label that must be printed on every package of grass seed. The information is often in small print but it is worth seeking. In fact, *the analysis label is the only really important printing on the package.*

On the label of a typical five-pound package of Kentucky bluegrass will appear the name Kentucky bluegrass and the statement that it is 90 per cent pure. This means that 90 per cent of the material consists of whole seed of Kentucky bluegrass. Such lifeless things as chaff, broken seed, dirt and other foreign but dead material are recorded as inert matter. If there is weed seed present, the amount must be stated. If there is seed of other crops, this amount must also be stated so that the total is 100 per cent.

One may well inquire why the package does not contain 100 per cent Kentucky bluegrass instead of a mixture of Kentucky bluegrass, useless material and perhaps unwanted seed. For a particular kind of seed, cleaning beyond a certain point becomes a losing proposition. Too much good seed would be discarded along with the foreign material. It might be possible to produce 100 per cent pure seed of such small-seeded kinds as bentgrass and bluegrass, but the cost would necessarily be very high and out of all proportion to any gain in real value. Home lawn owners can take consolation in the fact that seed from all reputable firms has been cleaned in about the same fashion and there is usually little merit in seeking the cleanest possible seed.

Weed seed mixed in the package with desirable grass seed is not nearly as much of a problem as most persons suppose. With modern cleaning procedures the amount of weed seed remaining is very small, and most of this weed seed is not from plants that will survive under lawn conditions. Finally, the amount of weed seed already present in most soils that have not been sterilized is so great in proportion to the tiny amount contributed by the grass seed mixture that no amount of grass seed cleaning would help particularly. The seedsman is often blamed for a weedy lawn or a poor stand of grass, when usually the fault is with the person who did not prepare and manage the new seeding properly.

There is another vital bit of information that the package analysis label must show. This is the germination percentage—that is, the proportion of the pure seed that will grow when it is placed under favorable laboratory conditions. In the case of Kentucky bluegrass, the figure might be 80 per cent germination. This means that of the 90 per cent pure seed, only 80 per cent will actually germinate. Thus the net is 72 per cent pure live seed, so a typical five-pound package of Kentucky bluegrass really contains about three and one-half pounds of pure live seed.

To compare values of two lots of the same kind of seed, the only matter of real consequence is the cost per pound of pure live seed. If you like arithmetic, multiply the germination figure by the purity and divide this figure into the retail price at which the seed is offered. Two lots of the same kind of seed that sell for the same price per pound of pure live seed will be, for all practical purposes, of equal value.

When grass seed is bought as a mixture of kinds, the matter can be quite confusing since the purity and germination of each kind of seed are stated. It is useless to try to compare a list of standards of quality with the kinds of seed in a mixture, for ordinarily most seed mixtures contain about the same quality of seed in terms of purity and germination. Hence the buyer can be reasonably safe if he merely trusts the seedsman to supply standard-quality seed in the mixture.

The really important points to be observed are the kinds and proportions of seed in the mixture. Ordinarily Kentucky bluegrass and red fescue are the grasses that will produce good turf for Northern home lawns. Almost everything else in the mixture is merely to lower the price or to give a quick show of green color that is reassuring but of no real value. A little quick-growing grass like ryegrass or redtop will cause no harm, but buyers should avoid lawn seed mixtures containing more than 15 per cent ryegrass or any seed at all of such coarse kinds as tall fescue. A simple rule for home lawn makers is to buy the right kinds of seed from a reputable seedsman.

Plant Grass in Fall

JOHN F. CORNMAN

LATE summer is the best time of year for planting new lawns and repairing old ones. After September 15 success is still possible, but difficulties increase with each passing day.

After the necessary topsoil is in place and well graded to give a pleasing effect and lead excess moisture away, organic matter is added. Granulated peat moss at the rate of three large (seven cubic foot) bales to each 1,000 square feet is a reasonable minimum. The peat should be spread evenly over the area to be planted.

If the soil is more acid than is desirable for turf grasses, as shown by a soil test, ground limestone at the rate of fifty pounds per 1,000 square feet should be spread on the peat moss. An adequate supply of nutrients deep in the soil is assured by a uniform application of about forty pounds of a 5-10-5 garden fertilizer over the peat and lime.

Then the peat, fertilizer and whatever lime may be called for should be worked thoroughly into the soil. This can be accomplished by repeated mixing with a rotary tilling machine. Mixing is not adequate until the entire top four to six inches of soil is uniform in texture. Layers of peat or similar organic matter anywhere in the soil are most damaging.

After the topsoil and soil amendments are thoroughly mixed, the area is raked smooth again. If the soil is fluffy so that footprints are deep, a few trips with a lawn roller and then reraking will firm the seedbed. The final raking should leave the seedbed surface smoothly graded and free of all large stones.

A second application of fertilizer, either twenty pounds of the garden-type fertilizer such as 5-10-5 previously used, or ten pounds per 1,000 square feet of 10-10-10, or one of the special lawn formulas, should be broadcast over the entire area. Now the lawn is ready for seeding.

The secret of choosing a good, economical seed mixture is to buy the most appropriate kinds of seed, even though they are relatively expensive, and use modest amounts. This method will give far better results than the usual heavy seedings of cut-rate mixtures of poorly adapted grasses.

An excellent choice for good soils in full sun is a seeding of two pounds per 1,000 square feet of one of the elite Kentucky bluegrass varieties or a mixture of several of them. Merion, Fylking, Pennstar, Adelphi, Windsor and Nugget are among the best of the varieties. Where there is some shade or where soils are less favorable, a planting of three or four pounds per 1,000 square feet of equal parts of an elite bluegrass and Pennlawn or Illahee red fescue is recommended. Top-quality commercial mixtures similar to the mixture just suggested will also prove satisfactory.

Even distribution of fertilizer, lime and seed are most important for uniform results. In broadcasting seed, fertilizer or lime, a wheeled distributor is desirable. Such work can be done by hand if care is taken, but a mechanical distributor does a good job quickly.

After the final fertilization and seeding, the soil surface should be raked very lightly with just the tips of the rake teeth to mix the seed into the top quarter inch of soil. Seed covered lightly in this manner will germinate more quickly. (If the seed is buried deeply or carelessly it will never sprout.)

Gardeners who find this final light raking difficult would do well to skip the operation. Nothing will be lost except a little speed in development. The final planting operation calls for firming the seed into the soil with a lawn roller half filled with water. If a roller is not available, the procedure can be omitted without large delays in development.

After the seeding is complete, the only concern for the next few weeks is to keep the surface of the soil moist at all times. Hand watering with a fine spray is required. Several waterings a day may be needed. Set sprinklers are not appropriate for this chore because the soil surface will soon be washed and gullied.

The very first watering can be delayed indefinitely, if desired. The dry seed will be secure except for trivial amounts that may be carried away by birds. Once the seedbed has been moist for a day or two, final success will depend largely upon keeping the seedbed moist continually.

In anticipation of the first cutting the mower should be sharpened and adjusted. The mower should be set to cut the grass at about one and one-half inches high. Mowing (at one and one-half inches) should be done on a continuous and regular basis from the time the first grass blades are tall enough to be reached by the mower until further mowing in the fall is impossible. New lawns need no protection from the weather. They should not be allowed to grow tall either before the first mowing, between mowings, or at the end of the season.

By following the program outlined here, there should be a solid cover of turf before winter. Then, with another routine application of fertilizer in late winter or early spring, followed by frequent mowing, a permanent top-quality lawn will be established.

Lime, a Vital Part of Turf

ALEXANDER M. RADKO

LIME is often regarded as a fertilizer; it is not. But lime is a vital part of turf culture and an understanding of its function in the soil will help make this clear.

Most soils in humid temperate regions are acid. Acid soils are common in all regions where rainfall leaches appreciable amounts of calcium and magnesium from the upper layers of the soil. Since these two chemicals are constituents of lime, the soil becomes lime-deficient or acid.

Acidity of the soil is measured by a numerical pH scale (pH simply means potential of hydrogen) which runs from 0 to 14. A reading of pH 7 is neutral; below that the soil is acid, above alkaline. Grasses in the temperate zone grow best in soils of pH 6 to 7. Soils rarely have a reading lower than pH 4, and a pH of 9 is equally rare. Actually the pH is an indication in a broad way, of the physiological condition of the soil.

An amateur can determine the pH of his soil by using one of the home soil test kits now on the market. Or he can take advantage of the services offered by agricultural experiment stations located at land grant colleges and universities within his state. Soil should not be limed unless a soil test indicates the need.

There are two principal types of lime for turf use—ground limestone and hydrated lime. Of these, ground limestone is the material most commonly used for home lawns. There are two kinds of ground limestone—high calcium limestone and limestone containing both calcium and magnesium; the latter is called dolomitic lime. Dolomitic lime is more costly and used primarily on soils low in magnesium. High calcium limestone is used on all other lawn soils. Either kind will raise the pH readings of soil.

How much lime should be applied to a given lawn area? Normally, ground limestone is used at the rate of fifty pounds to each 1,000 square feet every three years. This amount is usually required to maintain a pH level once a good level is attained.

If, to begin with, the soil pH reading is low, it is advisable to make yearly applications of lime at the rate of thirty-five to fifty pounds to each 1,000 square feet until the level is raised between pH 6 and 7. It is unwise to apply more than fifty pounds of ground limestone to each 1,000 square feet at any time, or even to make applications at this rate more than once a year. Heavier applications will tie up some of the minor food elements in the soil necessary to grass growth. Excessive liming also affects soil microorganisms adversely, particularly bacteria.

The gradual raising of a low pH level through proper liming will aid in the production of beneficial soil organisms. A sudden change in pH through very heavy lime applications will reduce the efficiency of soil bacteria, sometimes for several years. Bacteria are essential because they aid the conversion of nitrogen fertilizers into forms that can be used by plants.

Another important reason why a gradual rather than a sudden rise in soil pH is desirable is that lime reacts chemically with other elements in the soil. For example, although deficiencies of iron and manganese are not common, they do occur in certain soils, especially sandy soils and those that have been heavily limed. Excessive liming tends immediately to tie up iron and manganese into forms that plants cannot use. As a result, the turf becomes chlorotic and weak and may even die.

Aluminum in soluble form is toxic to many plants. In acid (low pH) soils, aluminum is highly soluble. Lime, therefore, will raise the pH and thereby tie up aluminum. Gradual applications will do the job and will not tie up beneficial elements such as iron and manganese.

Fungi (disease-causing organisms) can persist within a wide range of soil pH levels, but they predominate in acid soils. As the pH reading is raised, conditions become less favorable for fungi and more desirable for bacteria. This is further illustration of the fact that soil is a living system, and that proper applications of lime will help to keep it dynamic.

As mentioned, lime has a chemical effect on soils—it sets off a chemical exchange that aids in the release of certain elements while tying up others. In some soils this gives the appearance of a fertilizer application. This is why some gardeners have the idea that lime is a fertilizer. It is not, but it does put fertilizer to more efficient use. To substitute one element for the other would be a basic error in lawn soil care.

Lime can be safely applied to lawns at any time of the year if it is watered in thoroughly. Probably spring or fall is best to take advantage of heavy rains and thaw-heaving of the soil. Ground limestone is slow-acting and can be applied at the same time as fertilizer without danger of injury to the turf; the nitrogen will have been released long before the lime becomes active.

Hydrated lime must be applied separately. It is quick-acting and reacts with nitrogen fertilizer to form ammonia gas which is toxic to plant life. Thus hydrated (or burnt) lime is normally not recommended for home lawn use. If it is used, the rates of application should never exceed five to ten pounds to each 1,000 square feet at any one time.

Spring Lawn Care

JOHN F. CORNMAN

For a beautiful summer lawn gardeners must start work at the first opportunity in earliest spring. A thorough raking to clean off tree leaves, twigs and debris is the first project.

Opinions vary on lawn rolling. Many lawn experts believe that it is not necessary; others feel that it does have some beneficial effect if done carefully. If there has been a great deal of damage from frost heaving, the lawn may be rolled once as soon as the frost is out of the ground and the winter accumulation of debris has been raked off.

Lawn rollers usually can be rented from garden centers that provide this service. Put enough water in the roller so that the weight will just push the frost-heaved grass plants back into place. A single rolling in the spring is all the lawn needs. It can be omitted without any serious damage.

Two of the most important things for an established lawn are lime and fertilizer. Grass will not grow well in soil that is too acid. The only sure way to know whether the lawn needs lime is by a soil test. In case of doubt, apply limestone, for an unneeded lime treatment will do no harm if the lawn is fertilized adequately.

Every lawn needs fertilizer in early spring if it is to get off to a

Brisk raking and clean-up of debris are the first order of business for spring lawn care.

Nan Tucker

good start. If fertilizer was applied early last fall, as it should have been, the spring application will speed the growth of the new shoots of grass developed during the fall and winter. If not, then a spring fertilizing is essential.

A standard complete fertilizer, one containing all three of the major nutrients—nitrogen, phosphorus and potassium—is the most practical one to use. The fertilizers especially packaged for lawns are most convenient. The chief advantage of these products over less expensive kinds is that they are less likely to burn the grass if they are applied carelessly. Either type of fertilizer, properly used, will give consistently good results.

Before growth starts in the spring the chemical fertilizers are not likely to damage the turf. If the lawn has already started to grow, take care to spread the chemical fertilizer as evenly as possible and when the grass is perfectly dry. Use a wheeled spreader or distributor. A thorough watering immediately afterward will eliminate almost all possibility of grass injury. However, if the fertilizer is spread properly in the first place, that alone will be safety enough.

For most lawns a spring application of a fertilizer such as a 10–6–4 or a 10–10–10 should be made at the rate of about ten pounds to each 1,000 square feet. Any complete lawn fertilizer will be satisfactory if used at the appropriate rate, as indicated on the bag.

A Merion bluegrass lawn should be fed more heavily. Twice the rate suggested for ordinary lawns would be appropriate for Merion. If the fertilizer is of the non-burning type, it can be put on all at once. If a chemical fertilizer is used for economy, divide the required application in half and spread the second half a week or two after the first.

How much grass seed is needed for spring improvement of an established lawn? None at all unless there are completely bare spots, in which case each area should be prepared and seeded as for a new lawn. The common practice of throwing grass seed on an established lawn is sheer waste. The seedlings have no chance to get established to survive the summer.

If the lawn area is uniformly covered with grass but it is not thick enough, fertilization and better maintenance will restore it. Make the turf thick by strengthening the existing plants rather than trying to crowd in a lot of new seedlings. Fall is a much better time for lawn seed sowing, but if bare spots are not filled up with new grass now they are sure to become weed patches by summer.

Mowing begins when grass is about two inches high. The mower should be sharpened and adjusted. A lawn cannot look neat if mower blades are dull or if they are not set to cut properly. For a standard lawn of mixed grasses, set the mower to cut at least one and one-half inches high; this will leave the grass blades long enough to continue good growth. A Merion bluegrass lawn can be mowed a little shorter, but no closer than one and one-quarter inches. The cutting height selected should be retained all summer.

Mow the lawn frequently, particularly when growth is vigorous in the cool spring months. If the grass is allowed to grow tall between mowings, the tender, bleached crowns of the grass plants will be exposed to damage from the hot sun.

Most people judge their lawn success by the number of weeds they have, or the lack of them. Chemicals are available that can be used to kill almost any broadleaved weed without causing serious damage to the desirable grasses. Many of these chemicals are effective at almost any time during the growing season. Crabgrass requires different materials, and a single preventive treatment in early spring is the key to success.

Summer Lawn Care

RALPH E. ENGEL

MANY lawns will be saved or ruined in May and June. It is a season of rapid growth followed by hot weather—the most hazardous season for lawns in the Northeast. Right and wrong decisions during this period have great impact on the grass during the heat stress that follows. Some err in mowing or handling of clippings. Others feel compelled to fertilize the lawn improperly either because they neglected to do so earlier or because the good results of early spring feeding gave false encouragement.

Proper lawn maintenance includes regular mowing. The blades must be sharp and set at the proper cutting height for the type of grass.

Scotts Seeds

When summers are rainless, lawns should be watered thoroughly every week to ten days. Light sprinklings encourage weeds.

Gottscho-Schleisner

The late spring period is the start of the "downhill" season for Northern lawns. The first signs of crabgrass will appear, and there will be enough hot days to cause anxiety. Certain lawn efforts will greatly aid the lawn, while others will be a source of "danger." One simple set of rules will not cover all lawn types. Gardeners should observe the lawn regularly and be alert to changes in the grass.

If a stand of crabgrass plants appears, treatment with disodium methyl arsonate may give good control in late spring. Be careful, in following instructions at this season, to avoid turf injury. Crabgrass can be discouraged by high mowing and watering as infrequently as possible. This prevents rapid weed spread and tight growth which would crowd out the turf grasses. For the same reason, fertilization of turf containing crabgrass also is unsound.

Should the lawn be fertilized in late spring and early summer? Many lawns will benefit little or not at all from fertilization in warm weather. Color may be improved temporarily, but total growth response is relatively poor. Summer weeds are encouraged and the turf grasses are more susceptible to heat and drought. Lawns most likely to benefit from fertilization are those where water, disease and weeds are carefully controlled. In some cases, the excessively starved lawn justifies warm-weather fertilization.

When fertilizing the lawn in warm weather, materials with insoluble or non-burning characteristics are preferred. Intense stimulation of the grass is pointless. Usually it is desirable to use rates that give less than one pound of nitrogen per 1,000 square feet. Thus a 10-6-4 fertilizer would commonly be used at rates of five to ten pounds per 1,000 square feet.

By contrast, for Bermuda and zoysia lawns late spring and early summer is the ideal time to fertilize these grasses. Also, heavier rates would be used—ten to twenty pounds of 10-6-4 per 1,000 square feet.

Mowing procedures are critical in the summer months. Close mowing (under one and one-half inches) is ruinous for the Kentucky bluegrass-red fescue lawn. This weakens the grass, encourages weeds and increases heat and drought injury. If the lawn is prone to summer injury, a two-and-one-half or three-inch height of cut is recommended.

"How often should I mow?" is a common question of the home owner. Avoiding excessive growth which necessitates removal of one-half or more of the total top growth is a good rule of thumb. In terms of time interval, this can be every three to seven days in good growing weather or only every fourteen days in poorer weather.

Where lawns are of bentgrass, Bermuda grass or zoysia, mowing should be closer than for the Kentucky bluegrass lawn. Also, with these grasses, it becomes more important to avoid excessive top growth between mowings.

Should clippings be removed? In most cases, clippings can remain on the lawn without harm and provide some benefit. If clippings have a tendency to accumulate in piles during mowing, these should be scattered or removed. Also, if the clippings are unsightly or if the turf is very closely cut, remove the clippings.

Is watering desirable? The desire to water becomes second nature as soon as the grass shows first signs of discoloration. A lack of water is not always responsible for turf deterioration. Good lawn turf in the more humid sections will survive without watering. On very hot dry sites or in low rainfall areas, the use of water is very necessary.

In the Northeast, water rarely is required before late spring. Applying water before it is needed increases the need for water later in the season. Delay the start of watering until hot, dry periods have dried the soil to a depth of four to eight inches and the grass begins to show a "blue" color during the heat of the day. A healthy lawn, properly watered, seldom needs irrigation more frequently than once a week, even in dry, hot weather.

Water should be applied slowly and uniformly to rewet the full depth of dry soil. Improper watering is as bad or worse than no water, especially in the humid climates. Do not start to water and then abandon the turf to hot dry weather later in the season. This can cause more heat and drought damage than unwatered turf would experience.

Before starting a watering program, remember that in addition to the increased hazards from poor watering practices, watered lawns tend to be more weedy and more susceptible to disease injury. In some cases, these disadvantages outweigh the pleasure of a green lawn in dry weather.

An excellent chemical, 2,4–D, will easily eliminate dandelion, plantain and buckhorn. Spraying of the entire lawn with this chemical in summer is not good practice, as this can introduce enough 2,4-D to vaporize and injure sensitive ornamental plants. However, for safer application, spot spray this weed with a single gust from a mist bottle that contains a solution of this chemical and water. A brush or sponge attached to a broomstick can be used also.

Radical measures should be used rarely and never in warm weather. Also, this period is not a good one to experiment with all the new ideas or materials. Do not be so reactionary that proved materials such as 2,4-D for spotting dandelion are overlooked. Lean toward conservatism in lawn care, especially in the warmer months. This is a good season to cut the grass high, keep an observing eye on the lawn and relax. Before deviating from this comfortable approach, be sure that experience or professional knowledge supports the effort.

Solutions for Spring Lawn Problems

JOHN F. CORNMAN

NEW house in spring—no lawn—what to do? This is one of the most perplexing horticultural problems a new home owner has to face. For most persons there is really no perfect, economical answer. Here are the major possibilities:

1. Is sodding the answer? Almost ideal for any lawn problem is the lawn produced by an experienced commercial operator working with good soil and top-quality sod. The cost of such a contracted sodding job is about one-third to one-half more than a comparable contracted seeding job. Unfortunately, the price is beyond the average suburbanite's budget and far beyond the cost of a thorough do-it-yourself seeding.

2. How about planting a permanent lawn seed mixture in the spring after preparing the ground properly?

For crabgrass control, siduron can be used at seeding time without interfering with the germination of good grasses, so spring-planted lawns have some chance for success even where crabgrass has been a troublesome summer weed. Spring-seed lawns still require frequent watering and protection from traffic and at best will be a ground cover of seedlings rather than a dense, tough sod.

3. Would the usual commercial seed mixture containing plenty of ryegrass, or a top-quality bluegrass-fescue mixture spiked up with ryegrass do a better job? Certainly the ryegrass will show green more promptly. However, the slowly developing bluegrass and fescue plants will have to fight competition from the quick-growing ryegrass in addition to trying to hold their own against crabgrass.

The larger the proportion of ryegrass, the greater will be the competition. If the lawn survives the summer and then develops well during the autumn and following spring, scattered tufts of ryegrass will continue to disfigure the lawn for several seasons. Again, remember that the larger the proportion of ryegrass in the mixture, the worse the nuisance.

4. Should a temporary lawn of ryegrass be started in the spring, with a view toward rebuilding or renovating with permanent grasses in autumn? A heavy seeding of ryegrass will give a green cover in about two weeks. With careful tending it will begin to look like a lawn in a month or six weeks. Of course, this will not be a sod that can be walked on or used for badminton or other games, but it will give an illusion of a turf.

Just when the ryegrass might amount to something, it will be time to start all over again. A stand of ryegrass heavy enough to have functioned like a lawn will need to be turned under and the permanent lawn started from bare soil. If the ryegrass is thin enough to permit scarifying the surface and broadcasting good seed it could not have amounted to much as a summertime lawn.

Scattering seed of permanent grasses on the undisturbed ryegrass lawn will be useless. The surface should be loosened thoroughly with an iron rake or worked over with one of the new renovating machines. The effort and expense to prepare such a seedbed will be considerable. If seed is simply planted among the ryegrass, the same old ryegrass nuisance will irk the owner for the next several seasons.

5. All things considered, is a fall-seeded lawn the most logical

choice after all? An experienced turf-grass man would answer an emphatic "yes!" His course would be to spend spring and early summer in adjusting the grade of the land accurately and correcting depressions caused by gradual settling of the soil over filled areas. The placing of trees and shrubs and the preparation of good flower-bed areas bordering the lawn can be taken care of without danger of disrupting a new lawn seeding.

From the lady of the house a proposed program of this sort usually brings objections that the outside is a muddy mess from spring to mid-August and the children will track dirt into her new home. Even if seed were sown at once, the children could not be permitted to play on the tender seedling grass. Also, properly graded soil is neat in appearance, and since the children would be forced to stay on paved areas or play elsewhere, the dirt problem would be no different.

The choice for the family moving into a new home in late spring seems clear. Sodding solves the problem at once and meets all the objections except cost. The only economical solution is to accept a little inconvenience and delay while preparing for a top-quality fall seeding job that will pay dividends every year.

Weeds to Conquer

JOHN A. JAGSCHITZ

Do you encourage weeds to live in your lawn? You do when you neglect your lawn. Thousands of weed seeds lie in the soil ready to grow when grasses become weak and the sod thins.

Weeds do not cause poor turf; they are the result of it. The best defense against them is to maintain a dense, healthy, vigorously growing lawn. Do this by fertilizing, mowing and watering properly and by using adapted and improved turf grasses.

But if the weeds come, chemical weed killers, called *herbicides*, will control them. Good management must be coupled with the use of herbicides to encourage grass growth. If not, new seeds will invade and take over again.

Successful weed control depends on proper herbicide selection and application and precaution notes *supplied with the purchased material*. Correct application is extremely important. The correct amount of herbicide will kill the weed, while increases in the amount may injure the grass.

Herbicides can be applied as sprays or as granular materials to be used with a spreader. They should be applied when the wind is calm so they do not drift and damage other plants. With sprays, use low pressure and coarse spray because fine droplets will easily drift with the wind. Sprays are more efficient and less expensive for large turf areas, but home owners usually find granular materials more convenient.

Granular herbicides are often available in combination with turf fertilizers. These should only be used when there is a weed problem. Chemical treatment should be used only when there is a reason for it, and using it unnecessarily is a waste of money. Turf fertilizer-herbicide combinations are often misused as a fertilizer with no regard for the herbicide they contain. When used in gardens, flower beds and around trees and shrubs, the herbicide can cause severe damage. Another misuse is extra feeding by going around the tree or shrub twice with the spreader. The extra herbicide causes severe injury.

All herbicides should be considered *poisonous*. Handle them carefully and store them out of reach of children, pets and livestock. READ THE LABEL on the product. Do not contaminate foodstuffs or water supplies. Careless use is not the fault of the herbicide—it is yours.

Weed control can start before a lawn is actually seeded. There are fumigants that kill weeds and weed seeds in the soil. This reduces future weeds and eliminates those that are extremely difficult to control after grass is established. These weeds include annual bluegrass, bentgrass, nutsedge, quackgrass and tall fescue. Fumigants such as Dowfume (methyl bromide gas), Vapam or VPM (metham liquid) and Vorlex (liquid) are applied to newly prepared seedbeds prior to seeding.

After a waiting period of a few days to three weeks, depending on soil factors and the chemical used, grass seed can be planted safely. The disadvantage of fumigation is that (1) only experienced or professional applicators should do the job and (2) it can be costly. These chemicals must be handled carefully because they can be extremely harmful.

New lawns, especially those seeded in the spring, seem to have more weeds than grass. Most often these are annual weeds, such as ladysthumb, lambsquarters, pigsweed and ragweed, which come from seed in the soil. Many of them will be eliminated during the first two months by regular mowing. However, weeds that survive mowing, such as crabgrass, chickweed and dandelion, must still be controlled.

Most herbicides are not safe to use on seedling turf grass. Young plants are easily injured. After a lawn is six weeks old and has been mowed three or four times, it is usually safe to use herbicides. However, broadleaf weed control in spring-seeded lawns is best left until fall. Herbicides applied in the summer during hot, dry weather are apt to injure even mature grass. Lawns seeded in the fall are best treated the following spring.

Tests at the University of Rhode Island's College of Resource Development have shown that the herbicide called *bromoxynil* (Brominal, Buctril, and Nu-Lawn Weeder) can safely be used in seedling turf to control certain broadleaf weeds. It does best when applied to seedling weeds less than one and one-half inches across and four inches in height. It is less effective as weeds get older. Bromoxynil has successfully reduced heavy infestation of ladysthumb, lambsquarters, pigweed, ragweed and several other weeds. Within a few days the weeds turn gray-brown and become shriveled and dry. This should (1) improve grass seedling growth, (2) reduce the chance of grass being smothered and (3) make mechanical mowing easier. At present, several commercial sod growers are using bromoxynil.

Annual grasses in spring-seeded lawns, such as crabgrass, barnyardgrass, foxtail and goosegrass, are serious pests. Mowing does not kill them. They compete so severely with turf grass that by fall, after they die, they leave a sad-looking, thin lawn. There is an herbicide called Tupersan (siduron) that can safely be used in seedbeds and seedling turf to control crabgrass and reduce the invasion of other summer grasses. Tupersan should be applied to the surface of the seedbed after seeding and before crabgrass germinates and emerges. It will still do a good job if used before crabgrass plants reach the three-leaf stage or one-half inch in height.

For established lawns there are several herbicides one can choose from to control the common weeds. These include annual summer grasses, such as crabgrass, and a host of broadleaf weeds, such as chickweed, dandelion and plantain.

Crabgrass grows from seed each spring and dies in the fall, leaving a crop of seed for the following year. It is *easiest* and *best* controlled with a pre-emergent type herbicide. These are applied before crabgrass seed germinates and before the plant emerges from the soil. *They will not kill established plants.* Application is usually made in April or about the time of forsythia bloom and at the start of lilac bloom. Some herbicides provide good control even when applied in the fall. However, best results are insured by spring use.

Numerous herbicides have been evaluated for crabgrass control at the University of Rhode Island during the past several years. Three pre-emergent herbicides have consistently provided good control with safety to most turf grasses. They are Betasan (bensulide), Dacthal (DCPA) and Tupersan (siduron). Dacthal, however, when used on fescue lawns will cause some thinning.

As mentioned earlier, Tupersan is safe to use in new seedings. On lawns where Betasan or Dacthal have been used it is not safe to seed for about four months. Tupersan is effective when used on crabgrass plants up to the three-leaf stage. It also is safe to use on young grass being grown for sod and does not restrict sod rooting after transplanting.

Some herbicides show residual activity in lawns the year after their use. Betasan has the most residual activity, followed by Dacthal, then Tupersan. Half rations of Betasan and Dacthal can be used in the second year to provide good crabgrass control. Two years' use with good results should eliminate your crabgrass problem. Treatment year after year is unnecessary, can damage grass and is a waste of effort and money.

The best control of other summer annual weeds, such as barnyardgrass, foxtail, fall panicum or goosegrass, is again with pre-emergent herbicides. Goosegrass, however, is more difficult to kill than crabgrass. Recent tests provided only partial control. More information is needed about herbicides and their effects on these weeds.

Two new herbicides, A-820 (Amchem Products, Inc.) and Ronstar (product of Rhodia, Inc.) have provided good crabgrass control. The latter also showed good control of goosegrass. Future tests should aid in the search to find more effective and safer herbicides.

Several organic methanearsonate-type herbicides (DSMA, MAMA, MSMA) will kill established crabgrass and other annual summer grasses that one neglected to control with pre-emergent herbicides. They are sold under such names as Ansar, Clout, Crab-E-Rad, Dimet, Methar or simply "Crabgrass Killer DSMA." They work most effectively on young plants. Two or three applications, spaced about a week apart, are needed for complete control. Some turf-grass discoloration may develop. If the crabgrass plants are no taller than one inch and have not reached the five-leaf stage, a single application of Tupersan plus methanearsonate should be sufficient.

Annual bluegrass (*Poa annua*) is a weed that is very troublesome. Several herbicides are sold for its control. Most home owners will be discouraged with the results of these products. Annual bluegrass does not disappear as do other weeds controlled with herbicides. Results after several years can be disappointing. Possibly with careful and professional use some products may be effective. They do, however, require exacting and specific techniques, precautions and timing.

Pre-emergent herbicides have not proven successful to prevent broadleaf weeds in lawns. The weeds credited for control by specific herbicides are usually not found in mowed lawns. Lawns treated with Dacthal and Tupersan have been noted to contain fewer dandelions. However, control of dandelions is best left to the broadleaf weed-control herbicides that have been successfully used for years.

Broadleaf weeds such as dandelion, plantain, chickweed, etc., can be selectively controlled with herbicides. The best time for their use is in late September and October or in late April and May. The weeds and grass should be showing good growth and soil moisture should be ample. Avoid the use of herbicides during hot weather, as the grass may be injured. Do not mow or water for at least two days after the use of herbicides.

Most common broadleaf weeds, such as dandelion and plantain, can easily be controlled with 2,4-D. Some weeds, however, such as chickweed and clover, are not easily killed by 2,4-D. Herbicides such as Banvel (dicamba), MCPP (mecoprop) or Silvex are effective for these weeds. Broad-spectrum control (control of most all weeds), can be obtained by using a mixture of herbicides. There are numerous commercial products containing mixtures of 2,4-D with either one or two of the following—Banvel, MCPP or Silvex. Most of them can be expected to do a good job.

The combination of 2,4-D with Banvel is probably the most effective but requires caution under trees and shrubs. The mixture of 2,4-D with MCPP has a wide margin of safety, while Silvex plus 2,4-D has a smaller margin of safety, especially to bentgrass. A few specific weeds, such as knotweed, can best be controlled with Banvel, while spurge is best controlled with combinations containing Silvex.

Although herbicides will kill weeds, new weeds may appear in lawns from seed in the soil. Retreatment may be necessary after a year or so. If a dense, vigorously growing stand of grass is maintained and herbicides are used, weeds should not be a major problem.

PART V

PLACES
TO GARDEN

ARDENS APPEAR in all kinds of places. High above the bustling city streets can be found lush greenery where lofty shade trees grow and petunias billow over plant boxes. These are the penthouses and roof-top hideaways where urbanites escape the city's clamor in their own secluded havens. Although it is difficult to have a garden in the city, those who have been successful tell how in the following pages.

Some gardens grow by the sea, where daylilies and rugged roses defy the sand dunes, and banks of bayberries and beach plums face into the salty, misty winds. By the mountain lake cottage hydrangeas put on a summer show. Geraniums and lantanas bloom from window boxes on the porch. In the cool woodlands a wild garden grows. There the sprightly flowers of the forest floor and meadows thrive merrily in their new-found land.

Even at home there are ways to add something new to the garden. How about a shallow pool by the terrace where exotic waterlilies can glow in the heat of the day? What about the youngsters? They like to grow things, too. A plot of their very own to tend brings out qualities of responsibility and self-reliance.

A garden can be developed in many ways and in many places. Sometimes it just takes an idea and encouragement to get started.

(201)

Groundwork in the City Garden

ALYS SUTCLIFFE

MANY city dwellers with only a few square feet of planting space have the same enthusiasm for gardening as suburban home owners. Often their plans would do justice to a large estate, but eventually they are brought down to realistic proportions.

Like his country cousin, the gardener in the city has many things to consider. Drainage is a major factor. After a heavy rain, does the water sink into the ground quickly or does it stand in puddles for days? If there are to be flower beds, is it possible to dig the soil to a depth of at least eighteen to twenty-four inches? Is there sun in any part of the yard at any time of the day? For how long? On these vital factors depends the success of the city garden.

Most city gardens are not very big. More often than not they are surrounded by high fences which prevent air circulation. Also, high buildings cast heavy shade. City garden soil is often sour, particularly if the drainage is poor and the ground is fouled with deposits of dust, soot and oil fumes. In spite of all these hazards, fine gardens have been developed in the city, some at great expense and others by ingenuity.

The soil (assuming it is deep enough to support plant growth) should be tested to see what improvement is necessary. It can be improved by the addition of lime, peat moss and fertilizer in the right quantities. If there are only three or four inches of soil over clay, rubble or other fill, the gardener should consider excavating the area to a depth of eighteen inches or even two feet. He should make sure that the drainage underneath is good, then fill in with soil in which peat moss, leafmold or rotted manure has been added.

Sometimes it is better to raise the beds by building a wall about eighteen inches to two feet high. The height of the wall depends on the existing depth of soil and the type of plants to be used. The wall may be of brick or concrete, with seep holes about three feet apart along the base to give extra drainage.

A six-inch layer of coarse gravel or broken bricks should go in the bottom; next a two- or three-inch layer of partly decayed leaves or coarse peat moss, then the soil mixture. This should consist of soil mixed with peat moss and sand (one-fourth of each to the bulk of the soil). If the soil in the garden is not too poor, it can be improved by the incorporation of peat moss and sand to roughly the same depth. The addition of bonemeal (about one-half pound to eight square feet) will create a soil in which plants will grow. Lime should not be used in soil where rhododendrons and azaleas are planted.

Another vital factor for the city gardener to consider is light. He must determine the amount of sunlight the garden will get before he decides on the plants to be used. Light intensity may be increased by painting fences white.

A lawn in the city is a waste of time and money. It is better to have a flagstone or gravel area which, with an awning, will make a pleasant outdoor living room.

It may only be possible to improve the soil to a depth of three or four inches, which is deep enough for a groundcover of ivy or vinca (periwinkle). Then trees, shrubs and flowers can be grown in containers—the size depending on the root-space requirements of the plants. Small trees and large shrubs usually require containers two feet square by two feet deep.

Gay color can be obtained from spring-flowering bulbs such as crocus, snowdrops, daffodils, tulips and hyacinths; these may be planted among the ivy or periwinkle so that when they have finished flowering there still is a good green cover. It is well worth while to spend a few dollars each fall for fresh bulbs to insure good bloom each spring.

Potted flowering plants may be placed in the groundcover for summer color. Begonias, impatiens and fuchsias are good for shady gardens; geraniums, lantanas and petunias are fine in sun. City dwellers who are usually away most of the summer would do well to have only groundcovers and an evergreen shrub or two, with bulbs for

Restrained use of plant material, brick walls and flooring set off the ornaments featured in a Manhattan garden.

Gottscho-Schleisner

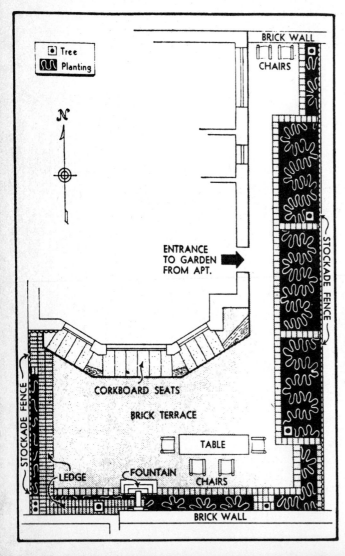

The plan is for an L-shaped city back yard, 40 × 8 feet on the east, and 30 × 15 feet on the south. Since shade was a problem and easy upkeep a goal, the green garden was designed with ferns, rhododendrons and ivy. Photo above shows the south wall.

Landscape by Leslie Larson

Mirrors cut in Moorish shapes reflect the simple charm of a city back yard, walled with cedar fencing.

Gottscho-Schleisner

spring color and a few potted chrysanthemums purchased in bud and bloom for a fall display.

General city garden maintenance calls for fertilizing once a year in late spring, after which the beds or containers should be mulched with peat moss or any similar material available. Trees and shrubs should be sprayed with a hose every day to keep them clean, but the gardener should avoid waterlogging the soil. Lime is applied as needed.

No matter how carefully the city home owner plans his garden, he still may encounter particular problems that can only be solved by trial and error. Thus, especially for a beginner, good advice is "go slowly—start small."

The Plants to Grow

NANCY GRASBY

THE city gardener should choose plants carefully. Trees, shrubs and herbaceous types must be able to grow in or at least tolerate poor soil, insufficient light and soot conditions. After some hunting, plus trial and error, I have found that there are many plants worthy of space in a city back yard.

High on the list of small ornamental trees are the flowering crab-apples (*Malus*) and cherries (*Prunus*), and the saucer magnolia (*Magnolia soulangeana*). Good, too, are the golden rain tree (*Koelreuteria paniculata*), the silk tree (*Albizzia julibrissin rosea*), Washington thorn (*Crataegus phaenopyrum*) and cockspur thorn (*C. crusgalli*).

Many varieties of Japanese holly (*Ilex crenata*), rhododendrons and azaleas grow well in the city. Other fine broadleaved evergreens are euonymus (*Euonymus radicans vegetus*) and Japanese andromeda (*Pieris japonica*). In the category of half-evergreen shrubs are the spreading euonymus (*Euonymus patens*), firethorn (*Pyracantha*), glossy abelia (*Abelia grandiflora*) and California privet (*Ligustrum ovalifolium*).

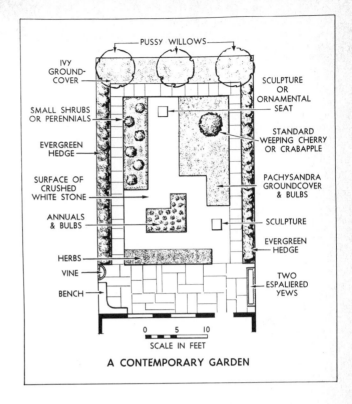

A small, city back yard lends itself to a tidy formal design which is traced by paving, groundcovers and crushed stone.

Design by Nancy Grasby

Labels in diagram:
PUSSY WILLOWS
IVY GROUNDCOVER
SMALL SHRUBS OR PERENNIALS
EVERGREEN HEDGE
SURFACE OF CRUSHED WHITE STONE
ANNUALS & BULBS
HERBS
VINE
BENCH
SCULPTURE OR ORNAMENTAL SEAT
STANDARD WEEPING CHERRY OR CRABAPPLE
PACHYSANDRA GROUNDCOVER & BULBS
SCULPTURE
EVERGREEN HEDGE
TWO ESPALIERED YEWS

0   5   10
SCALE IN FEET

A CONTEMPORARY GARDEN

Valuable deciduous shrubs include rose of Sharon (*Hibiscus syriacus*), forsythia, spirea, hydrangea, winged euonymus (*Euonymus alatus*), flowering quince (*Chaenomeles japonica* and *C. lagenaria*), Regel's privet and common barberry (*Berberis vulgaris*).

Certain perennials are more amenable to the city environment than others. Dependable kinds are hosta, daylily, bearded iris, *Sedum spectabile*, chrysanthemums and plumy bleeding heart (*Dicentra eximia*). There are several good annuals, plus tender perennials grown as annuals; among them are zinnias, petunias, marigolds, impatiens, flowering tobacco (nicotiana), spider plant (cleome) and four o'clock or marvel of Peru. All are valuable where indifferent light prevails. For gardens on terraces, the list is much longer.

Groundcovers, both annual and perennial, are vital to city gardeners. The familiar evergreen pachysandra is splendid for outlining beds. Plants should not be allowed to dry out. Rooted cuttings should be planted close together. Myrtle or periwinkle (*Vinca minor*) is almost evergreen; the lilac-blue flowers are delightful in early spring.

(207)

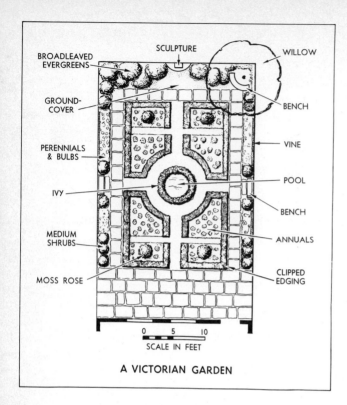

BROADLEAVED EVERGREENS

SCULPTURE

WILLOW

GROUND-COVER

BENCH

PERENNIALS & BULBS

VINE

IVY

POOL

BENCH

MEDIUM SHRUBS

ANNUALS

MOSS ROSE

CLIPPED EDGING

0   5   10
SCALE IN FEET

A VICTORIAN GARDEN

An elaborate garden pattern for a city back yard can be planned by using a pool as a focal point. Tidy beds of annuals and clipped hedges provide summer color.

Design by Nancy Grasby

Annual groundcovers are very useful around the edge of a lawn and near rocks. Outstanding kinds to grow from seed are the creeping zinnia (*sanvitalia*) with tiny golden flowers and the black-eyed clock vine (*thunbergia*) with pretty yellow or creamy white flowers. The common strawberry (*fragaria*) makes a splendid groundcover and edging plant. The mock strawberry (*Duchesnea indica*) with small fleshy red fruits is very pretty and survives autumn's first frosts. It may be hard to find.

Several sedums, notably *Sedum acre*, are excellent perennial groundcovers. Creeping charlie or moneywort (*Lysimachia nummularia*) spreads rapidly and hugs the ground, forming a light green, glossy carpet. Planted in a terrace box, it drapes the sides. Violets will take over an area in sun or shade and are indifferent as to soil. Virginia creeper (*Parthenocissus quinquefolia*) is wonderful for filling in large bare spots and twining over walls.

Vines also play many roles in a city garden. Boston ivy (*Parthenocissus tricuspidata*) does not need support and is wonderful for

(208)

draping a brick wall. It is good combined with evergreen English ivy (*Hedera helix*). The small-growing variety of Boston ivy known as Lowi is best for delicate tracery on a low wall.

Wistaria vines of great age are to be seen all over the city. Wistaria should be trained horizontally for best flowering. It pays to buy a well-grown specimen.

Grapes make a most satisfactory vine for fences and arbors and may produce fruit. Morning glories are foolproof annual vines, but the gardener should consult a catalogue and try other kinds of vines. Moonflowers supplement morning glories with fragrant white blooms at night.

Among the roses, hardy climbers such as Blaze, Paul's Scarlet, Dr. Van Fleet, New Dawn and City of York are often splendid in the city. Certain hybrid perpetuals, hybrid musks and floribundas may also be grown with considerable success. The Fairy, a spreading, bushlike, pink polyantha rose, is spectacular in some gardens.

There are other interesting and unusual plants to consider. Lan-

Bamboo, ivy and andromeda stand out against a backdrop cedar fence.
Molly Adams

(209)

Concrete lattice panels screen a city pool garden that features cotoneaster and crabapple.

Molly Adams

tana makes quick, shrublike woody growth. It will stand rough treatment and quite a lot of shade. It does not seem to be particular about soil. The flower color range is remarkable. Potted plants must be set out each year.

A fig tree is unlikely to reach full size without winter protection, but it makes strong seasonal growth. The large distinctive leaves contribute greatly to a garden's texture pattern.

Ivy can be grown as a groundcover, a wall covering or a hedge. Trained over a heavy-gauge wire form, it is a splendid substitute for a broadleaved evergreen shrub. It can also be trained on supports against a board fence, in a variety of designs, to make a year-round pattern.

Rue, a woody perennial herb with tough blue-green foliage, is almost a must in a city yard. The large-leaved sweet basil is an annual herb, lettuce green in color. It grows easily from seed. Besides being good in salads, it is a delightful little filler plant, fresh-looking to the end of the season.

An Almanac for City Gardeners

HAL LEE

March and April

1.   On the first warm week-end, sweep up the winter's accumulation of incinerator ash, soot, etc., from the terrace or rooftop. Hose down the tile or brick several times.

2.   Paint plant boxes, fences, gates and windbreak supports with a good grade of metalized outdoor house paint or enamel. Paint trellises or arbors before vines sprout.

3.   Plant a flowering crabapple tree on a south or east terrace while it is still dormant. Water the branches several times daily (top to bottom) and the tree may blossom this spring.

4.   Build one or two new plant boxes eight feet long by two feet wide and deep for trees and tall shrubs. Boxes eight by two to two and one-half feet wide and one foot deep hold flowers and small shrubs. Boston ivy is planted at the extreme back of the box. When new pink shoots are four to six inches long, train them onto the brick or stucco wall with small dabs of modeling clay. They will soon grip the wall unaided.

5.   Planter boxes require a topsoil mixture that will hold moisture (peat moss, manures or compost). Enrich the soil mixture with bonemeal. For good drainage place gravel, sand or coal clinkers in the bottom of the box.

6.   Seed of annuals and perennials may be started in a sunny east or south window. An early start indoors is also good for tuberous begonias and caladiums.

May and June

1.   During the first week of May plan succession bloom for summer and fall. This is more difficult in the small rooftop garden, especially if most of the planter boxes are filled with spring-flowering bulbs.

After they bloom, the leaves must be allowed to ripen. If the tallest growing spring bulbs are placed in the back of the flower boxes (as they should be) the ripening leaves can be screened with a planting of fast-growing dusty miller, set four to six inches in front. Another alternative is to discard the bulbs after flowering and buy new ones each fall.

2. Early May is a good time to plant broadleaved and needled evergreens: yews, hybrid rhododendrons, azaleas, boxleaf holly, andromeda and mountain laurel. These plants grow better in semi-shaded and less windy sites, but the holly and andromeda in particular are perfectly able to endure the environment of a terrace or rooftop. All of them will respond to monthly feedings of cottonseed meal from May to August; some gardeners prefer to fertilize with ammonium or aluminum sulfate.

3. May 15 is accepted in the Northeast area as a safe time to take potted house plants outdoors and "plunge" them in the soil. Harden off the plants by placing them in an open window on warm days in late April and early May. Some plants are unpotted and planted in soil. But always leave the amaryllis in its pot; insert a stake and tie up the leaves. Then feed monthly with a teaspoonful of 5-10-5.

4. When frost danger is past, begin transplanting home-grown seedlings to the garden or planter boxes. But it will be another six weeks or so before these come into bloom. If earlier flowering is desired, buy some geraniums, petunias, dwarf marigolds, ageratum, lobelia, sweet alyssum, impatiens, portulaca, lantana and verbena.

5. Chrysanthemum or aster seedlings or transplants may be purchased now to grow for fall bloom. If space is limited, buy ready-to-bloom plants later on. Zinnias and marigolds are easy to grow from seed sown outdoors after May 15. Remember that all plantings, including bulbs, may be placed twice as close together as is usually suggested. This is because of the extra rich and friable soil used by wise urban gardeners. Rooftop and terrace gardeners should have good luck with annual and perennial flowers because of the ample exposure to full sunlight.

July and August

1. Except for occasional weeding and spraying, easy does it. On week-ends, when non-gardening city dwellers take their cars (and carbon monoxide) out to the beaches and suburbs, you can relax and get a sun tan in a garden deck chair or chaise.

2. Evening is watering time, when the terrace tile has cooled off. Water everything from top to bottom including the trees as well as the vines on the walls. Remember that it takes an inch of water to penetrate one foot of soil in the flower boxes and two inches for the two-foot-wide tree and shrub boxes. Once the plantings are well established, remove the nozzle from the hose and let the water flow into the soil slowly until it drips out of the drainage holes at the bottom of the boxes. Terrace and rooftop plantings need this deep watering several times a week when July and August provide little rain.

3. In areas where incinerator ash is voluminous and makes flower beds and other plantings unsightly, everything should get an early-morning spray except hairy-leaved plants such as gloxinias and African violets, and possibly roses in bud and bloom. Clean leaves and flowers seem to be a more important consideration in city gardening than the questionable risk of water damage in the sunlight. City rooftop and terrace gardening may be thought of as an extension of hydroponic gardening because of the need for such large quantities of water.

4. Early July is a good time to feed roses, after their June bloom. Careful examination of the leaves will indicate whether they need a good rose dusting powder. Climbing roses are useful for terrace trellises, moon-gates and even on closely woven colonial picket fences which serve as windbreaks. They should have a south or east exposure. Started roses are available in quart cans and may be planted almost any time of the year, although early spring is usually preferred.

5. Chaste tree (*Vitex agnus-castus*) is a wonderful plant which is covered with blue blossoms in late July and August when floral color, especially blue, is scanty. This is best planted in November. Heavenly Blue morning glories climbing over an arbor are a lovely sight in midsummer. But morning glory vines are annuals and they

(213)

leave tenacious dead stems which have to be hand picked from trellises sooner or later. Better to train them up on green twine in front of the arbor or trellis. Then, when their bloom is ended, simply cut the strings and throw the vine away.

September and October

1. Plant Oriental poppies in early fall, also the early flowering bulbs. Throw out the geraniums and other annuals after they stop blooming. For most city gardeners it is not worth the trouble to carry geranium cuttings over the winter. Mid-September to October 1 is the best time to lift house plants from their outdoor beds and bring them indoors. If they are pot-bound, replant in the next larger size pot.

2. September is the hurricane season and high winds are the greatest enemy of a rooftop gardener. If a hurricane is on the way, "batten down the hatches." Tall poplars, willows, honey locust trees—any plants ten feet or higher—are most vulnerable on a rooftop. Of course, six-foot windbreaks all around the terrace garden are a big help. Trees may be tied to them with clothesline.

November and December

1. All the spring-flowering bulbs should be planted before cold weather makes outdoor work unpleasant. November is the ideal month for planting deciduous trees, hedges and some perennials and biennials. These cooler and less harried fall months also are good for building and filling another planter box or two.

2. Warm fall days are a good time to "put the garden to bed" for the winter. All dead leaves, weeds, stalks of withered annuals, etc., should be thrown into the compost heap. Do not apply mulches. It is important, especially with evergreens, to keep the soil moist until the first hard freeze of winter.

January and February

1. Stay inside by the fireplace, and look forward to getting the new seed catalogues shortly after New Year's Day.

2. Give some thought to making the living room or bedroom more suitable to house-plant culture. The average home temperature

is fine for most tropical plants: 72 to 75 degrees in daytime and 60 to 65 degrees at night. However, the heat usually is too dry. Small and decorative electric recirculating fountains are available for less than $50. They plug into a wall socket and will add considerable humidity to the air.

3. Then, too, most indoor gardens have improper lighting. Inexpensive fluorescent lighting may be installed behind valances. Window sills can be tiled so pots will not mar the paint. The same thing can be done beneath and behind floor boxes or room divider plant boxes, to avoid damage to hardwood floors, rugs or walls.

Penthouse Landscaping

PHILIP TRUEX

CONTAINERS come first in planning the city roof garden. Standard narrow window boxes are used for the tiny balcony, while raised masonry beds are appropriate for the spacious penthouse. But for the average-sized roof garden, wooden terrace boxes and tubs are suitable.

The terrace box is made of one-inch or one-and-one-half-inch board and may range from twelve to eighteen inches in width and depth. A length of four to five feet is most practical. The box is raised slightly from the terrace floor to aid drainage.

Drainage is no problem if three-quarter-inch holes are bored into the bottom of the box, one per square foot. Then a layer of drainage material can be placed on the bottom, either gravel, coarse cinder or pot shards (broken clay pots).

The soil mixture is the next most important consideration. It must be of top quality.

For each cubic foot of box space a good mixture can be made from approximately twenty-five pounds of topsoil, ten pounds of leafmold or humus, two quarts of peat moss and two quarts of vermiculite, which is handy and light for improving soil texture. Into each batch of this mixture a small handful of superphosphate or bone-meal and a large handful of dehydrated cow manure is added. A too-fertile mixture can result in coarse leaf growth and few flowers. Liquid fertilizer should be applied monthly, however.

Pot-grown annual bedding plants provide most of the summer color in the average terrace box. There always is a wide selection of trailing foreground plants available in spring. These are planted in the front of the boxes. Verbena, balcony petunia and ivy geranium are all colorful, but none can rival lantana. Lantana is more rooftop tolerant than any other trailing annual. It reaches its peak at chrys-anthemum time.

For the middle of the box there are many medium-sized annuals. These include French marigolds, dwarf zinnias, ageratum, snap-dragons and zonal geraniums for full sun, and wax begonias, coleus, impatiens, torenia and fragrant stock for semi-shade.

Tall plants are usually needed for the background. Cleome, giant African marigolds and giant zinnias are good for full sun, and nicotiana (flowering tobacco) blooms in semi-shade. The marigolds and zinnias produce a fine mass-color display, while the cleome makes a stately accent planting for the far end of the terrace. Nicotiana should be placed where its delightful fragrance can be appreciated.

City roof gardeners can plant annuals unusually early. Daily temperatures in the city often are ten degrees or so higher than those in surrounding suburbs. The soil volume in terrace boxes thaws rapidly in spring into a workable condition. Most annual plants can be set out the first week of May. Seed of annuals also can be sown a week or more ahead of the suburban schedule.

Annuals grown in terrace boxes can be spaced closer than usual. In fact, their root systems thrive on close quarters, provided that moisture and nutrient needs are met. Background vines and fore-ground trailers will not rob growing space from plants set in the middle of the boxes. Young seedlings, however, should not be sur-rounded with full-grown plants; they cannot compete. In fall, when the annuals are waning, they should be pulled up so tulips, daffodils and the little bulbs can be planted.

Perennials can be combined with summer-flowering bulbs. The most dependable trailing perennials for the edge of boxes are sedums (S. *spurium* or S. *hybridum*), or creeping charlie (*Lysimachia num-*

Rocks point up the curved planters and lend a naturalistic touch to a city penthouse garden.

Gottscho-Schleisner

Castor bean and privet form the backdrop for a sitting area on a city rooftop.

Molly Adams

Roses will bloom freely on a penthouse if they are planted in deep boxes with well-drained soil.

Gottscho-Schleisner

mularia). The latter is considered a pesky weed in lawns, but in roof gardens it is a real boon. In a short time creeping charlie will completely cover the side of a terrace box, giving the impression that the plants are growing out of a mossy bank. The bright yellow flowers in June are a bonus.

Medium-sized perennials which grow on a rooftop include gaillardia, Stokes's aster, dianthus, coralbells and pot-grown chrysanthemums; all of these are for full sun. Good choices for semi-shade are daylilies, hosta, bleeding heart and columbine.

Early spring planting of container-grown perennials, spaced well apart, can provide a series of blooms all season. For a real color display, however, it pays to interplant the perennials with summer bulbs in May and June. Ideal where background height is important is the quick-growing Peruvian daffodil (ismene) with its enormous white flowers. Where space is cramped, gladiolus corms can be tucked in between perennials to give a burst of color in midsummer.

Giant dahlias are usually too overpowering for terrace boxes, but the dwarf Coltness and Unwin hybrid dahlias are very valuable. Young plants can be used to fill in. Their brilliant blooms continue

(218)

well into fall, when they blend with the 'mum display. For fragrance, tuberoses can be included; they are roof-garden tolerant and take up little space, especially the variety Dwarf Pearl.

It may surprise some city gardeners to find that the spectacular climbing gloriosa lily (G. *rothschildiana*) does so well in a roof garden. The effect of its exotic scarlet and yellow flowers, borne on a stocky four- to six-foot vine, is really exciting. It is an expensive bulb, but this is compensated for by the fact that it is easily divided and carried over the winter, even in a warm apartment.

With their handsome foliage, caladiums are ideal summer bulbs for the shaded area of the terrace. Tuberous begonias are not a good choice, however.

After one of the perennial boxes has become overcrowded, the plants can be divided in spring and replanted in another box. The soil of the former perennial box is then reconditioned and fertilized, in preparation for the planting of annuals. The soil in the various boxes never becomes used up if the plantings are alternated like this every few years.

Roses can be grown in a terrace box, but best results will be achieved only if the entire box is devoted to them. Also, it is easier to give the roses uniform care if they are all in one group. A foot of soil depth is adequate; more is preferable.

Climbing roses such as red Blaze or pink Dream Girl do yeoman service when trained on a fence or trellis. Among bedding roses, the compact floribundas such as Summer Snow, Garnette or Pink Bountiful will grow much better than the hybrid teas. They can be planted closely—little more than a foot apart. Other good choices are the small-flowered polyantha rose and, for edging, the miniature or fairy roses.

Deciduous or evergreen hedges can also be grown on the roof. The easiest hedge to grow is privet. Other possibilities include winged euonymus (E. *alatus*), flowering quince (*Chaenomeles lagenaria*) and even Lombardy poplars, where a tall screen is needed. The most dependable evergreen hedge plants are upright yew (*Taxus*) or Japanese holly (*Ilex crenata*).

LEFT: A wire grill container, sphagnum moss, flat of seedlings and trowel are the basic ingredients for soilless planter gardening. RIGHT: The container is planted by filling it with successive layers of moss and plants. Seedlings are set at a slightly upward slant.

Moss Planters
for Soilless Gardening

GEORGE A. CARLE

DRAMATIC new effects can be achieved by growing plants in containers of sphagnum moss or peat. These soilless containers are ideal for limited planting areas, to cover posts and to create privacy by building plant walls.

The seedhouse of G. R. Vatter of Bern, Switzerland, originated the idea of moss-wall gardening in 1944. The façade of the store was decorated with columns of sphagnum moss, covered with flowering plants.

Actually, this method of plant culture is another form of hydro-

LEFT: The container is watered thoroughly with a liquid fertilizer solution after it is planted. Foliage should be syringed afterward to remove the fertilizer residue. RIGHT: Begonias flourish in a wooden wall planter.

George A. Carle and Louis Buhle

ponics, the growing of plants in chemical nutrient solutions. But instead of having the root systems immersed in water, sphagnum moss is used to support the plants in the container. The moss is water-retentive, which allows it to absorb and store nutrients necessary for plant growth. It also acts as a buffer in preventing an overconcentration of salts due to overfertilizing.

Construction of containers suitable for soilless plant culture is simple. Size and shape can vary. The skeleton of the container can be constructed of wood (cypress or redwood, for example) or metal. Treat the wood with a rot-resistant, non-poisonous preservative. If metal is used, treat it to prevent rust and corrosion from fertilizing materials.

The frame construction should have all sides open, making it possible to plant all areas; then the container can be used as a center-piece. A container with a solid back can be hung or placed against a wall.

Wire grill, metal rods or wood bars are used to retain the sphagnum moss in the container. The material is set around the open sides and fastened to the frame. If wire grill is used, heavy staples will fasten it to the frame. The top of the container is left open, as in a soil-type planter. If the container is for indoor use, a small tray should be attached to the underside to catch excess water.

Of course, other materials can be used in place of sphagnum moss. Some plantings have been made with fine peat moss in the center and a coarse, fibrous peat moss used as the outer wall. Osmunda or orchid peat is another possibility. All materials should be moistened before planting.

When planting, a layer of sphagnum moss (or other material) is placed at the bottom of the container to a depth of about one inch. The plant is then inserted between the openings of the vertical wall. It is advisable to place each plant deeply and at a slight upward slant. Successive layers of plant material and sphagnum moss are built up until the top of the container is reached.

Where the container is open on more than one side, all sides should be planted at one time. The sphagnum moss should be packed firmly to prevent later settling.

The number of plants needed will depend upon the kinds used. Place them close together. They will not spread as in horizontal beds. Although more plants are used in moss than in soil culture, the cost is offset by the size of the plants needed. Rooted cuttings or seedlings in two-and-one-half-inch pots are recommended. They are easy to plant and adapt faster than larger plants.

After planting, the container should be watered thoroughly and placed in a sheltered location for about a week. Syringe the foliage occasionally. Generally, one watering is sufficient until the container is put in its permanent spot.

The gardener will find watering is a simple chore. If the moss feels damp, no watering is necessary. However, in hot sun or exposed, windy locations care should be taken to prevent the sphagnum moss from drying out. Plants will respond to an occasional syringing with a fine spray.

Often the watering and feeding chores can be done at one time. If watering is indicated prior to fertilizing, be thorough and saturate the sphagnum moss. Wait a day or two and then fertilize.

Fertilizing should be started as soon as the containers are placed in their permanent locations. A complete water-soluble fertilizer, including trace elements, should be used every seven to ten days. At the start the solution can be half the strength recommended by the manufacturer for house plants; increase or decrease the amount as necessary. The moss should be damp to facilitate penetration of the nutrient solution. (This might mean watering the container the day before fertilizing.)

Whenever possible, fertilize on a cloudy day or late in the afternoon to prevent foliage burning. Use a sprinkling can with a fine rose for measuring the amount of solution and applying it evenly. Hanging baskets should be laid on the ground and left there so that the nutrient solution can penetrate. A light spray after fertilizing is beneficial and will remove fertilizer residue from the foliage.

Many types of plants have been grown in sphagnum moss containers—ageratums, geraniums, begonias, pansies, lantanas, dwarf marigolds and coleus. In addition, zebrinas, *Asparagus sprengeri,* alternantheras, strawberries, lemon balm, chives, water cress and mints have done well. Many of the small, compact annuals can be used. In fact, it would be a challenge for the gardener to see if he can grow other plant materials in this new applied form of hydroponic culture.

Landscaping the Apartment Plot

JOHN R. REBHAN

MANY garden apartment developments now offer small plots where tenants with green thumbs can stake a garden claim. Imaginative use of flowers and shrubs can transform even a small patch of ground into a garden gem.

Thanks to easily installed fences, inexpensive garden ornaments and plentiful plant material, gardening in a small area—even on a short-term lease—can be rewarding. A bold and simple planting plan can be designed for a rectangle only twenty feet by thirty feet, a fifteen-foot square or for a triangular patch.

For example, such plots might be centered with a lawn or gravel panel and bordered with three-foot-wide planting beds. Low-flowering shrubs might be set out along one or two sides. Annuals and perennials can be planted in the remaining beds, backed by a temporary fence or the wall of the building. A square or rectangular plot might be divided into four beds separated by narrow paths. In the center of each bed a flowering shrub becomes a focal point for surrounding flowers.

There are many design possibilities. Of course, the gardener should keep in mind that an obvious ground pattern is essential, since space does not permit an adequate enclosing planting. Free-flowing borders become lost and meaningless in a tiny garden. A star, a circle or a diamond of flowers placed in the center of the plot does not make the best use of space.

It is possible, of course, to go to the other extreme and cover the entire area with rows of flowers. However, without open space or paths within the garden area the result is merely a flower patch and not a garden.

Ornaments are useful in highlighting the design of a small garden. Large white flower pots overflowing with petunias can be placed at the corners of each bed. The pots are an inexpensive, yet effective device. A simple bench or a bird bath strengthens the garden design. A pole swathed in morning glories which were started from seed or a pole used to support bright climbing roses is eye-catching.

Shrubs are important in the small garden, for they help to point up the design. There are several low-growing flowering shrubs for gardens that receive at least six hours of sunlight a day; except where noted, they grow about three feet tall and wide. It is important to select those which thrive in average soil and are not gross feeders. Then annuals and low perennials may be planted close to them.

Slender deutzia (*Deutzia gracilis*), which is covered with white blooms in May, may be used for accent or as an enclosing hedge. A pink variety also is available.

Anthony Waterer spirea (*Spiraea bumalda*) is an old favorite, with rose-colored flowers from midsummer until fall. It is a good informal hedge. Glossy abelia (*Abelia grandiflora*) is semi-evergreen. Pale pink, arbutuslike flowers appear all summer. An excellent hedge or accent shrub, glossy abelia can be sheared. However, it is more handsome when allowed to develop naturally. Glossy abelia is not effective the first summer after planting, as are the other shrubs mentioned. If time is not the important factor, it is worth waiting for.

Marigolds, zinnias and daisies add gay bloom to a garden apartment plot.

Gottscho-Schleisner

Blue spirea (*Caryopteris incana*) is noteworthy for its powder blue flowers from August to frost. It makes an attractive foil for petunias. Or blue spirea can be used as a hedge, as a single specimen or in combination with other shrubs.

St. Johnswort (*Hypericum*) is a wonderful choice for yellow to dominate the garden. There are several low varieties which bloom all summer. A patented variety, Sungold, grows only two feet tall and the top growth is quite hardy. However, should top growth winterkill, the dead portions are cut off and the plant rejuvenates in early spring.

Floribunda roses are a happy choice in the small garden. Not only do they make delightful informal hedges or create beautiful effects with other plants, but the blossoms are fine for arranging. Worthy of trial are award winners Vogue, Circus, Fashion and White Bouquet.

Mockorange (*Philadelphus*) can be grown in the small garden. There are several low-growing species available. A new variety, Frosty Morn, grows only forty inches high and produces large, fragrant white flowers in late June just like its full-sized counterpart.

Cinquefoil (*Potentilla*), another genus with several low-growing

(225)

species, bears flowers from June until October. A named variety to look for is Gold Drop, which has yellow flowers and rarely exceeds two feet in height. It must have full sun to flower prolifically.

Flowering quince (*Cydonia*) no longer has to be omitted from small gardens. Nurserymen have introduced several low-growing hybrids, such as Knaphill Scarlet and Rowallane. Even a tiny garden now can have its share of brilliant scarlet in early spring.

Remember to include a few evergreens in the planting scheme for an attractive wintertime picture. Small upright Japanese yews or columnar junipers can be kept in scale for years with an annual shearing. Just one evergreen at the center or at each corner of the garden is all that is necessary to focus attention on the garden design.

Dwarf mugo pines might be used to mark the intersection of two paths. English ivy or periwinkle, confined by shearing, can be used to edge the beds; these evergreen groundcovers also are dramatic on the winter landscape.

After shrubs and evergreens have been selected, the gardener turns his attention to flowers. Annuals are generally first choice. They are easy to grow from seed and flower beautifully all summer, if the plants receive several hours of sun a day.

For backgrounds sow African marigolds, cosmos, zinnias, four o'clocks and bachelor buttons. Good medium-tall annuals are blue salvias, dwarf nicotianas, Unwin dahlias, calendulas and French marigolds. Along the edge of a border try sowing seed of dwarf marigolds, sweet alyssums and nasturtiums. Set out plants of petunias and verbenas.

Perennials also have a place in the small garden. For shaded areas try hostas and daylilies. Tubers of caladiums and tuberous-rooted begonias bring splashes of color to the shaded garden.

Dwarf iris, coralbells, Shasta daisies, phlox and dwarf asters are but a few of the many sun-loving perennials suitable for the small garden. A dozen or so gladiolus corms grouped together will provide an interesting display of color, or the spikes may be picked for use indoors.

When space is limited, gardeners are tempted to crowd plants together. Nothing is gained; growth is spindly and the plants do not bloom well. Restraint in the quantity of plants grown is as essential as good design, if a tiny garden plot is to be enjoyed to the fullest.

Planting by the Sea

F. F. ROCKWELL

A SUMMER cottage near the sea presents a charming picture when framed by a colorful garden. Even a moderate amount of plant material can provide bright blooms.

Before deciding what to plant, the gardener should consider how to provide some degree of protection in extremely exposed sites. By far the most serious problem in every seaside garden is strong, persistent wind.

Beach plums and Rugosa roses can be used to start a hedge or screen that will afford considerable protection to low plants growing in their lee. A good temporary shelter belt may be established with woven wire fencing, over and through which seaweed is draped and interwoven. Sand driven against this fencing by the wind will quickly establish a protective artificial dune. Often an inexpensive wood or picket fence will serve as a support as well as a wind shield for honeysuckles or rambler roses.

The next big obstacle to overcome is extremely porous sandy soil—the kind which, as gardeners say, allows rain to go faster after it hits the ground than it did before. Humus must be added. There is nothing better than peat moss. A layer at least two inches deep, and preferably three or four inches deep, should be dug into the soil to a depth of six inches. Animal manures, if they can be obtained, add considerable humus as well as available plant food.

For a long-term improvement, any green crop, such as rye or perennial ryegrass, should be sown at the end of the season (any time after Labor Day until hard freezing). The grass crop will provide green manure which can be dug under in spring. Kelp or other seaweed, dug under, also is excellent.

(227)

Marigolds, dianthus, coreopsis and petunias thrive in a sunny border by the sea.

Paul E. Genereux

Most seashore soils, especially along the Eastern coast, are likely to be very acid. A soil test for acidity is desirable, but even without one, an application of agricultural lime (five to eight pounds per hundred square feet) is a safe recommendation. Wood ashes also can be used.

Fertilizers should be applied "little and often" to avoid loss by leaching. The new slow-acting nitrogen plant foods are effective.

The gardener should keep in mind that seashore sunshine is more intense than it is inland. All plants which, even to a slight degree, are shade lovers should be kept from full exposure to the sun.

Many trees will do well in the seaside cottage garden. Well-prepared planting holes, generous mulching and adequate staking until new roots are developed (two to three years) are important in getting trees established. Suitable species include red cedar (*Juniperus communis*), pitch pine, Japanese black pine, Chinese elm, birch, pepperidge, red maple, hawthorn, moraine locust, poplar, willow, sassafras and mulberry.

Low-growing twiggy shrubs with small flowers will withstand shore winds. Good choices are smoke tree, Russian olive, tamarisk, brooms, euonymus, and roses such as *Rosa rugosa* and *R. carolina*. Among the worthwhile native plants are bayberry, winterberry, inkberry, wild and hybrid blueberries, beach plum and shadbush.

The low-growing perennials are best, especially if there are no dunes to offer protection. The gardener might try dwarf hardy asters, bellflowers, allium, daylilies, echinops, erigeron, gloriosa daisy, dwarf iris, gaillardia, coralbells, rudbeckia, lythrum, silene and yucca. Creepers that will thrive include arabis, creeping phlox, iberis and *Alyssum saxatile citrinum*.

Annuals that thrive near the sea are brachycome, Swan River daisy, chrysanthemum, cosmos, California poppy (*Eschscholzia*), lupine, poppies, petunia, saponaria, scabiosa, sweet alyssum and calendula. Other fine annuals are ice plant, *Phlox drummondi*, lantana, dwarf marigolds, nicotiana, portulaca, verbena, *Vinca rosea*, zinnia and candytuft.

Flowers for the Summer Cottage

BARBARA M. CAPEN

W<small>HEN</small> the days lengthen and school vacation time draws near, thoughts turn to the summer cottage tucked away in the mountains or in the valleys. Fortunate is the home owner who can spend a few spring week-ends at the cottage, preparing the soil or doing some early planting.

Nevertheless, those who vacation so far from home that early spadework is impossible may still plan to have summer bloom. Even those people who only rent a cottage for a short period can have some flowers.

To give gardeners a head start, most nurseries and many roadside stands feature a variety of plants growing in baskets, pots and cans. This is a most welcome innovation which is particularly useful to short-season gardeners.

Plants for the summer garden may include vines, shrubs, perennials and annuals. The selection depends on the location of the property and the home owner's personal taste. But since flowering shrubs need a minimum of care, they should be considered wherever possible.

Along coastal areas the blue hydrangea is a popular shrub for its long season of bloom and large floral clusters. Although it is not difficult to grow, a fairly moist soil (or frequent watering) is essential. To retain the vivid color of the blooms, the soil must be acid, with iron present in some form. In an alkaline soil the flowers are pink. Hydrangeas, combined with groups of pink or yellow floribunda roses, will provide a striking display most of the summer.

Inland the rose of Sharon, smoke bush (*Cotinus coggygria*), butterfly bush, abelia and chaste tree all may be combined for a summer-flowering shrub border. In wooded areas the sweetbay rhododendron will bloom in part shade during July, while the shrubby St. Johnswort and the sweet pepperbush flower in part shade during August.

Summer-flowering vines may be chosen for their decorative value, but more often they are needed for shade. Fast-growing annual vines, such as morning glories and scarlet runner beans, have showy flowers. They lend shade on a lattice or trellis, or will quickly cover a bare fence.

The old-fashioned rambler rose Dorothy Perkins is useful to cover a farm fence or rough stone wall. The large-flowered, repeat-blooming climbers, such as Dream Girl, Temptation and New Dawn, may be trained to grow on the cottage or garage where space permits. These roses also will provide shade for a terrace or outdoor sitting area.

A few perennials should be featured in the summer garden. Many types may be planted in May. These include phlox in white or shades of pink, lavender and red (purchased in clumps); Wonder of Staffa (*Aster frikarti*), a pale blue, and cushion chrysanthemums in pink, white and buff (purchased as rooted cuttings).

But annuals with their variety of shapes and colors really are the mainstay of the summer garden. Some may be grown from seed planted outdoors until June 1. For example, zinnias, French marigolds, sweet alyssum, annual gaillardias and early cosmos will bloom by the end of July. Other annuals, such as petunias, snapdragons, African marigolds, seedling dahlias and ageratums, must be purchased as plants; they may be set out until July 15.

Geraniums, lantanas, heliotropes, Boston daisies, impatiens and petunias all do well in planters filled with good garden soil. And rosebushes—especially the low-growing floribundas and polyanthas—may be grown in boxes at least twenty-four inches deep. Monthly feeding with a soluble plant food is advised.

For the new gardener, there are a few essentials to be learned before buying any plants. Will there be adequate sunlight, protection from wind and good soil on the property? The home owner must first try to improve growing conditions.

Wind sweep is an important factor to consider. Few plants will survive direct and continuous wind blowing from the water. Breezes that whip around mountain tops and drafts that come from the valley may also affect plantings. Windbreaks should be built in the form of fences or hedges of wind-resistant plants, such as Russian olive, privet and red cedar.

Hollyhocks and nasturtiums adorn the picket fence that separates the garden from the lakeside.

Gottscho-Schleisner

Finally, the soil may need extra attention. Moisture-holding materials, such as peat moss, leafmold and shredded cattle manure, must be added to sandy soil, in addition to a complete fertilizer.

In the mountains rock ledge is sometimes a problem. The gardener may have to try several locations before finding a pocket of soil deep enough for planting. In a woodsy area the soil may be too acid for most plants. Hydrated lime, dusted lightly over the soil and turned under, will temporarily make it slightly alkaline.

No matter where the summer garden is located, a refined planting should not be superimposed on a natural setting. Garden flowers should be kept in the open area around the house or terrace, rather than placed at the edge of a woodland. And in some cases it may be necessary to limit the cottage garden to plantings in a few tubs, boxes or large pots placed on a porch or terrace.

Planters may be constructed easily of scrap lumber treated with a copper naphthenate preservative. Handsome redwood boards will make an attractive planter, too. The boxes may be simple, reinforced squares, rectangles, triangles or shaped to fit a corner of the house or terrace. They should be at least six inches deep. Planters twelve to eighteen inches deep are more satisfactory because the plants will have greater root space. A deeper box also retains more moisture.

A Pool for Waterlilies

G. L. THOMAS, JR.

WATERLILIES lend bright color as well as an exotic touch to the home landscape.

The latest development in water gardening for beginners is the prefabricated fiber glass or polyethylene pool. It is available in different sizes and shapes. The pool is simply set into a precut depression in the lawn, and then filled and planted.

A newly poured and set concrete pool should not be planted or stocked with fish immediately. The pool shell releases considerable free lime into the water, which will kill goldfish and retard plants. In my opinion, the quickest and best method of neutralizing or "curing" a newly poured and set concrete pool takes ten days.

Fill the pool to the brim, and let the water set for five days. Drain, refill the pool, allow to set for five days, and then drain the water again. Mix a quart of ordinary kitchen vinegar with ten quarts of water. Use an old broom or stiff brush to scrub the pool floor and walls with this solution. It may bubble a bit as the vinegar works on the free lime, but this will not weaken the concrete.

Rinse out with a brisk spray from the garden hose. When the pool is filled again, the water will remain neutral and sweet. For this final fill, prop the garden hose into position and set the nozzle to throw a strong, heavy spray. It will take longer to fill the pool this way, but it aerates the water, which is good for the fish.

An informal-shaped pool, placed where the sun shines brightly, provides a place for waterlilies to flower.

Paul E. Genereux

Hardy waterlilies can be set out as soon as it is comfortable to work outdoors—about mid-April. Tropical waterlilies should not be planted until hot weather is fully established, usually the first or second week of June.

The hardy waterlilies bloom early, and finish with fall's first frost. The so-called tender kinds start blooming late, but have a long season.

It is better to underplant than to overplant a pool. Much of a water garden's charm depends on the reflection of flowers and trees in free water. Therefore, do not cover much more than half of the water surface with lilies and lily pads.

Most catalogues list waterlilies as extensive, medium or small growers. Roughly, with the hardy types, extensive growers' leaves cover from ten to twelve square feet of surface, medium growers cover eight to ten square feet, and small growers about four square feet. The foliage of tropical waterlilies is half again to twice as large as that of the hardy kinds. Tropicals do best with about eight inches of water covering the crowns; hardies need a foot of water.

Hardy waterlilies require about a cubic foot of earth per rhizome. Tropicals need half again that much, and lotus twice to three times that much. These plants may be given more room, but never less.

A heavy garden loam, mixed with fertilizer, is best. Lighter soils produce much foliage, but little bloom. Swamp muck and leafmold appear nutritious, but they usually sour. Heavy clay, mixed with fertilizer, can be used, although plant roots find it difficult to penetrate.

Well-rotted cow manure—one part to three parts of soil—is the best fertilizer to use. Dry cow manure should be applied more sparingly—one part to eight or ten parts of soil. Never use lime or fresh cow manure.

Dry commercial fertilizers, especially the 10-10-10 mixes, help produce fine waterlilies. Mix a generous double handful of these fertilizers to one planting container of soil. Blood meal—one quart to a bushel of earth—gives satisfactory results; it should be mixed three weeks ahead of planting time.

A hardy waterlily, planted in the minimum cubic foot of soil, needs new soil and fertilizer every spring. Planted in half again or twice that much soil, it can be left in the pool two or three years, or even longer without repotting. It will winter well between blooming

An openwork brick pattern fence provides a perfect background for a formal garden pool setting.

Gottscho-Schleisner

Pots of gay geraniums highlight the setting for a rectangular pool.   *Molly Adams*

seasons if set upon the pool floor, below the freezing line. Most water gardeners look upon tropicals as annuals and discard them at the end of the season.

If scrawny foliage and lack of bloom indicate insufficient fertilizing, do not move a waterlily in the middle of a growing season to replant it. Make a "vitamin pill" of bonemeal, as large as a grapefruit, with just enough clay to bind it. Thrust the "pill" into the planting box soil so that it touches the rhizome gently. Large plants should get two "pills."

If the pool produces few blooms, double-check the amount of sunlight it receives. A minimum of four or five hours a day of sun is needed.

Casual day-to-day grooming keeps a pool beautiful. Discard excess foliage. Cut or pinch off leaf stems near the rootstock and remove dead blooms.

Waterlilies are subject to fewer diseases and have fewer insect enemies than most other flowering plants. If small colonies of insects are discovered on blooms or foliage, wash them into the pool with a stiff spray from the garden hose. The fish will quickly dispose of them.

A comfortable fish population for the home waterlily pool can be estimated by water volume or by water surface area. Allow one inch of fish (measuring from tip of nose to tip of tail) for every gallon of water. For the brood of one mated pair of goldfish, allow 300 gallons of water. (In computing pool capacity, figure seven and one-half gallons of water to the cubic foot.) I prefer to estimate from water surface—one inch of fish for every twenty square inches of surface. Thus a one-inch fish would require a four-by-five-inch area. In figuring water surface, do not subtract those areas covered by waterlily pads. The more exotic fish—veiltails, moors and calicos— require a little more room; allow about a quarter more by volume or by surface area.

Children Like to Garden

WINIFRED H. STRAKOSCH

WHEN children have the gardening urge, parents may think they will have to dash out and rescue a section of the garden. But by giving children a spot of their own to grow plants, their interest will prove a rewarding experience for parents and youngsters alike. Even though a special garden will not always guarantee hands off the grownups' plants, it should give children respect for the efforts of others and provide happy activity.

Unskilled hands and immature judgment on the needs of plants cannot always make a garden grow. Parents who are eager for their children to have green thumbs must count on joining in the fun.

In any case, youngsters need coaching in the techniques of planting, cultivating, weeding, irrigating and—perhaps most important—how to keep off growing plants. Children will learn to like gardening if their plots are a success rather than a jungle of weeds. Parents can count on supervising and maybe they will have to do patch work.

The young gardener will want to grow everything. The list I received from a five-year-old included watermelons, corn, potatoes, tomatoes, beans, sunflowers, morning glories and all the pink flowers in the catalogue.

Older children won't use much more restraint. It will be up to the parent to keep the choices within reasonable limits. Starting with small shrubs and potted plants has a real advantage—there is immediate satisfaction. Also, plants already well grown can take much rougher handling than tiny, four-leaved seedlings.

House plants such as coleus, impatiens, geraniums and begonias can be moved outside for the summer. Small plants of azaleas, boxwoods, Japanese hollies or cotoneasters might be purchased for a permanent addition to the child's spot.

One, Two—Small hands can easily grasp the large vegetable seed. String acts as guide for straight rows.

The New York Times

Let's see now—Tomatoes taste good but peas and carrots are prettier. I think I'll let Mommy decide.

A. Devaney

. . . the biggest beets of all.

Steve Schapiro

(238)

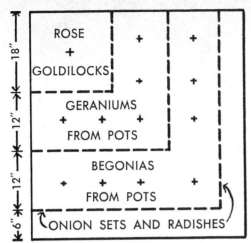

The littlest gardeners can raise roses, geraniums, begonias, onions and radishes on a 4 × 4 plot that is easy to maintain.

Plan by Winifred H. Strakosch

Even a three-year-old can dig a very good hole. He will delight in filling it with water, then a plant. With a bit of help the littlest gardener can get a begonia into a hole right side up and firmed into place. You can be sure that the three-year-old will never run his tricycle over that plant.

If the child is old enough to handle seed, then let him plant vegetables. They are quick to grow and nothing tastes quite as good. Beans, radishes, beets, Swiss chard and kohlrabi will produce a crop in less than two months. Also, this seed is large enough to be handled one at a time. This is the best way to plant seed, since thinning is not a skill children learn readily.

Crops such as watermelons, corn and cucumbers take two and one-half to three months to grow to maturity. They are all right for veteran gardeners who have learned patience. The young novice wants quick results. In addition to the five vegetables mentioned, onion sets and tomato plants are good choices for the child's plot if there is room to let plants sprawl.

A garden means flowers to a youngster. Plan for at least one or two annuals to grow with the vegetables. Dwarf French marigolds and the small-sized zinnias, such as Lilliput, Cupid and Tom Thumb, are easily grown from seed. Seed of such favorites as pansies, petunias, red sage or snapdragons is difficult for youngsters to handle; plants are recommended to insure successful bloom.

Choice of the garden's spot is very important. It can determine the success or failure to a large degree. Let sun, soil and prestige guide selection. Sun is essential for vegetables and most flowers to grow well. Soil must be well worked and enriched, especially for the vegetables to bear good crops.

Prestige? Try to avoid the natural urge to keep the beginner's garden in the background. Too often, the inconspicuous site has the least sun and poor soil. The child will do much better if he is not pushed back into a corner. It is much more fun to be working near the grownups. This also will make it easier to supervise the project.

The idea to start out on a small scale cannot be overemphasized. A few plants growing well and maturing quickly will provide a thrill of satisfaction to a youngster. If there is too much to care for he might become discouraged. Short-term goals help maintain interest to keep the work going.

The garden plans shown here can be started and finished in two to three months. If the child has had fun and his enthusiasm and patience will last through the summer, then a second planting of flowers can follow the vegetables he harvests.

For children over six years of age, the garden is planned with some succession cropping. In the first row the onion sets and radishes will be pulled out approximately three weeks after planting. Marigolds can fill in the space. Plants are thinned to six or nine inches apart. Swiss chard and beets will occupy their rows until July. A second sowing is made. One plant of tomato Tiny Tim should bear from August until frost. After the bean row is spent, chrysanthemum plants are suggested for fall color. And if there is a fence or post near the garden, morning glory vines could be trained on it.

Special rewards for really good gardening might include the privilege of more space to grow the "big" crops, or some novelties such as Indian corn or strawberry popcorn, gourds, or yellow tomatoes and plum tomatoes, bells of Ireland and snow on the mountain. Come fall, the child may want to put in bulbs and even help with shrub and tree planting.

Whatever guidance effort is involved for the parents, it is more than compensated by the pleasures of teaching and helping youngsters. Parents should expect to help make decisions and teach the techniques of growing. They will want to check on the completeness of the child's efforts. Keeping the plants alive is the main concern. Helping in this way does not spoil the child or make him irresponsible. It will just nudge him along the path to complete responsibility for the project. He will get the feel of it before too long.

Getting Started with Wild Flowers

JUDITH-ELLEN BROWN

In choosing a section of the home garden as a site for a wild-flower patch, the gardener should, of course, try to duplicate as closely as possible the setting in which the plants thrive. The majority of woodland natives suitable for home culture like a protected, semi-shady, well-drained site.

The degree of shade required by different species varies. However, most woodland plants need some light and few will grow in a really dark spot. Moisture needs differ, too. Most woodland species must be assured some moisture during hot spells. It is only denizens of swampy or boggy areas—marsh marigolds, for example—that will flourish in constant dampness. Protection from wind, especially the warm, dry winds of summer, also is needed.

The gardener should analyze the soil in his prospective wild-flower preserve. Naturally, plants which do well in light, thin soil—bird's-foot violets and wild columbines—cannot be expected to flourish in heavy, soggy soils. Those which are found in the acid earth of evergreen forests—bunchberries, wintergreens and the like—will not survive in a limy locale, and vice versa.

Some modification of the soil can be made, such as adding peat moss or sand to lighten heavy soil, or digging in quantities of leafmold to enrich a sparse soil. However, it is usually impractical to try to convert a distinctly limy soil to one that will accommodate acidloving wild flowers.

The best time to start a wild-flower garden is in early spring or fall. Before planting, the ground should be cleared of weeds, grass and rubble. Soil is enriched or lightened as needed to make a porous, woodsy mixture. If actual woods soil is unavailable, equal parts of

(241)

Star flower is a delicate woodland plant that blooms in summer.

Gottscho-Schleisner

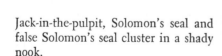

Jack-in-the-pulpit, Solomon's seal and false Solomon's seal cluster in a shady nook.

Gottscho-Schleisner

sand, garden loam, peat moss and compost should be dug in to a depth of a foot or more. Chemical fertilizer should not be used.

A good time to plant wild flowers is on a cool day, preferably in early morning or late afternoon. This prevents excessive wilting. In the new garden plants usually will be obtained either by purchasing nursery stock or by collecting specimens from nearby woodlands. In the latter case, permission must be obtained from property owners. Never remove species protected by conservation laws.

For effective display, it is advisable to plant at least three specimens of any sizable species (trillium and wild geranium, for example), and six specimens of smaller kinds, such as spring beauty or squirrel corn. Shrubs and larger plants should be set in position first.

Plants should be watered well and mulched with an inch or two of peat moss or similar substance. Daily watering is recommended until the plantings become reasonably well established.

The gardener who develops his wild-flower garden in a spot where some native plants are already established has an easier job than one who starts from scratch. The former merely has to clean up neglected areas and add new plantings which will be compatible in character and cultural requirements with those growing on the site.

Once the wild-flower garden is established, maintenance will be relatively simple. Cultivation is not only unnecessary but may actually be harmful. The mulching effect of groundcovers and fallen leaves (which are left undisturbed) keeps weeding and watering chores to a minimum. Spraying is seldom if ever needed.

It should be noted that, although most wild-flower gardens are devoted to plants of our native woodlands, other types of wild-flower gardens may also be developed. In a sunny open spot, flowering plants of the fields—asters, lupines, butterfly weeds—may be used. In areas resembling our damp, open meadows, such species as bluets, Turk's cap lilies, blue flags and camassias may provide still another type of garden. The property which boasts a natural bog offers an opportunity to grow some of our loveliest and most difficult natives. Attempts to construct an artificial bog or to grow true bog plants in ordinary damp soil are usually unsuccessful.

Whatever type of wild-flower habitat the gardener chooses to establish, it is a sound plan to start out with easily grown plants. As he gains experience, he may attempt the more demanding species.

In addition, he may wish to experiment with such projects as growing wild flowers indoors in winter and raising wild flowers from seed.

Of course, there are many wild flowers that can be started easily from plants. These include meadow rue (*Thalictrum*), wild strawberry (*Fragaria virginiana*), woodland phlox (*Phlox divaricata*) and wild ginger (*Asarum canadense*). The trillium species, such as snow trillium (*Trillium grandiflorum*) and purple trillium (*T. erectum*), also are good for the novice to try.

The following wild flowers are only for the gardener who is experienced in plant propagation. The striking fringed gentian (*Gentiana crinita*) and eastern lupine (*Lupinus perennis*) can be raised from seed. More tricky varieties that can be started from plants include bearberry (*Arctostaphylos uva-ursi*), painted trillium (*Trillium undulatum*), shortia (*Shortia galacifolia*) and galax (*Galax aphyllia*).

Also for the experienced gardener to start from plants are trailing arbutus (*Epigaea repens*), twinflower (*Linnaea borealis*), and the lady's slippers—moccasin flower (*Cypripedium acaule*), showy lady's slipper (*C. reginae*) and yellow lady's slipper (*C. pubescens*). Of course, many plants are impractical for introduction into the home wild-flower garden, such as arethusa (*Arethusa bulbosa*), grass pink (*Calopogon pulchellus*), calypso (*Calypso bulbosa*) and most fringe orchids (*Habenaria*).

Wintergreen carpets the ground where moccasin flowers bloom in late summer.
Gottscho-Schleisner

PART VI

FRUITS
AND VEGETABLES

ALMOST EVERYONE who has a plot of ground, be it large or small, finds space somewhere for growing a favorite vegetable or fruit. Nothing tastes so good or is eaten with more pride than home-grown apples, peaches, tomatoes or lettuce. Fruit and vegetable growing can be designed to suit a family's tastes exactly. The family with a small garden or numerous leisure-time activities may satisfy its urge to reap a harvest by setting out a simple edging of lettuce or radishes by the flower border. The clever cook can tuck a few herbs by the kitchen door where they will be ready to flavor her specialties. A few tomato plants take up little space yet provide an ample crop for salads and sandwiches. Some families may like to plan elaborate vegetable plots and maintain vast fruit plantings to supply a steady fare for the table with extra quantities for freezing and canning.

The dwarf fruit trees are ideally suited to the suburban property. They are compact in size for easy care and picking. The harvests are generous, too. Bramble fruits do not take up much room and they can double as property dividers or screens. A grapevine can serve a dual role by shading an arbor and providing late summer fruit.

Those who decide to be fruit growers must remember that a modicum of pruning and spraying is necessary to realize full harvest. But these techniques are simple to acquire once the gardener becomes a fruit or vegetable tiller.

Decorative Roles for Vegetables and Fruit

NANCY R. SMITH

INGENIOUS home gardeners are doubling the value of certain fruits and vegetables by using them decoratively in the landscape. The results are neither bizarre nor impractical, and the ideas are especially welcome on small properties.

For example, a home owner in my neighborhood created a beautiful effect by planting a row of assorted dwarf fruit trees to replace an ungainly privet hedge. Another gardener revamped a sloping back yard by installing brick terraces and planting them with everbearing strawberries—a startling change from vine-covered soil.

Vegetables may seem the least likely to be successful as decorative plantings. However, many gardeners have been using a kind of tucked-in planting for years. I now plant cucumbers in hills along a fence. I discovered that tying the vines to a support saves space, keeps the fruits out of the soil and simplifies harvesting. The curling vines and large foliage add an unusual note, too.

Curly parsley fronds are another of my favorite touches along the kitchen walk. The plants grow in company with dill, chives and three pepper plants as well as radishes and leaf lettuce in early spring.

Another likely place for an early crop planting of salad greens might be the edge of the flower border. By the time the annuals and

Strawberries edge a small patch of lettuce and cabbage.   *J. Horace McFarland*

perennials are ready to make a show, most of the greens will have been harvested. Parsley, chives and dill, however, would occupy the ground all season.

Window boxes or similar containers made for porch, terrace or patio use could be used for a salad garden. Large containers would support tomato plants which, if staked, can supply the table moderately well. Three plants of the cherry, plum or pear types of tomatoes will give an ample harvest for the average family.

A sunny strip of ground along the garage or house can also be utilized for vegetables. Rhubarb is another favorite of many gardeners. With lush foliage it forms an attractive dividing line between drive and lawn or flourishes as a trimming for the kitchen entrance. Planter barrels have become almost standard garden equipment. They can be filled with a variety of edibles from herbs to strawberries.

If there is need, or room, for a hedge, several kinds of bush

Planter boxes are perfect for salad greens where space is limited.

Mason Weymouth

fruits will give double satisfaction. Improved varieties of blueberries are compact, extra-fruitful and as handsome as any ornamental. They also make a fine corner planting. For barrier-type hedges, nothing keeps out strays—both two and four-footed types—more effectively than blackberry bushes.

Grapes are versatile; they grow equally well over a fence, arbor or trellis. One of my neighbors grows them on a trellis on the sunny side of a garage. An ingenious hinging arrangement permits the support to be lowered when painting time comes.

As with any type of decorative planting, fruits and vegetables must be used according to a plan. The results will be less interesting if the plants are just dotted hither and yon. This is true of both fruit and vegetable plantings, but it applies particularly to fruits, for they are a more permanent investment.

Vegetable Garden Primer

F. C. COULTER

THE home owner who has never had a vegetable garden will be agreeably surprised by how many dividends can be had from even a small one. In addition to fresh, succulent vegetables the gardener will have invigorating outdoor exercise, a profitable hobby and the good glow that comes with honest agricultural dirt on the hands and shoes. The home vegetable plot also can provide vegetables close to the kitchen door that seldom if ever are found in the market.

The needs of the plants are simple: suitable soil, sunshine and moisture. Vegetables need plenty of sun. They will not thrive where the shadow of the house falls on them, or close to trees where, in addition to lack of light, they will be robbed of food and water by tree roots. Nor should the gardener choose a site where pools of water stand in early spring. Although vegetables must always have water, they need good drainage.

The soil should be neither too acid nor too alkaline, and it should be well supplied with plant food. These factors can be determined by a soil test. Lift a section of soil by driving a trowel down vertically. Send the sample to the state experiment station with a note saying that a vegetable garden is planned and ask for recommendations. (If the address is not in the telephone directory, the local seedsman or garden center will have it.)

After sending in the soil sample, the gardener's next step is to make a plan of the plot and the crops to be raised. The size of the plot will be determined by the area available, the number of persons in the family and the amount of time the gardener can devote to cultivating it. The novice is almost certain to make the plot too large. A well-planned and well-tended small plot will yield as much as a larger one which has become a burden to the gardener and an eyesore because of weeds and untidiness.

For the first experimental year a plot of fifteen-by-twenty to twenty-five-by-twenty feet will probably be ample for an amateur gardener with a small family. The easiest and most popular vegetables to grow are beans, tomatoes, lettuce and summer squash. Sweet corn could be added to the list, but it takes a lot of space for a very small yield.

In making the plan, put the tomatoes at the back of the plot, each plant three feet apart both ways from the next. Each should yield about ten to fifteen pounds of tomatoes over the season. Bush beans will come next. Plan on having two or three rows, spacing them about three feet apart. The plants should be set three to four inches apart in the row; five to ten feet should be seeded each week-end for a continuous supply.

Lettuce should stand twelve to fifteen inches apart. I suggest the loose-head type from which the gardener can take a few leaves at a time, instead of the solid types where the whole head must be lifted. Squash should be three feet apart; six plants should suffice, provided the fruits are picked when they are small.

The space that is left can be given to vegetables of your preference—cress and chives for salads or carrots because they can be harvested when they are finger length, tender and sweet. Herbs such as mint, parsley, sweet basil and sage can be added. For cabbage, broccoli, asparagus, spinach, melons and cucumbers it is better to rely on the stores where they are plentiful and cheap.

Only a few tools are needed for vegetable gardening: a spade or fork for digging, an iron-headed rake for pulverizing and smoothing the soil, a hoe, a trowel and a length of line with two stakes for marking the rows. Do not begin working the soil too early in the season; you lose nothing by waiting until spring has taken over from the frosts and rains of winter.

Clear out all large stones and bits of builders' trash; work in uniformly any lime that may have been recommended in the soil test report. Apply fertilizer a week later, when pulverizing with the rake. Make a smooth seedbed in which the plant roots can ramble for food and form a good anchor. Finish by firming down the soil to avoid air pockets.

Beans, squash and carrots are grown from seed sown in the row at the rates shown on the packet. Lettuce and tomatoes can be sown directly in the row, but plants started indoors will gain weeks of time.

To save space, cucumbers can be grown on a fence.

Molly Adams

Seed can be sown indoors in a sterile medium in small fibrous pots. Afterward, when the weather is warm enough, set pot and all in the garden row. This avoids the root damage and shock that may be caused by raising seedlings in flats and transplanting them.

Salad Greens

RUTH TIRRELL

THE most popular salad green is lettuce. In the Northeast, it can be picked for six or seven months, often more. But it takes planning and the right variety.

Lettuce is a cool-weather crop. Loose-leaf kinds, which grow fast and resist heat, are best for the beginner. Loose-leaf alone can satisfy almost anyone's needs.

For a head start, I sow seed inside in early March, then transplant seedlings outside a month later (or whenever the ground can be worked). On that same April day, I sow more lettuce in a row outside. The first lot comes along faster in spite of the setback of transplanting.

Lettuce transplants rather well. Be sure that only the root goes below ground—none of the leafy portion. The seedlings seem wobbly at first but soon sit firm on the ground. Be sure to encircle spring seedlings with paper collars as protection against cutworms.

Some gardeners sow lettuce the previous fall, protecting the seedlings over winter with mulch. The lettuce starts growing again early in spring. I often make two more small sowings at intervals through spring—skipping early summer—then a last sowing in mid-August. Loose-leaf becomes full-size in about seven weeks.

In rich soil, Salad Bowl may spread a foot and a half or more, a full-blown rosette of layer upon swirling layer of wavy leaves. Its open heart may not taste as icily crisp as head lettuce, but it's as tender and more delicious.

Other varieties of loose-leaf are Burpee's Greenhart and Slobolt; both stand a long time without going to seed; both are suitable for winter greenhouse forcing. Oakleaf, a good all-round lettuce, is heat-resistant. Ruby's red frilly leaves add color to salad. The old favorites, now improved, are Grand Rapids and Black Seeded Simpson.

Butterhead lettuce—distinct but loosely folded heads—and crisp-head or iceberg kinds—tightly folded heads—are considered much more difficult crops than looseleaf. For one thing, they take far longer to grow—eight to ten weeks for butterheads and ten to thirteen for crisp-heads. They must be started inside; later sowings are not practical for most home gardeners. To make quick unchecked growth, head lettuce needs the richest soil and abundant moisture. If the heads have to form in hot weather (usually they do), they need shade of some sort—a netting canopy. Where spring comes late with summer close behind and there is no long, cool growing season, it is an achievement to grow fine head lettuce.

An improved, heat-resistant variety of butterhead lettuce is Buttercrunch, whose thick heart (rather than a tight head) has finest quality. The flavor is sweet and delicate; the texture crisp and "crunchy." Buttercrunch resembles the famous Bibb but is larger and resists heat.

Summer Bibb and Burpee Bibb, somewhat smaller than Buttercrunch, have the same quality and slowbolting tendency. Tom Thumb is the smallest lettuce, but right for tiny gardens.

Other butterheads are: Dark Green Boston, which was developed in England and has few peers in quality, but must be on its way early in spring and Deer Tongue, or Matchless, an upright plant with all-green leaves of unusual shape.

A delicacy among lettuces is cos, or romaine. The plants grow upright (ten inches high); the leaves are self-folding about the heart. Parris Island Cox has dark-green leaves and a more open, less blanched heart than the well-known Paris White. The flavor of cos is more piquant than most lettuce. Start cos early; it takes almost as long to grow as iceberg.

Lettuce may provide the main bulk of a salad but leaves of other greens add strong or unusual flavor. Snippets of sorrel, for instance, offset the blandness of lettuce—but an all-sorrel salad might seem too sour.

I started the perennial French sorrel (*Rumex acetosa*) from seed. Six permanent plants take up little room. They begin growth early in spring and produce past the first frosts. Keep flower stalks cut off in summer or the leaves get bitter. A loose mulch in winter protects without smothering. Another French sorrel, *Rumex scutatus*, has narrow, arrow-shaped leaves, a little more acid.

Several plants of a different genus, but the same mustard family, bear the common name "cress." All have a pungent flavor.

Not everyone can grow fine watercress, *Nasturtium officinale*. The best site is close to a pure, gently moving stream or a spring.

It is possible to grow watercress in soil kept damp in a garden, windowbox or greenhouse, but it means a lot of tending and may not seem worth the bother.

A child can grow peppergrass or peppercress (*Lepidium sativum*). Though not so succulent as the finest watercress, peppergrass has a good sharp taste.

Sow seed first in a box inside; sow outside early in spring and again and again until hot weather, when cress tends to bolt and turn bitter. Sow in fall, too. Cress grows fast and is ready to eat in ten days. The curly kinds make a good garnish like parsley or chervil.

With the melting snows of February come the bright, shiny-green rosettes of wintercress, or yellow rocket (*Barbarea vulgaris*). It was once cultivated in England as a salad crop and probably still is, but not as a rule. Here yellow rocket grows wild, though not a weed.

Quite different plants may have the same common name. Besides yellow rocket and the spring flower, sweet rocket (*Hesperis matronalis*), there is another rocket, *Eruca sativa*, a salad plant.

I once grew rocket under the French name *roquette*. Its somewhat coarser leaves tasted much like yellow rocket (wintercress) which grows free for me on the edge of a nearby field. So I didn't need *roquette*. But it is a good choice for a strong, sharp, rather spicy green to counterbalance lettuce.

Sow rocket in spring and again in midsummer for a fall harvest. Young plants can be potted for use inside. Rocket will self-sow, but letting the creamy-yellow flowers bloom and go to seed makes the leaves tough and bitter. Seed for rocket can be bought in this country under the name "Mediterranean rocket."

Rocket-*roquette* is closely related to the Italian salad green, which goes variously—according to the region of Italy—under the names *ruca*, the diminutive *ruchetta*, *rugola*, or *arugola*, or *rucola*. All derive from the Latin *eruca* (colewort or mustard).

A friend on Long Island grows arugola from seed that has come down in her family since 1921. (The original plant grew in the province of Salerno.) Arugola can grow as a perennial. It can be cut again and again and should be, to keep most plants from going to seed. It stands summer heat better than lettuce and can be picked into October. A dozen plants is a good number. The flavor is "mildly pungent"—but not like a hot pepper. A favorite salad of mine is arugola leaves, sliced tomato, some minced garlic, and olive oil.

Another Italian salad vegetable is *Cicoria catalogna*, or asparagus chicory, also called *radichetta*. For salad, use the dandelion-like leaves and the tender shoots (really young seed stalks). Later, the thicker stalks are cooked the same way asparagus is done.

Sow the French leafy vegetable "Maches" in early spring and again in late summer. A hay mulch prolongs the season into early winter. Use the young leaves for salad, the big, coarse ones for "greens."

(256)

As a main salad vegetable, endive can substitute for lettuce in fall. Endive is hardiest and can survive for at least three weeks longer than lettuce. Sow the seed around July 4; endive takes about three months to grow full size. It can be sown, too, in early spring, but plants mature better in cool weather.

Endive has a characteristic bitterness, but blanching the heart makes it sweet and tender. A few weeks before harvest, tie the outer leaves about the inner, making sure they are dry or rot will set in.

Chinese cabbage is also for fall. Sow the seed in early July. If sown in spring, Chinese cabbage "bolts" without forming its firm, elongated head. It is self-blanching—the leaves folding layer upon layer about the inner heart. The innermost ribs, wide and almost white, crisp and tender, can be sliced raw like onions into a salad. The flavor is sweet yet spicy, not as strong as common cabbage.

Corn salad, or Lamb's Lettuce (sometimes called fetticus), has large round leaves of a mild flavor. It does best as a late fall or early winter crop—and may, if mulched, of course, last until spring in a usable state. Broadcast the seed in late August in a raked-over area where an earlier crop has been pulled up.

Fancy and costly, Witloof chicory, or Belgian endive, is usually flown here from abroad. It is not a difficult crop for a home gardener, but a long growing period must precede the final winter delicacy.

Sow the seed in late spring in soil that is loose and free of stones. (The aim is to get long, straight roots like parsnips or carrots.) The top foliage, coarse and bitter, is not used during the outdoor growing season.

In late fall, after a freezing period, the tops are cut back, and the roots lifted, during a thaw, packed into boxes of sand or soil, and brought into a moderately warm (about 60 degrees) dark cellar, garage or closet. There must be little or no light.

In a few weeks, the pale pointed shoots of folded leaves—like goatees—emerge, delicate and delicious. One shoot can serve a person. They are best raw in salad, with grapefruit sections, perhaps; but they can also be braised. Belgian endive is really, of course, an endive-like growth on a chicory root.

Roots left in the ground can be used for early spring greens; later, they get bitter. If allowed to mature, a plant stands four feet tall with an equal spread. Dozens of chicory-blue blossoms resemble the related roadside wildflower.

Tomatoes to Grow

CARL D. CLAYBERG

WHEN seed catalogues arrive, home gardeners spend many happy hours reading through them to select the tomato varieties that are most appealing. Only someone with a large garden, however, can grow many varieties of a single vegetable to find the ones most suitable for him. This is especially a problem with the tomato. More than 300 varieties are currently available.

Last summer I grew some fifty new and old tomato varieties to evaluate their relative merits. As my tomato-breeding work primarily concerned early varieties, I selected only early and mid-season types for the trial.

Late varieties usually have stems that grow to indefinite lengths, producing in regular alternation a flower cluster, three leaves, another flower cluster and so on. These are called indeterminate varieties.

In contrast, most early varieties, and all varieties described here unless indicated otherwise, are determinate. They have shorter stems which end in flower clusters and have less than three leaves between the flower clusters. This growth habit leads to a concentrated early set of fruit low on the plant, so staking is unnecessary. Determinate plants also should not be pruned. They usually are small enough, and pruning can markedly reduce their fruit yield.

Over the years plant breeders have developed varieties resistant to serious diseases or pests not easily controlled by the home gardener. If the home gardener has been unable to grow healthy tomato plants, resistant varieties may be the answer. Resistance to fusarium and verticillium wilts and to nematodes is especially valuable. Such resistance is noted in the varieties described below. Also given are average fruit weights, based on the results of the trial.

Those who cherish having the first ripe fruit of the season will be interested in three small-fruited varieties that were particularly early. They ripened fruit in only three months from seed planting. Two had small plants that produced fruit for a few weeks and then were finished for the summer: Early Cherry (average fruit weight 1.0 oz.) and F_1 Early Salad (1.2 oz.). Red Sugar (0.4 oz.) was a large, prostrate-growing, indeterminate variety with very sweet-flavored fruits.

Slightly later than these was one of the best varieties in the trial, All-America winner F_1 Small Fry (0.8 oz.). Small Fry has especially good flavor, yields prolifically for most of the season and is resistant to fusarium and verticillium wilts and to nematodes.

Some gardeners feel that tomatoes are simply not worth growing unless they have large fruits. The earliest large-fruited varieties are about two weeks later than the earliest small-fruited ones. The standard of this type is still Fireball (4.6 oz.). It is a fairly small plant that fruits for only a few weeks. New Yorker (5.2 oz.) is similar in most respects and is resistant to verticillium.

Two others as early but with even larger fruit are Early Bird (6.4 oz.) and Starfire (6.0 oz.). Early Wonder (7.8 oz.) is a few days later but has the largest fruit of the early varieties tested.

Four excellent mid-season varieties were equally good. All are resistant to fusarium and verticillium wilts: Campbell 1327 (8.6 oz.), with considerable resistance to fruit cracking; F_1 Pearson Hybrid No. 9 (9.4 oz); F_1 Jet Star (10.4 oz.), an indeterminate type; and F_1 Terrific (10.0 oz.), also indeterminate and resistant to nematodes.

The variety Burpee's VF (8.4 oz.) ripened its first fruits at the same time as the mid-season varieties but continued to produce them for a much longer period. It could also be considered a late variety. This fusarium- and verticillium-resistant variety is indeterminate and a heavy foliage producer that should be staked and pruned. A dry summer with rain at the end of the season will cause much fruit cracking in late tomatoes. These conditions have been common in recent years. But Burpee's VF was among the most crack-resistant varieties tested.

One last point should be stressed, whether the gardener grows his own plants from seed or buys them from a bedding plant dealer. Even if only a few plants are grown, they should be of different maturities so that fruit is produced throughout the season. Two plants each of early, mid-season, and late varieties, for instance, will suffice for the small garden.

A border of mixed herbs provides leaf textures
for the garden and flavorings for the kitchen.
Gottscho-Schleisner

Herbs by the Kitchen Door

NANCY R. SMITH

My favorite culinary herbs are planted in a small bed along the
kitchen patio. Here their fresh leaves can be snipped at will, rain or
shine. Herbs love the sun, require little pampering and thrive in
many types of soil. They withstand heat and drought and are not, as
a group, susceptible to disease.

Borage, dill and savory are three annual sorts a beginner might
try. Borage seed is large, and germinates quickly after being pressed
firmly in the ground. The leaves have a faint cucumberlike flavor.
Borage will self-sow if the pure blue flowers are allowed to go to seed.

Summer savory also grows readily from seed. The plants are
rather floppy in habit. Pinching back the tops promotes better growth
and denser foliage. Succession sowings insure a ready supply through
the season.

Dill, one of my favorite herbs, grows quickly from seed. Although the flower heads and seeds are invaluable for pickling purposes, I prefer to use the tender young foliage. Cut in sprigs as needed,

(260)

the leaves can be added to soups and salads. A second sowing is advisable. Seedlings do not transplant well. Sow seed sparingly. Extra plants are pinched off at ground level.

Chervil has a flavor similar to French tarragon. Like dill, it germinates easily but does not transplant well. Sowings can be made in spring and again in late summer. Plants do best when somewhat shaded from the burning sun by taller-growing species.

Seed of sweet basil germinates in less than a week after sowing. Pinching back the tops of the plants helps produce neat little bushes. Its clove pepper taste is useful in many dishes. *Ocinum basilicum* is the most generally used of the basils.

Just for fun, as well as for the aromatic seeds, the herb gardener can plant caraway seeds. The seed germinates readily and, once established, the plants will self-sow year after year. This biennial herb produces plants that resemble Queen Anne's lace. Starting it in summer means that the crop can be harvested next year. Some gardeners sow seed in early fall and harvest the seed crop the next season, too.

Parsley seed will germinate more quickly if soaked in water for twenty-four hours before planting. If sown in spring, the parsley can be used in summer. A sowing around August 1 will yield plants that

Spokes of the wheel provide pockets for a few favorite herbs.
Gottscho-Schleisner

have a better chance of wintering over. These young plants also can be potted for the window sill. Because of the uncertain weather in my area I sow parsley annually.

Chives are true perennials. Clumps of the hardy bulbous little plants are relatively inexpensive, and so it does not pay to grow them from seed. Every third spring the sturdy clumps will need division to prevent overcrowding. The delicately onion-flavored leaves can be cut freely, but the entire plant never should be sheared off continually.

Sage and thyme are two other perennial herbs that are kitchen favorites. Sage is very long-lived. Older plants should be cut back to a couple of shoots to promote new crown growth.

Thyme seed is finer and should be covered with finely sieved soil. Plants have a tendency to winterkill. The crowns should be protected so that they do not collect moisture.

Using kitchen herbs in their fresh state, at the peak of quality and flavor, is an unforgettable experience. However, provision can be made from the same plantings for winter use, too. Herbs can be dried and stored in tightly closed glass containers, which are kept out of strong light.

Fruits on a Small Scale

ERNEST G. CHRIST

FRUIT growing can be a satisfying pastime for the gardener who wants to relax and enjoy producing a few choice apples or pears or quarts of berries. He will do well to concentrate on growing a small quantity of fine fruit because the production of bushels of tree fruits and crates of berries requires hard work and often is disappointing.

A knowledge of the basic principles of fruit culture will help eliminate many difficulties experienced by the amateur fruit grower. Plants are most productive when grown in full sunlight. Unless one has an area exposed to sunshine all day, fruit gardening is not recommended. Even the blueberry, which is sometimes considered a shade plant, yields more berries when set in a sunny location.

Where space is limited, small fruits such as strawberries, brambles, blueberries and grapes are practical. As few as twenty-five strawberry plants and their runners will yield twenty-five quarts of berries the second year. Do not overcrowd the area with too many plants. Blueberry rows should be no closer together than eight feet and the plants four feet apart in the rows. Grapes should be set in rows six feet apart and a trellis is required for best results. Plant dwarf trees ten to twelve feet apart each way or six to eight feet apart in rows spaced fifteen feet apart.

Dwarf trees are popular today because few small home gardens have room for the standard thirty-foot apple or sweet cherry trees. In addition, the dwarf varieties are relatively easy to spray.

Insects and diseases that attack fruits must be controlled if the plants are to survive. Tree fruits need a rather exacting spray program. Treatment has been simplified with the introduction of improved spray materials. Single-package or all-purpose mixtures are available to protect the trees; a popular spray contains malathion, methoxychlor and captan.

Improper planting can cause permanent damage. Dig a hole large enough to accommodate the entire root of the fruit plant. Roots that are cramped and bent at planting will never straighten.

All the tree fruits—except the peach and sour cherry—require cross pollination. Not all varieties are compatible. For example, the Seckel pear and the Bartlett pear will not pollinate each other and the Bing, Lambert and Royal Ann sweet cherries will not pollinate each other. Japanese plum varieties will not pollinate European types.

If the gardener has two types of trees that are not compatible he can achieve pollination by obtaining a few flowering branches from a compatible tree. The branches are placed in a bucket of water a few feet above the ground near the tree to be pollinated.

Grapes and small fruits generally are self-fruitful. There is one exception in grape varieties and that is Brighton. Blueberries that are cross-pollinated will ripen earlier and are a bit larger than those not cross-pollinated.

Fruit plants require annual pruning in early spring. Strawberries should be thinned so that runners are spaced at least four inches apart. Grapes do best when pruned to the cane system rather than the spur system. Four or six long canes with ten or twelve buds per

Dwarf-sized fruit trees are especially suited to a small plot. They usually begin to bear crop one or two years earlier than standard-sized trees.

Gottscho-Schleisner

cane should be left on the plant. Tree fruits respond best to moderate pruning, while severe cutting delays fruiting and results in rank sucker growth.

The gardener should select fruit varieties recommended for his particular area of the country. For example, strawberries grown in Florida or North Carolina are not suited for New Jersey or New York plantings. Grapes that succeed in New Mexico and California do poorly in the East. Tree fruits are more adaptable but even these should be selected carefully.

Unless the soil is exceptionally rich, some fertilizer will be necessary for fruit plants. Spring is the best season for application. From late March to early April is an excellent time to do the job. For most efficient use of the fertilizer, apply it before the particular plant begins to bloom. Use the mixture on the soil over the spot where the roots are concentrated. A good fertilizer proportion would be 5-10-5 or 8-8-8. Higher analysis mixtures such as 10-10-10 also are satisfactory if used carefully. Liquid or soluble fertilizers also give good results.

Nitrogen is the most important of all nutrient elements. It must be used wisely. An excess of fertilizer (which means too much nitrogen) will result in soft or poorly colored fruits and rank vegetative growth with reduced yields.

During severe drought periods water often is required to mature the crop. Apply water at weekly intervals to soak the ground thoroughly down to the roots. A daily spray of a fraction of an inch of water is of little value.

All fruit plants respond to mulches of straw, hay, grass clippings, pine needles or leaves. Mulches add organic matter and nutrients to the soil and retain moisture. However, some mulches can become a fire hazard in dry weather. In addition, they sometimes harbor field mice that can feed on roots and tree trunks.

Barrels, Pyramids and Tubs

ROBERT HENDRICKSON

THE strawberry lends itself well to space-saving planting and thrives in anything from a jar to a large pyramid planter or a strawberry barrel. Recommended varieties are the new and prolific Geneva or any of a number of everbearers that will produce all summer long.

Probably the oldest of all strawberry planters is the strawberry jar. These clay, terra-cotta-colored containers are not easy to obtain but are well worth looking for. The attractive ceramic jars have openings or "pockets" in the sides as well as room for a few plants on top. They can be set outside, or in a sunny window, and require very little care.

If you can't obtain a strawberry jar, a small box, two by two feet or longer, will serve just as well for the patio or a sunny window. Either find the right size box, or build one to your own specifications. Fill the container with a rich soil and plant a dozen or so everbearers for a refreshing treat all summer long. Place a large stone in a corner of the box that you can run the hose against when watering the plants.

(265)

A strawberry barrel is a space-saving method of growing fruit.

Roche

Strawberries can also be grown on the patio in hanging baskets suspended from tree limbs, in tile flues filled with soil and in decorated gallon cans attached to a fence. Old tires, scalloped along the edges with a sharp knife and colorfully painted, can serve as strawberry as well as flower patio planters. For a really unusual effect, try inserting a few plants in soil-filled natural crevices of old logs.

The strawberry pyramid saves far more space than it will occupy on a front lawn or in a backyard. Prefabricated aluminum pyramids with sprinklers and protective coverings are available from numerous manufacturers, but it might be worth your while to build your own from sheet metal or lumber.

The metal pyramid is simply a series of three tiers, the bottom one generally six feet, the second about four feet, and the third about two feet in diameter. To make a strawberry pyramid from aluminum, use corrugated lawn edging sheets, which are the necessary six inches or so wide.

Build the first tier, setting it on the ground and filling it with soil. Then add the second and third tiers, filling each when it is set in place. A piece of perforated three-inch pipe can be inserted from the top to water through, or a sprinkler can be placed at the top.

To construct a square strawberry pyramid from lumber, use two by eights coated with wood preservative and precut in whatever dimensions you desire—one tier might be five feet square, the other three and a half feet square and the last two feet square. Join the boards for each tier frame with one-half-by-three-and-one-half-inch corner braces, using 16d nails, and place each frame as with the circular pyramid.

Either of these terraced planters will hold about fifty plants. They'll even hold more than on a level bed if you drill holes in the sides of the wooden or aluminum tiers too, planting strawberries therein, and they are far more convenient to tend.

The old-fashioned strawberry barrel is another great space-saver and is portable as well. Berries grown in this way will always be clean and will ripen evenly. Strawberry barrels can be made out of anything from a wooden nail keg to a steel oil drum. Starting at the bottom, simply drill from two-to-four-inch-diameter holes in circles around the barrel.

Stagger each circle of holes six to twelve inches from the preceding one. Make the holes in each circle six to twelve inches apart from center to center. Finally, drill holes in the bottom for drainage, and paint or decorate the container so that it can be set on the lawn or patio.

When ready to plant, place stones or gravel in the bottom for drainage, fill with soil and insert a piece of perforated drainpipe that has been cut to the height of the barrel.

Fill the drainpipe with sand, set the plants in the holes and at the top of the barrel and water through the drainpipe. For better air circulation, place the barrel on wooden blocks.

The best soil for strawberry planters is a mixture of equal parts of rich loam, manure, compost and sand. When any of these containers are used, all strawberry plant runners should be removed, and plants should be replaced every few years. The plants can be fed with a water-soluble fertilizer. Protect them from birds during fruiting time by covering the plants with cheesecloth netting.

Raspberries

GEORGE L. SLATE

THERE are so few commercial raspberry plantings these days, raspberries are scarce on the market. A home planting would provide fruit for dessert, jams, canning and freezing.

Raspberries are easy to grow. The crop ripens in July after the strawberry season and harvest continues for four weeks. The autumn fruiting varieties produce berries from early September until frost.

There are three types—black raspberries, red raspberries and purple raspberries, which are hybrids between the black and red varieties. The black raspberry is jet black in color and richly flavored. The canes arise from the crown without the sucker plants which cause the red varieties to wander away from the mother plant. Dundee and Bristol are standard varieties, but New Logan and Blackhawk are grown in the Middle West.

The red raspberry produces many sucker plants. Eventually, if those suckers outside the fruiting row are not removed as they appear, the planting will become a thicket with little value for fruit production. The fruiting row should not be over a foot wide.

September is the earliest variety. Other good sorts are Milton, Taylor, Newburgh and Latham. Amber is the best flavored of all and amber in color. It ripens late. September also produces a fall crop on the tips of new canes. North of Massachusetts the fall crop of September may be too late; in those regions Durham may be useful as the fall crop, since it is a few days earlier.

The purple varieties grow like the black varieties, but the berries are larger, dull dark red in color and rather tart. The fruit is excellent for jams, canning, freezing; many like it for dessert. The purple raspberries bear heavier crops than the black and red varieties. Sodus and Marion are good varieties.

Raspberries need fertile, well-drained soils far enough away from large trees to avoid their shade and root competition. Good air circulation reduces damage from fungus diseases.

Plants may be set in the spring and fall in rows seven feet apart with the plants three feet apart in the row. The plants should be cut to the ground after planting and not allowed to fruit the first year. No fertilizer should be used at planting time, but a small application may be made later after the plants are well started. Those who have not grown raspberries previously should know that the canes sprawl on the ground the first year; thereafter they grow erect.

Summer care is mostly cultivation and hoeing to contol weeds. If any quack (witch) grass is present, it must be completely eliminated the first summer or it will be a nuisance for the life of the planting.

Raspberry plants are shallow-rooted and respond to mulching. Hay, straw, sawdust and tree leaves are good mulches; peat is satisfactory but expensive.

Nitrogenous fertilizers may be used, particularly on the lighter soils. Ammonium nitrate, one-half pound to 100 square feet, is enough. With 5-10-5, three pounds is needed for this area. On light soils sulfate of potash may be needed, especially if the lower leaves of the new shoots become brown at the margin in summer. Mulches and manure may help to correct potash deficiency.

Raspberries must be pruned each year. Raspberry canes are biennial; they grow one year, fruit the following year and then die, being replaced by a new set of canes from the root system. The canes which produced the crop are removed after fruiting.

In the spring before growth starts, the weaker canes of the red raspberries are removed and the remainder are thinned to about ten canes to four feet of row. The tips are cut back about one fourth.

With the black and purple varieties there are branches. The

branches of the black varieties are cut back to eight to ten inches in length. With the purple varieties the branches are left about a foot long. The weaker canes are removed, but usually all the stronger canes may be saved.

The tips of the new shoots of the black and purple varieties should be cut off in June at eighteen inches for the black types and twenty-four inches for the purple. Unless this is done the canes grow very long and are not easy to manage. This should be done as soon as the shoots reach the desired height.

Fruit Tree Espalier

HENRY P. LEUTHARDT

ESPALIERED or trained fruit trees are filling important roles in landscaping by providing design and color for contemporary gardens. The meticulously trimmed branches form leafy patterns against buildings and fences with added features of spring bloom and fall fruit.

Espalier training is based on several horticultural principles. When understood, it is easier to plan tree care. Symmetry of pattern is of utmost importance. An even flow of sap aids in the development of bearing fruit spurs.

The open exposure of the plants to sunlight results in large fruit. Tree varieties must be selected carefully, since certain kinds grow best in horizontally trained shapes while others thrive when trained vertically. Proper understocks must be used for espalier; a small root system is desired. Also, the proper understock limits the size of the tree by slowing its growth and encouraging early bearing.

There are several basic espalier forms. Palmette Verrier is used only for trees with symmetrical shape without a middle branch issuing from the main trunk. This is true mainly of apples and pears. The Palmette Verrier consists of parallel upright branches and was named for the French university professor who developed the form in the nineteenth century. He believed that upright training contributed

Lush spring growth on an espaliered apple tree should be thinned out in summer.

A triple-U espalier is pruned back to tidy four-inch shoots leaving fruit buds to develop.

If there is a fruit bud on an espaliered tree shoot, cut the stem about two inches above it.

Cutting of a shoot above a potential bud will encourage the fruit to develop.

A latent fruit bud, which appeared last year, bears young apples for harvest.

Sy Friedman

immensely to symmetry and production. The Palmette Goucher espalier is distinguished from the Verrier in that it consists of several U-shaped arms in two-fold, three-fold or four-fold espaliers.

The horizontal cordons are recommended for those fruit varieties which have a natural drooping tendency such as Yellow Delicious apple or Bosc pear. The cordon consists of one, two, three or more tiers of long branches trained fifteen to eighteen inches apart. The English use the fan shape pattern widely throughout their gardens. Peaches, nectarines, cherries as well as apples and pears grow well in this pattern.

Pruning, spraying, proper support and fertilization are essential to espalier care. The espaliered trees must be supported to prevent the branches from being blown by the wind or broken under the weight of the fruit. A wooden trellis may be built in the basic form of the espalier. Wire fastened three to six inches away from a wall also may be used. To tie the tree to the support, raffia or plastic strips should be used. Wire or string is not recommended since they would cut into the bark as the tree grows. A tree that is supported properly will retain its original shape.

Pruning will maintain the shape of the tree and rid it of excessive growth. Pruning also develops fruit buds and bearing spurs. Apples and pears bear primarily on spurs. Peaches and nectarines bear fruit on one-year-old shoots. A bearing spur is a shoot or twig of limited growth with short internodes (distances between the leaves).

Espaliers are pruned at least twice a year—during the summer in June and once during the winter. The winter pruning is done to cut out dead wood and excessive shoots.

Summer pruning helps to keep the plant in its proper shape. Espaliered fruit trees have sent out shoots mainly from the point at which the arms connect with the trunk. These shoots should be pruned back flush with the trunk and arms or pruned to encourage fruit bud formation. When an espalier has reached the desired height, it is easily kept at that height by pruning the tops of the vertical branches.

Fruit buds are made or differentiated in late June and continue developing throughout the summer. A latent fruit bud is a bud with four or five leaves around it. A leaf bud is found under the axil of a single leaf. If the shoot on which the fruit bud appears is pruned an inch or two above the latent fruit bud, this bud will develop into a fruit bud.

Occasionally a tree will shoot out excessively after it has been pruned in June. These shoots may have to be cut back again during the summer if growing conditions are extremely favorable. All shoots should be kept to about four inches. Since peaches bear fruit primarily on one-year-old shoots, some of these shoots should be left for next year's fruit. A peach is very vegetative, however, and it is best to remove one-third to one-half of last year's shoots during the winter.

A good spray program is essential to good fruit. Scale, scab, aphid and leaf hoppers are the principal pests in apples. Pear psylla, scale blister mite and fire blight attack pears. Peaches and nectarines are susceptible to brown rot, red leaf curl and peach borer. Most of the pests are controlled with the application of miscible oil during the dormant period, and one of the general-purpose fruit sprays should give sufficient protection during the summer. For specific controls of pear psylla, sprays should be applied at the end of July and during August. A spray of malathion applied to the trunk and branches of peach trees from mid-July to mid-August should control the peach borer.

Mulch First, Plant Second, and Vegetables Grow

BEVERLY FLEMING

AFTER one season of vegetable growing—a frenetic, endless summer of unlimited aches and ridiculously limited results I was ready to throw in the trowel. Then I discovered gardening can be remarkably easy and thoroughly rewarding.

The revelation came as I began to know some of my new neighbors. Farmers who had worked the Connecticut soil all their lives. Women who filled their freezers with home-grown vegetables. Some who even had surplus enough to start roadside stands. Amused by my novice problems, they began to share their shortcuts and simple earthy wisdom.

Local advice was consistent and consistently simple. My complicated city ways, they claimed, had caused me to overspend, overwork and overreact. "Relax," they scolded. "A vegetable garden is supposed to serve you!" I, with my city-bred suspicions, viewed their ideas as a bit simplistic. Was it really possible to eliminate all those weeds, diseases and wiggly intruders without fences, fertilizers, fungicides and all of the accompanying effort?

Trying to relax and believe, I began to compile the local wisdom and plan for next year. Every step that I put down in my garden book seemed so natural, so logical that I soon did feel relaxed, at least on paper. Today, of course, many of these methods have become popular as part of what we now call organic gardening. And the delicious, nutritious results are well known. But even the best organic processes can be complicated. My neighbors had no fancy name for their procedures. If they had had time to think about it, I suppose they might have come up with something like "organic gardening made easy."

I began in the fall, after the first killing frost. All weeds were pulled up (for the last time, I might add). Diseased plants were removed and burned. Whatever else remained—corn husks, cabbage leaves, squash vines—was tossed right back on the garden. This was the beginning of one of my neighbors' greatest labor-saving ideas (no more hauling matter to the compost pile, then eventually hauling it back). No shredding or treating the compost. In time, nature takes care of all that.

The garden became my compost pile. I mulched it with all available material: grass cuttings, leaves, hay, what cow manure the neighboring farmers could spare. (Even cow manure becomes unnecessary after a few seasons, when the soil is rich enough.)

Then came the kitchen mulch: all kinds of fruit and vegetable peelings, lettuce leaves, scraps of leftover vegetables, eggshells. Everything except meat and other foods which might attract animals. I became an impassioned collector of this potential garbage, rushing out daily to feed my treasures to the garden. Before the cold weather came, my garden mulch stood about ten inches high. Through the winter, I continued to add kitchen waste, even tossing it on top of the snow. Not very aesthetic-looking, I admit. But neatness definitely doesn't count when you're making this bountiful patchwork cover, designed to accomplish three important things: (1) to keep the ground soft and moist, (2) to encourage a naturally rich soil, (3) to prevent the recurrence of weeds.

In the spring, because of this mulch, there was no need to turn the soil over, no artificial fertilizing, absolutely no pre-planting preparation! Instead of all the torturous work of the previous season, I simply rolled back the mulch just enough to plant my rows of seed. When the stalks grew large and sturdy (and they did!), the mulch was spread back and carefully arranged around each plant. All during the growing season, I continued to add both kitchen and hard waste, trying to maintain a five-inch thickness. This eliminates two of the endless summer chores: weeding and cultivating. And, except for the most drastic dry spells, a nice moist mulch even makes watering unnecessary.

The next step in setting up a no-work summer was to pest-proof the garden the natural way, eliminating all those unpleasant chemicals and other so-called deterrents. My new pesticides were flowers and herbs. Besides being highly effective, they also add beauty, fragrance and charm to a vegetable garden.

The star in my new cast of defenders was the lovely marigold. I planted these colorful annuals around and between the tomatoes, string beans and eggplant to eliminate nematodes. To keep the cucumbers free from black aphids, I used nasturtiums, plus a few marigolds to help ward off cucumber beetles. For corn, either sunflowers or sweet geraniums are effective in repelling all sorts of corn predators. Other flowers, seemingly odoriferous enough to repel a variety of vegetable garden pests, are cosmos, asters and chrysanthemums. I scattered these general insect repellents throughout the garden.

In the herb family, sage watches over my broccoli, although mint or rosemary is equally good at fighting the deadly cabbage moth. Radishes are great around cabbages, too, fending off root maggots. For anyone planning to grow potatoes, their savior is horseradish, an excellent way to repel the Colorado potato beetle.

Probably the most practical herbal protectors are garlic, onions and chives. Grow them everywhere and generously, for their function is threefold. Besides guarding your lettuce against carrot flies and aphids, they actually contribute flavor to growing plants. Later on, these staunch friends will help you again in the kitchen.

As for moles, cutworms and Mexican beetles, nothing seems to work as well for me as mulching. My thick, protective blanket has virtually eliminated these annoying intruders.

Once flowers, herbs and vegetables are all living in happy, well-mulched harmony, here's an extra bit of protection: take a flour sifter and sift a layer of flour over everything. Actually, anything white seems to repel creatures of the night. I use flour because it's handy and harmless. However, this ploy must be repeated after every rainfall. Should you still have trouble with any really stubborn creatures, try tossing a few dishpans of soapy water on your garden. It won't hurt the vegetables, but watch the bugs disappear.

As for birds, the simplest solution I've found is to tie a couple of foil pie pans to a stake in the middle of your garden. With a little wind, they'll clash like cymbals, keeping your vegetable path bird-free.

Finally, if you have any unusual regional problems: next to your friendly neighborhood advisers, a gardener's best friend is the local County Agricultural Agent listed in the telephone book under county government. He is thoroughly trained in plant diseases and insect control. And he is ready to serve you with free advice on almost any gardening subject. Part of his service is to issue a variety of bulletins and leaflets on what may be current or impending problems in your area. These are also free, on request.

My first disastrous summer now seems nightmares away. I can even laugh about all the cultivating, weeding, fertilizing, fencing, spraying, worrying. With all my beautiful, aromatic, labor-saving devices working for me day and night, vegetable gardening has become easy, inexpensive and abundantly rewarding. Sometimes I almost feel guilty about reaping so many benefits from so little effort. But it's hard to feel guilty when you're so relaxed.

ANY WOODY PLANTS can be propagated quickly at home and the cutting method is one of the easiest to learn. The average suburban plot has abundant resources of tree and shrub cuttings and each piece when rooted will mature into a plant exactly like its parent. This method is not only an economical source of plant material but a practical way to increase stock of valuable specimens. Cuttings can be gathered in summer when growth is green or propagating can be delayed until fall when new wood has hardened.

Seeding, another way to increase plants, is basic with all gardeners. Once success with sowing grass, annuals and vegetables is achieved, there are perennials, biennials and wild flowers to grow. To sharpen the adventures of wild-flower gardening, fresh seed often can be gathered from fruits and berries during woodland hikes. Or many seed houses stock assorted supplies of wild flower, perennial, biennial and even some tree and shrub seed.

New Plants from Tree and Shrub Cuttings

R. R. THOMASSON

PROPAGATING plants in the home garden by means of cuttings or layering is a practical phase of gardening. Home propagation can come to the rescue when the budget for nursery stock is exhausted. Also, it is possible to trade favorite plants with a neighbor.

Some woody plants are difficult to propagate. However, many of the common shrubs may be readily increased from cuttings or layering. I have started pussy willow, red-twigged dogwood, bush honeysuckle, euonymus, forsythia, mockorange and numerous others by merely sticking cuttings eight or ten inches long into ordinary garden soil.

Those who were too busy to take cuttings in the spring have a second chance in the summer. For summer propagation softwood cuttings are taken. This is wood of the current season's growth which is firm enough to break under pressure with a snap. I make the cuttings two to six inches long; the bottom cut is just below a node or leaf bud. If more than one cutting is made from the same stem, the top cut should be just above a node. Always keep cuttings moist until they are set in the rooting medium.

The cuttings may be rooted in sand, vermiculite or a mixture of sand and peat moss. This medium may be placed in a coldframe, box, flower pot or in a special bed in the garden. Humidity is important. Also, cuttings need protection from the midday sun.

To insure uniform humidity, a covering of polyethylene plastic is a great help. Three or four stiff wires are fastened over the box of rooting medium after the manner of the "bows" on a covered wagon. A sheet of polyethylene is then folded over the wires and under the box to make it reasonably airtight. The plastic keeps moisture in but allows gases to escape.

For plants that do not root readily, such as magnolia and holly, the use of one of the root-promoting hormone chemicals is desirable. Follow directions on the package.

Since soil moisture is vital, it is well to start the cuttings where they may be easily reached with the hose. A generous mixture of peat moss or compost in the soil, plus a mulch of the same material, will help hold the moisture.

Many a splendid rosebush has been grown from a cutting taken from a bouquet and stuck in the ground with a glass jar turned upside down over it. A blossom stem four to six inches long with three nodes makes the best cutting. Some shade and ample moisture are essential. While rose cuttings can be rooted in ordinary soil, they will have a better chance in a medium of sphagnum moss or sand and peat moss.

The gardener should not lose sight of the fact, however, that rosebushes purchased from a nursery are more vigorous than the ones that grow on their own roots. Nursery plants are budded or grafted onto strong understocks such as the rugosa, multiflora and dog rose.

Another popular method of increasing plants in the home garden is layering. Cut a vigorous young branch or shoot partway through, bend it down and cover it with an inch or two of soil. I mix peat moss with the soil to improve the moisture-holding capacity. The cut area of the stem will produce roots. Then the new plant can be severed from the parent branch and planted separately in the garden.

A variation on this method is air layering, an ancient Chinese system. It is especially useful for tree and shrub cuttings which do not strike roots readily. Cut partway through the branch and wrap a ball of damp sphagnum moss around the cut. The ball of moss is then wrapped in polyethylene which is tied at each end to make it as nearly airtight as possible.

In considering inexpensive ways of increasing plants at home, do not overlook the pleasure of planting seed gathered on hikes through the country. Tree seeds such as acorns, buckeyes, elm or red maple seed may be planted.

1: In May, after the azaleas have flowered, six-inch cuttings are taken from the new growth. The cut is made below a node.

2: Root inducing hormone powder speeds propagation. The cut ends are dipped into the powder and excess is tapped off.

5: The flat is tightly sealed and set in a shaded site for eight to ten weeks. Additional watering should not be necessary.

6: Of the twelve azalea cuttings inserted in the flat, nine developed fibrous roots in eight weeks. Other evergreens are propagated similarly.

3: Treated cuttings are placed into a clean flat containing half-sand and half-peat mixture. It is soaked the day before planting.

4: The entire flat is covered with a sheet of polyethylene which is supported by arched wires. Moisture is retained.

7: Rooted cuttings are planted in pots, or if their root systems are substantially developed, they may be set directly into the garden.

8: Pots of rooted azalea cuttings are stored in a coldframe during the winter months. Plants in the garden should also be protected.

Herman Gantner

(283)

Dogwood, persimmon, Juneberry, sweet gum, yellow wood or tulip tree seed will have to be stratified. Stratifying means storing the seed in moist sand, soil or sawdust at temperatures above freezing. Some seed is improved by freezing, however. It can be gathered in fall and stored over winter. Among these are seed of golden rain tree, yellow wood, flowering dogwood and redbud.

If it is not possible to take cuttings during the summer months, gardeners can postpone their propagating until fall, when many professional nurserymen take cuttings. They cut eight- to ten-inch pieces of tree or shrub twigs and bundle them. The cuttings are buried in the ground, deep enough to prevent their freezing.

I usually wait until April to take such cuttings. I select the previous year's growth and take cuttings about eight inches long. They should be as thick as a lead pencil. The length and size of the cuttings can be varied, however, with no marked effect. These cuttings are placed in rows in full sun, eight or ten inches apart. By the following spring, they are ready to be spread apart to grow.

Propagating with Hardwood Cuttings

KENNETH MEYER

MANY deciduous shrubs and some trees can be easily propagated from hardwood cuttings taken in fall. This method has been successful to start dozens of mockoranges, several specimens of *Deutzia gracilis*, a white wistaria and two Concord grape vines, to name a few.

October and November are the best months for taking hardwood cuttings. Generally speaking, it is well to wait until after a few frosts, when the plants have dropped their leaves and become dormant.

The cuttings are taken from healthy stems or canes of the current season's growth. Each should be seven to nine inches long and of approximately lead-pencil thickness, with at least three or four buds or nodes (leaf joints).

The base of each cutting should be cut straight across and just below a node. The tip usually is cut off on a slant, so it will be easy to distinguish from the base later on. Exceptions are rose of Sharon and weigela, which should be propagated from tip cuttings. The basal part of each stem is best discarded, as it is usually too hard and thick to root readily.

Cuttings of each kind of shrub are tied with soft wire or tarred string in separate bundles of ten to twenty-five each. The butt ends are kept together. Be sure to attach a weatherproof identifying label to each bundle. Thus prepared, the cuttings are ready for winter storage; during this time they form calluses (protective tissue on the cut surfaces) which are conducive to root formation the following spring.

The bundles of cuttings may be buried in a coldframe. Equally good is a deep box filled with slightly damp soil, sand or sawdust; the box is stored in an outbuilding or unheated cellar where the temperature remains around 40 to 45 degrees. The material around the cuttings should not be too moist. It should neither exude water nor absorb vital moisture from the cuttings. It must not be allowed to freeze.

A simpler way to handle hardwood cuttings is to bury them below the frost line in a well-drained garden location where there is no danger of standing water. A trench is dug deeply enough to accommodate the bundles standing vertically (with butt ends up). Horizontal storage is satisfactory, too. To insure good drainage, a layer of coarse sand about two inches thick is spread over the bottom.

After the cuttings are in place, sandy soil is used to fill in the trench and form a mound over it to a height of a foot or more. With the approach of severe weather, pile a thick mulch of straw, salt hay or litter on top of the mound; this will further help to preclude temperature fluctuation caused by the sun. Such insulation is also a wise precaution when a coldframe is used as the storage place. A labeled stake driven into the ground at each end of the trench will serve to mark the spot; otherwise it is difficult to locate the cuttings in spring.

Nothing more need be done until spring, except to prepare the ground in the intended garden site so it will be ready for spring planting. The soil should be spaded deeply, left rough, and allowed to settle over winter.

In April or May, when the soil is dry enough to be worked, it should be hoed, raked, and made ready for planting the same as any other garden bed. The best way to plant the cuttings is to dig a narrow trench at least seven inches deep, with one side nearly vertical and the other sloping.

Do not use chemical fertilizer, but mix liberal quantities of humus or screened compost into the trench. To be on the safe side, place an inch-deep layer of sand in the bottom for good drainage.

Space the cuttings, butt ends down, six or eight inches apart against the vertical side of the trench. The tip of each cutting should be only a couple of inches above the ground. Fill in with good sandy soil and tamp it firmly around the base of each cutting. Leave a slight depression to catch rain water.

Do not let the cuttings dry out while the planting is in progress. The callus is soft and dries quickly when exposed. Wrap the cuttings in a damp cloth while working.

There is some difference of opinion about treating the cuttings with a root-inducing hormone before planting. Some gardeners have found it unnecessary, but such treatment might be of considerable value with hard-to-root species. The chemicals are available in various strengths. A simple test can be conducted by treating a portion of the cuttings and then checking the rooting results against the untreated cuttings.

Once planted, the cuttings require no special attention beyond shallow cultivation and a good watering twice a week in really dry weather. By the end of the first growing season most of the cuttings will have developed into husky plants, one to three feet tall, with two or three stems.

Among the many popular plants which may be propagated easily from hardwood cuttings are beautybush (*Kolkwitzia amabilis*), cotoneaster, shrubby honeysuckle, kerria, forsythia, flowering quince, elaeagnus and certain spireas. The viburnums are also good plants for rooting this way, as are euonymus, currants, gooseberries, climbing roses and trumpet vines.

Wild Flowers from Seed

JUDITH-ELLEN BROWN

RAISING wild flowers from seed can be an absorbing project for the hobbyist. He will achieve a sense of satisfaction which will repay abundantly the patience and effort involved.

Admittedly, raising certain wild-flower species from seed is unduly laborious. For example, native creepers such as wild strawberries and partridgeberries are propagated more readily by stem cuttings. Propagation by division of established clumps is considerably easier with native iris, wild ginger and many other varieties.

However, with plants that resent being disturbed—such as butterfly weeds and lupines—collecting and planting the seed is a practical method of establishing them in the home garden. And, with the fringed gentians, seed propagation is about the only way the home grower can raise plants successfully. Needless to say, this is definitely not a suitable species for the beginner to attempt.

In general, the gardener who wants to grow wild flowers from seed must be prepared to collect his own, since few nurseries offer seed for sale. Packet collections of wild-flower seed are not recommended; they may contain a high percentage of weed seed.

One point to remember is that most wild-flower seed should be planted as soon as possible after it has ripened. Although some species may be held until the following spring, delay usually results in slower germination. Trillium, for example, may take an additional year to germinate if not sown promptly. On the other hand, liatris (blazing star) may perform better if seed is held over for two or three years before sowing.

The beginner will find it a good plan to start out with varieties that are easy to cultivate. Eventually, as his knowledge increases, the novice may progress to exacting plants such as arbutus.

As a start it may be wise for the new wild-flower gardener to experiment with seed that can be sown directly in the ground. Species that may be planted directly outdoors are those which, in nature, seed themselves freely. In this category are meadow rue, violets and mayapples.

Seed of such readily propagated woodland varieties should be collected when ripe and planted in a cool, shady site. The gardener should try to duplicate the natural habitat. Some winter protection—a mulch of leaves, twigs, etc.—is desirable, but such cover should be removed before the seedlings come up in spring.

Other varieties which may be sown directly in the garden are native to sunny, open areas. These types—which include the butterfly weed, the monardas (Oswego tea and wild bergamot) and native larkspur—are easy to grow from seed. The seed is collected when ripe and planted in an open spot in the fall. The site should be cleared and the soil prepared in advance. Cover the newly planted area with burlap over the winter.

In most cases seed will sprout by the following spring. Seedlings may be transplanted during the first fall and can be expected to bloom the second summer after the original sowing. In fact, the monardas may start to flower during the first year after planting.

Most wild-flower species, however, require more effort if they are to be raised successfully from seed. The seed should be planted in flats or pots. Use soil that simulates the plant's natural environment. If possible, it is a good idea to take some earth from around the original plant at the time the seed is gathered. If this proves impractical, seed may be sown in a mixture of one-third leafmold or peat moss, one-third clean garden loam and one-third coarse sand.

For acid-loving plants the proportions should be altered to about two parts of oak leafmold to one part of sand and one part of loam. After sowing, press the seed lightly into the soil and cover with a thin layer of soil or sand.

Pots (or cans with holes punched for drainage) are recommended for smaller seed. For extremely fine seed, a layer of dried sphagnum moss, vermiculite or similar substance may be placed over the soil; the seed then may be sown on this sterile surface and a thin covering of the same material scattered lightly on top.

After sowing, the soil should be watered very gently to avoid

Trilliums are one of May's show-iest wild flowers.

Judith-Ellen Brown

displacing the seed. Naturally, seed of moisture-loving varieties, such as marsh marigold, must be kept wet—either by standing the pot in a dish or pan of water or by sinking it into the moist soil near a brook or pond.

To prevent the seed from washing out, a piece of burlap may be laid directly on the soil. Glass darkened with newspaper also may be used. Covers should be removed in the spring. The young plants may be given the necessary shade by setting the containers under trees or shrubs or by placing them under lath frames.

When the seedlings are ready for transplanting they may be placed in plant bands or set in rows in flats. They should be kept moist and shaded during this period. Seedlings should be mulched during the following winter.

The plants usually can be moved to their permanent location by the second spring, although this will vary with the sturdiness of the species. Blooming time will vary, too, depending on the variety. A few kinds of plants may begin to blossom their first year after sowing. Some wildlings will not come into bloom until their second year, while others may take three years.

Of course, the over-eager gardener will be disappointed if he chooses wild flowers that are difficult to grow from seed. To be ruled out—for beginner and expert alike—are such exacting plants as arethusas, the fringed orchids and calypsos. Their stringent requirements make them practically impossible to maintain in the home wildflower garden, even if collected seed can be germinated successfully.

Biennials to Sow in Summer

MARY S. GREEN

Pansies, forget-me-nots and English daisies are the old reliable biennials that provide a burst of cheerfulness in the spring garden. For real distinction in the flower border, though, three others are needed—foxgloves, wallflowers and Canterbury bells. And a fourth sweet william, is a very dependable filler for almost any border. Seed sown in midsummer will bloom the following spring, since biennials are plants that require two years to reach maturity.

The gardener-in-a-hurry can find almost all these plants for sale at local garden centers. Growing one's own plants from seed, however, is a much more satisfactory way of providing a dependable supply of particular varieties.

Mixed pansies (*Viola tricolor hortensis*) make joyful spring arrangements. Blue Boy is a pale blue variety, Lake of Thun a deep, rich blue, and Coronation Gold, a golden yellow. These varieties combine well with the colors of spring daffodils and tulips.

The Oregon Giants produce flowers three to four inches in diameter, and in rich blends of colors. The only drawback is that the blooms are so large, they tend to hang their heads slightly.

Blue, white and pale pink forget-me-nots (*Mysotis alpestris*) can be used to carpet spots between the bulbs and other larger plants in the border. English daisies (*Bellis perennis*) have flowers that are white or in varying shades of pink to red. Like forget-me-nots, English daisies self-sow but the seedlings come mixed in color.

If only for their fragrance, wallflowers (*Cheiranthus cheiri*) would be worth growing. Unlike most of the early-blooming plants,

Tall foxgloves lend stately accent
to the June garden.

Jeannette Grossman

Pansies are easily raised from seed
sown in late fall or early spring.

J. Horace McFarland

wallflowers are comparatively tall, to eighteen inches. The variety
Primrose is pale yellow and Cloth of Gold a deep, glowing gold.
Vulcan is bright red and Blood Red a deep, dark red. There also are
bronze and orange-toned varieties.

Sweet william (*Dianthus barbatus*) is another medium-height
biennial that blooms after the wallflowers have finished. Flowers come
in solid colors—white, red or the bright salmon of variety Newport
Pink—and are marked by an eye or ring of contrasting color.

Foxgloves (*Digitalis purpurea*) are especially useful at the back
of a wide border where big clumps of three to five plants can be
grouped together. The new Excelsior strain has flowers all around the
stem instead of just on one side as with the older sorts. Blooms are
in shades of purple, pink, apricot, cream and white. The tall spikes
are particularly effective against a wall or a shrubbery background.

Last of the biennials to bloom are the Canterbury bells (*Campanula*). The *Campanula* medium varieties have graceful spires of bloom, but the cup-and-saucer types (*C. medium calycanthema*) give a much more massive display of color. The flowers, which come in cool pinks, whites, blues and purples, are long lasting. After the faded flowers are picked off, the plants bloom again.

When growing biennials from seed, exactly the same technique is used as for growing annuals—only the timing is different. One can wait until August to sow seed of pansy, forget-me-nots and daisies for bloom the following spring. But for the other biennials, June or early July is none too early to start next year's plants.

Perennials from Seed

OLIVE E. ALLEN

ONE advantage of raising perennials from seed is that it is possible to have the named varieties and exact colors wanted. Another advantage is economy; clumps from a nursery can be expensive if many are needed.

Perennials will flower the year after seed is started. Among the easiest for the home gardener to grow are delphinium, lupine and columbine. However, pinks, perennial candytuft, yellow *Alyssum saxatile*, gaillardia, baby's-breath, pyrethrum, Shasta daisies and Oriental poppies are well worth sowing.

It pays to buy fresh seed, which is available in July. This is especially important for delphinium. When ordering, remember that one seed packet will produce quite a few plants. So unless there is room for a lot of perennials, it is wise not to buy too many packets. Separate colors or named varieties are preferable for the color-conscious gardener. One or two colors or varieties sown each summer will soon build up a fine display.

One kind of seed should be sown to a pot and labeled. Soil is composed of sifted compost, sand and peat moss or humus. Cinders go into the bottom of the pot for drainage, then the soil mixture, then a thin layer of sterile vermiculite or sifted sphagnum moss. Water and press the seed into the top layer of vermiculite or sphagnum moss and cover lightly.

A coldframe is an excellent place for pots of seed, for it will give protection from drying sun, wind and too much rain. Soil in the pots must be kept moist but never soggy. Too much water or poor drainage will cause seed to rot. Perennial seed may take as long as three weeks to germinate.

When the young seedlings have developed their second pair of leaves, they are transplanted into a place where they will have more room to grow. Transplanting can be into individual small pots, into flats, into rows in the coldframe or to a protected place in the garden. Seedlings should be spaced at least two inches apart, and the soil into which they are planted should be enriched with a little 5-10-5 fertilizer.

Again, seedlings must not be allowed to dry out, yet they should never be overwatered. This is the stage when damping-off, a fungus disease, will cause young seedlings to fall over and shrivel up. This occurs if the soil is kept too moist or contains spores of the disease. To control damping-off, the soil can be saturated with a special chemical for the purpose before planting.

In August, when the sun is strong, I like to lay a couple of old

Columbine, foxgloves and Oriental poppy fill a corner with summer-time bloom.

Gottscho-Schleisner

wooden shutters across the coldframe. Light filters through the shutters but the plants are not scorched. The cover of the coldframe, of course, is left off all summer.

It will be necessary to weed regularly. Weeds grow so vigorously under these ideal conditions that they would soon choke out the seedlings, if left to grow. Pull weeds carefully without disturbing the fine roots of the seedlings.

Slugs and cutworms as well as plant lice or aphids are apt to be pests when the plants are small. Slug bait is effective and nicotine sulfate or malathion will kill plant lice. Rabbits, woodchucks and even mice may nibble the succulent green leaves. Turkey wire laid over the top of the coldframe will keep out these pests.

As the seedlings grow into recognizable plants and clumps, they may be transplanted into their permanent places in the garden. However, if winters are likely to be severe, with constant freezing and thawing of the ground, the newly transplanted clumps may be heaved out of the soil before spring.

I prefer not to transplant young perennials to a permanent site until spring. They are left in the coldframe with the cover in place all winter and transplanted when the soil has thawed out and warmed up a bit. This transplanting can be done early. Bloom may be a little later than normal.

The Versatile Coldframe

KENNETH MEYER

THE coldframe is adaptable to so many uses all year round, it now is almost as essential for good gardening as the mower is for proper lawn care.

It is an ideal place for growing high-grade seedlings. The frame need not be pretentious. I have at times grown hundreds of excellent plants in nothing more than a heavy wooden box with the bottom knocked out and an old window sash laid on top.

Nowadays there are various kinds of prefabricated frames available, some finished and others all ready to be put together. Anyone handy with tools can build one to suit individual requirements.

Some of the ready-made frames, especially those of aluminum or copper, come equipped with electric soil-heating cables and a thermostat for regulating temperatures automatically. This equipment can be installed in a home-built frame, too. The prefabricated frames sometimes have sash covers of various transparent plastics instead of glass, which seems to make no difference to the plants.

Whatever kind of frame is decided upon, the first step is selection of the best possible site for it. Facing south is best; east is acceptable. There should be adequate protection from cold sweeping winds, especially from the west; this may be furnished by a building, fence or hedge. Also, the spot chosen must have good drainage. Nearness to a water supply is important. Some advance thought given to these details will insure good results from the coldframe. Above all, do not select a site where snow from a sloping roof can pile up on the frame.

Next in importance is the soil. My preference is for a well-prepared and friable sandy loam, into which a little well-rotted manure and a small amount of bonemeal have been incorporated. The surface layer of soil should be extra light and fine so that tender seedlings can penetrate easily. I keep a container of such sifted soil at hand when sowing seed, and use it for covering them.

If the soil in the frame is naturally heavy, its texture can be improved and porosity increased by mixing in sand and humus such as finely granulated peat moss and sifted leafmold.

Seed may be sown in soil-filled flats or directly into the soil in the coldframe. Kinds that need special attention, and those that should be started earliest, such as petunias, snapdragons, verbenas and salvia, are best sown in flats or low clay pots called bulb pans so they can be moved around as desired. Marigolds, zinnias, asters, cosmos and other rugged kinds can be sown in the open soil.

Most seed is sown about one-eighth to one-quarter of an inch deep. One-half inch is usually deep enough for even the larger kinds. Extra fine seed like petunia need only to be pressed in lightly. Guard against sowing any kind of seed too thickly. Crowded seedlings become spindly.

A southern exposure is the best location for a coldframe.

Molly Adams

Hardy seed may be started in early spring in a coldframe.

Roche

Assorted cuttings of woody plants can be rooted in the coldframe.

Gottscho-Schleisner

The proper time for seed sowing varies with local climate, but generally speaking seed can be sown in a frame from four to six weeks sooner than out in the open, especially if a little artificial heat is supplied. However, I have raised many very early plants in a frame with only the sun's heat, and they were large enough to set out by the time one would ordinarily be sowing seed in the open ground.

The gardener should not make the mistake of trying to push growth too rapidly. Regular attention to properly controlled conditions of air and moisture inside the frame will produce stocky plants with heavy root systems.

After seed is sown and, in fact, until garden planting time, the main points to watch are temperature, light, moisture and ventilation. A small thermometer hung in one corner of the frame is helpful.

When the frame cover is closed, little or no watering is required during cold cloudy weather. When the sash is raised slightly to admit fresh air, watering may be necessary every day.

The gardener should keep an eye on the sun, especially if his frame has soil-heating equipment. At times the full sun will be much too strong for young plants and they must be shaded. A lath screen provides convenient shade; it is easily made by nailing plastering lath to two strips. Space the lath about one and one-half inches apart.

The sash cover should be left on the frame in cold weather, but on sunny days it is opened an inch or two—even wider as outside temperature rises. Proper ventilation is most important. Lack of it, together with insufficient light and too high temperature, encourages the damping-off fungus disease which attacks and kills seedlings at the ground line.

The recommended average temperature inside the frame is around 50 to 60 degrees. This is approximate, of course, and varies with other factors. Some early seedlings thrive with less heat than others. On cold nights, or if the temperature outside drops suddenly, the sash over the frame should be covered with some form of insulation to conserve warmth. I use a couple of old quilts for moderately cold nights, and a discarded wool rug for severe weather. Specially made mats can be purchased for the purpose. Sometimes old wooden shutters or boards are used to provide additional insulation.

After plants have formed their second set of leaves, they should be transplanted carefully to two-and-one-half inch pots or plant bands, or into larger flats, for further growth. They may also be reset into the soil in the frame an inch or two apart. Certain kinds of plants —snapdragons, for example—will be encouraged to branch if the tips of their main stems are nipped out as they develop.

When most of the plants have been set in permanent locations outdoors, the coldframe becomes an excellent place to sow seed of biennials such as English daisy, pansy, sweet william and foxglove. Perennials, too, can be started then—from seed or cuttings—to provide sturdy clumps for fall planting.

PART VIII

HOUSE PLANTS

TENDING A SPRAWLING philodendron that ekes out a new leaf every so often is a modest way to grow plants indoors, but at least it is a start. The next venture may be chives on the kitchen window sill, then an African violet in the den.

House plants do not require a great deal of care, but some are more particular than others. All of them need proper light, moist air and good soil.

Those requiring minimum attention are the foliage plants that dominate indoor plant collections these days. Their green pattern softens the stark lines of interiors and they grow with little sunlight. By contrast, those plants with shining flowers—geraniums, begonias, gloxinias, orchids, to name a few—need frequent watering and feeding, which they reward with gay blooms.

Gaining in popularity is artificial light gardening. This new phase of growing transforms basements, unused nooks and even closets into indoor oases. Any number of kinds of plants are successful under fluorescent lamps and as improvements occur in equipment, the scope will be broadened.

Actually, when it comes down to it, there really are very few kinds of plants that cannot be grown indoors. The challenges and rewards of success make the house-plant hobby thrive year-round.

Fancy Foliage
of the Indoor Ferns

F. GORDON FOSTER

AGAIN, as in the Victorian period, there is a growing interest in ferns as house plants. Along with other things in a fast-changing world, fern selection has been updated and is no longer confined to the Boston fern with its endless variants.

House ferns, mostly of tropical origin, do best with moderate day temperature of 72 degrees and cool night temperature of 65 degrees where reasonable humidity is supplied by a humidifier or by hand spraying. With a few suggestions on choice and some tips on culture, fern culture can be as easy and successful as flower growing.

Ferns vary greatly in size and character. Some, like the golden polypody (*Polypodium aureum*) are large and robust in color and texture. Others, especially the smaller maidenhairs, are delicate in shade and soft to the touch.

Several holly-ferns grow throughout the world. Two favorites from the Orient are excellent for the home. Start with the Japanese holly-fern (*Cyrtomium falcatum*), which has dark, waxy green leaflets. Each leaflet has sharp prickly spines, suggesting Oregon holly rather than fern. Select if possible the variant, *Rochefordianum*.

Fortunately, Japanese holly-fern tolerates dryer atmosphere than many others, and its strong leaflets can be cleaned with a damp cloth. If a small plant is selected, it probably will have only three or four three-lobed leaves. As it grows, subsequent leaves will become more and more like holly, ultimately reaching heights of twelve to twenty-four inches.

The Tsus-sima holly-fern (*Polystichum tsus-simense*) is much smaller. This plant, with fernlike leaves, is slower-growing and good for the terrarium. With the higher moisture of the glass enclosure, it is compatible with native woodland plants.

(302)

Boston ferns have never lost their foothold in the American home. Originally a mutation of the wild swordfern of Florida, *Nephrolepis exaltata*, Boston ferns have maintained first position in sales since their inception in 1894. The earlier varieties had pendulous leaves six or more feet long, like those of their ancestors, and required a high pedestal or planter to keep them from touching the floor. Subsequent horticultural treatment has produced smaller and bushier plants which are more desirable for the home.

Originally Boston ferns were sold with complex names. Nomenclature has been greatly simplified until now such mundane names as Fluffy Ruffles can be found in florists' shops. Reversion to ancestral form is frequent, and leaves on one plant may range from a lacy-cut pattern to a pinnate pattern that resembles our native Christmas fern. While there is great similarity in the leaf pattern of these two ferns, there is no generic relationship.

Large Boston ferns currently cost between five and seven dollars. I prefer smaller plants in three- or four-inch pots. Three small plants may be placed in a large pot and packed with damp peat moss. Grouping smaller plants gives better appearance than one large one. Later the plants can be used individually or placed in a table planter.

Bird's-nest fern (*Asplenium nidus*) makes a delightful focal point when placed on a low windowsill or bay. Here is a fern with simple, tonguelike, glossy green leaves that is not only handsome but requires less attention than other plants. Its leaves uncurl from a central mass of heavy black scales, and by maturity each will have developed a strong dark midrib which contrasts nicely with the green. Where unfolding leaves have chewed edges, be on the alert for tiny greenhouse snails. While the leaves are still in the tightly coiled stage, these pests operate beneath the protective black scale covering.

Maidenhair ferns are always admired. Actually there are about 200 species of maidenhairs growing throughout the world, mainly in warmer areas. Most have delicate leaves reminiscent of the ginkgo tree. All have characteristic, prominent forking and reforking veins.

The best maidenhair selections for the home are Venus maidenhair (*Adiantum capillus-veneris*) and rosy maidenhair (*A. hispidulum*). Venus maidenhair has soft, light applegreen leaves and is more popular. Croziers of rosy maidenhair are rose-colored, and as the leaves come to maturity the color changes to a dark reddish-green shade. A close look will reveal tiny spines on the stipes and surfaces of the leaves.

Ocean Spray and Pacific Maid maidenhairs are also good and have overlapping leaflets of light green. These bushy plants are fine for the fern dish or small planter. All these ferns are fast-growing and for continued healthy growth should be divided and repotted each season.

Some ferns are epiphytic and grow in trees or over rocks. These plants, when grown in hanging baskets or mounted on cork-bark plaques, do well in the home. One of the easiest epiphytes to grow is golden polypody (*Polypodium aureum*). Like so many ferns of this group having long, climbing, fuzzy rhizomes, it is indiscriminately called "rabbit's-foot fern."

The plant is a native of Florida and commonly appears on the latticelike bark of the cabbage palmettos. The first leaves of young plants may have only two or three lobed segments. Subsequent leaves develop large multi-segmented blades and have long dark stipes. With favorable growing conditions, the plant may reach a height of twenty-four inches in the home.

A more interesting plant than the native golden polypody is the horticultural variant Mandaianum. This variety has deep wavy-edged leaves, and with its powdery blue-green surfaces the fern becomes quite showy. Both polypodys do well as potted plants or in hanging baskets.

Button fern (*Pellaea rotundifolia*) is a native of New Zealand. A good house plant with dark green, almost round leaflets, it is as unusual as it is unfernlike. While generally grown in pots, it can be grown in an open hanging basket or wire ball to facilitate root moisture and proper drainage.

While Davallias have long been my favorites, I think that the New Zealand mother-fern (*Aspleninum bulbiferum*) is my second choice. This fern normally thrives in deep, damp ravines where its green feathery leaves reach lengths of six feet. Sometimes referred to as "viviparous" or "live bearing," this species, in addition to reproducing by spores, is capable of producing offspring by vegetative budding in. Long before the plant reaches full stature, small plants may be seen budding from the parent leaves.

In their native habitat, the mother-fern leaves become so heavily

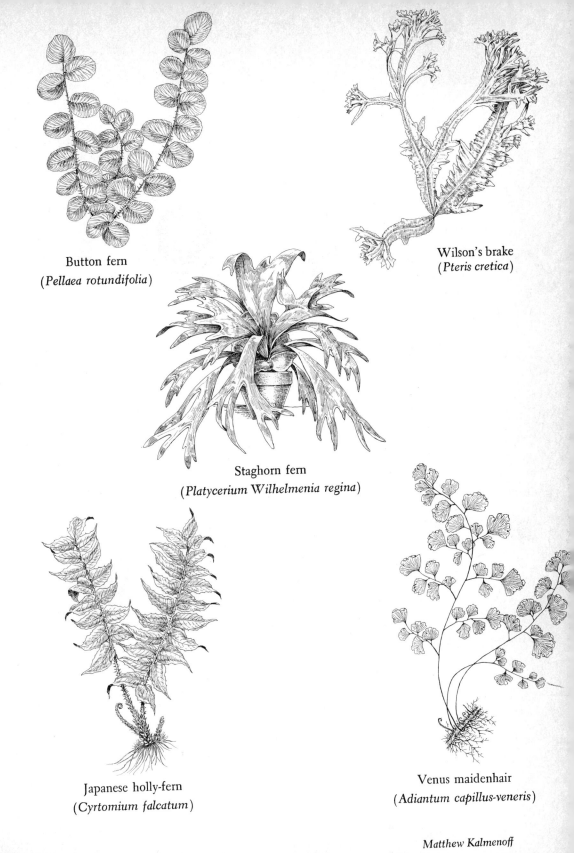

Button fern
(*Pellaea rotundifolia*)

Wilson's brake
(*Pteris cretica*)

Staghorn fern
(*Platycerium Wilhelmenia regina*)

Japanese holly-fern
(*Cyrtomium falcatum*)

Venus maidenhair
(*Adiantum capillus-veneris*)

Matthew Kalmenoff

laden with offspring that they touch the ground, allowing the young plants to root and become independent. In the home, new plants are quickly propagated by placing the budded leaves on damp peat moss. It takes about three months in a moist growing chamber to get a little fern ready for planting. Plantlets from ferns only three or four months old are common.

Those who have leftover Christmas poinsettias in all probability have two or three small ferns growing at the base of the tall plant as green filler. These ferns generally are the fast- and easy-growing *Pteris cretica*, sometimes called Cretan brakes, natives of the Mediterranean area and many other warm countries throughout the world.

Before discarding the poinsettia, remove the ferns and replant them in smaller pots. Chances are that you have a Victorian brake, a fern with dark green and silver variegation. This plant has dimorphic leaves, that is, differently shaped sterile and fertile leaves. The sterile leaf is prettier; the fertile leaf carries spores along the edges of narrow, elongate leaves.

Another likelihood is the ribbon brake, a fern having leaves with cream-colored bands running along the midrib. Fanciest of all is Wilson's brake, a plant with leaves ending in ornate finger tassels.

Staghorn ferns, with their antlerlike leaves, are really curios of ferndom and never fail to gain attention. These epiphytes are native to faraway tropical countries and, contrary to popular belief, they can be grown in the home. Staghorn leaves are good examples of dimorphism as the long antlerlike leaf is fertile and the round leaf or shield is sterile.

Living in trees, these ferns tightly wrap the shields around the irregular bark, catching and holding both rainwater and decaying organic material needed for growth. Staghorns may be grown in well-drained pots but all appear more realistic when mounted on cork bark plaques. Water plants thoroughly and allow them to become almost dry. In addition to reproducing by spores, this group also propagates from its "pups," small plants peeking out from behind the sterile leaves.

During the winter months, ferns do best in sunshine. If the light appears too strong, it may be tempered by curtains or Venetian blinds. For years I have used fluorescent lamps, two forty-watt tubes about eighteen inches above the plants, clock-controlled, for fourteen hours each day.

For successful fern culture, moist atmosphere is essential. Grow plants over a pebble tray kept wet. In lieu of a humidifier, use a hand or tank sprayer at least once each day. Common with most plants, roots must never come to full dryness, but avoid overwatering as a soggy soil will eventually kill a fern.

Be willing to repot plants when needed. Generally late summer is best as the roots become adjusted before the winter months. Commercial African violet soil is a good mix. For those requiring a greater quantity, mix equal parts of screened topsoil, humus and sand. Soil for maidenhairs is improved by adding ground oyster shells. Limit the soil mix for epiphytic ferns to humus or leafmold blended with chopped fir bark. I avoid fast-working fertilizers but occasionally use a sprinkling of bone meal. During the winter, one application a month of dilute fish oil emulsion is beneficial.

Ferns are relatively pest-free although it is best to guard against the white, waxy mealybug and the various turtleback scales. Most ferns are killed by commercial insecticides. It takes time, but it is better to control these pests by touching them with isopropyl alcohol applied with a Q-tip. Flush the leaves at the sink for plant cleanliness and to remove any of the insects' sticky residue.

Scented Geraniums

MARY ELLEN ROSS

ONE of the fondest memories of my childhood summers is the faint odor of peppermint from scented geraniums growing in the corner of a screened-in porch.

Scented geraniums come in a variety of forms and shapes as well as leaf colors and fragrances. Most of them have small blooms; some are quite colorful, which adds charm to the beauty of the foliage.

Blooms may be sparse indoors unless the night temperature falls to 55 degrees or slightly lower. Scented-leaved geraniums need full sunlight for best growth but will tolerate partial shade, especially the peppermint-scented variety. Water plants when the soil approaches dryness.

Rapid growers, geraniums need trimming and pruning frequently. Use fertilizer once a month. Ordinary garden soil or regular potting mixture is best. Geraniums are prone to aphids and white flies, but these pests can be controlled with an aerosol spray or malathion.

Among the scented geraniums are several with lemon fragrance. *Pelargonium crispum* has the strongest odor and is most desirable. Prince Rupert Lemon and its variegated form with larger leaves are stronger-growing types. The variegated form is highly favored for its decorative green and white foliage.

Most popular is old-fashioned rose (*P. graveolens*), which is used in jellies, cakes and teas. Rober's Lemon Rose may be more fragrant and even better to use in cookery than the old-fashioned rose, but it does not have the same beautiful foliage. Rose geraniums also come in variegated forms—Lady Plymouth, Grey Lady Plymouth and *P. graveolens variegatum*.

Peppermint-scented geranium has large velvety leaves and strong scent. A rank grower, it should be pruned severely to keep a shapely plant.

A basket variety with small leaves is apple geranium (*P. odoratissimum*), which has the scent of apples. Small round leaves send out runners that bear fluffy white blooms. *P. grossularoides*, also a hanging-basket variety, has the strong scent of coconut. It has small dark-green round leaves and many pink blooms.

Strawberry (*P. scarborviae*) is similar to the *crispum* with very small dentate leaves, which smell like a basket of strawberries. Other scented geraniums smell like lime or ginger. The oak-leaf varieties are labeled as pungent-scented. Then there are the pine-scented varieties of the *Denticulatum* group with sticky foliage like the pitch of pine.

A Moss-stick for Climbing Plants

WALTER SINGER

INDOOR gardeners can achieve interesting effects with climbing plants, particularly philodendrons, by providing them with naturalistic supports. For philodendrons, the best supports to use are moss-sticks or moss-poles, either of which can be made at home. The plants' roots grow into the moss, which keeps them moist but not wet.

There are two ways to make moss-sticks with sphagnum moss. About two pounds of dry moss should be enough to make one moss-stick two and one-half feet long. Fresh, long sphagnum moss is best.

A moss-stick is made of a one- or one-and-one-half-inch wooden stick, preferably long-lasting redwood or cedar. About two to two and one-half feet is a good length. For greater sturdiness, nail a four- to five-inch piece of wood of the same thickness to the bottom of the long stick.

Moisten the moss thoroughly and spread it on a piece of strong wrapping paper. The paper should be about eighteen inches in width and the same length as the main stick. Place the stick on the moist moss and roll the moss around the stick by rolling the paper with the moss. When the moss is evenly wrapped around the stick, tie the moss both criss-cross and spirally with thin copper wire.

Another kind of moss support is the moss-pole. It is based on a cylinder of one-quarter or one-half-inch mesh wire (hardware cloth). A piece twelve inches wide and twenty-four or thirty-six inches long will be needed.

Roll the mesh wire into a cylinder, overlapping the edges about one-half inch. This will make a cylinder with a diameter of about three and one-half inches. Fasten the overlapped seam at six- or seven-inch intervals with wire.

To make the cylinder sturdier in the pot, push two sticks (about five inches long), crossing each other, through the bottom of the cylinder. These crosspieces will firmly anchor the pole in the flower pot or tub. Fill the empty cylinder with moist sphagnum moss; use a stick to pack the moss compactly.

Then the moss-pole or moss-stick can be placed into a pot or tub with ample drainage material in the bottom. Fill the container with a good, porous soil mixture, tamping it slightly around the moss-stick or moss-pole up to three-quarters of the height of the container.

For best results start with small philodendron plants which can be easily trained to grow on the moss. A young plant growing on a moss-stick or moss-pole will produce much larger leaves than a plant which has been started without such support.

A combination planting of a large-leaved philodendron with several small-leaved vine-type varieties is very attractive.

Under Lights

GEORGE A. ELBERT

Decorating the home with plants is no longer confined to a few indestructible tropical foliage specimens. Decorating with flowers is no longer restricted to short-lived florists' gift plants or cut flowers.

With artificial light, the darkest corner of a house or apartment becomes a growing area superior to a sunlit windowsill. In a "light garden," every day is sunny and there are no seasons.

The popularity of this type of gardening grows and grows as amateurs learn how simple and successful it is. Many things have been learned along the way. Here they are, to date.

Plants. Fluorescent light kept burning for fourteen to sixteen hours a day, where temperatures are much the same summer and winter, changes the natural habits of plants. A growing list of exotics, many unknown to horticulture only a few years back, will bloom under lights practically every day in the year with little attention. Most of them are not found at the local florist but at specialist mail-order nurseries or at some local growers. "Light" gardeners call them "miracle plants." They really are. African violets everyone knows, as these were the first plants known to flourish under lights. Now amateur growers are becoming familiar with such gems as *Oxalis regnelii, Cuphea hyssopifolia,* Columneas (Goldfish Plants), *Hypocyrtas* (Candy Corn Plants), *Streptocarpus* (Constant Nymph), *Euphorbia Bojeri* and *Gesneria cuneifolia.* Sinningias, relatives of gloxinias, with daintier flowers, are available in a number of ever-blooming hybrids with names like Dollbaby, Pink Flare, Poupee, Freckles, Bright Eyes and the extraordinary Cindy, which, on a small plant, produces an endless stand of flared slipper flowers. The white throat is painted in a precise pattern of purple dashes and dots.

Even some of the annual plants from the garden do well for months at a time, including portulaca and Thymophylia (Dahlborg daisy), both of which prefer full sun in the garden. These plants are relatively compact and fit easily under the light fixtures.

Herbs. There is a new craze for apartment-grown herbs. French small-leaf basil, chervil, winter savory, marjoram and rosemary are a few of the possibilities. A two-tube, twenty-four-inch fluorescent unit with reflector hung under the kitchen cabinet provides sufficient growing space for all these, and more, delectable cooking herbs. Recently, we had a good-size salad of our own apartment-grown Bibb lettuce.

Lights. New types of floodlights are useful in keeping large living room style foliage plants (dracaenas, scheffleras, dieffenbachias) in shape. They also act as supplemental light for blooming ones. General Electric's Cool Beam spot directs heat rays backward so that the light reaching the plant is relatively cool. All the large bulb manufacturers now have "grow bulbs" which serve the same purpose, over a smaller area, as do fluorescent tubes.

Among the fluorescent tubes, there has been an improvement in the intensity of the light that is very beneficial to plant growth. More and more amateurs are experimenting with Very High Output and Super High Output tubes for orchids and other light-demanding plants. Because of much higher wattages, these tubes require special fixtures.

Of the "growth" tubes only Vita-Lite, made by Duro-Lite, is relatively new. Cactus and succulent growers are enamored with the tube, because it appears to be the first of the artificial lights which

This fluorescent-lighted terrarium in a fireplace provides ideal climate for unusual gesneriads to flower.

Gene Maggio

has what it takes to keep their plants thriving. Similarly, bromeliad growers choose Optima (Naturescent), also by Duro-Lite.

Less demanding plants, which constitute the majority of good indoor bloomers, are satisfied with ordinary commercial fluorescent tubes, in such combinations as Warm White and Daylight or Natural. These sell for less and are available in most electrical supply stores.

Combating Glare. Until very recently, a valid objection to light gardens in living areas has been the exposure of tubes, which results in an objectionable glare. A major breakthrough has been made by the use of para-wedge parabolic section louvers, one form of which looks like the plastic crate used in the ceilings of elevators. These louvers eliminate glare at an angle of forty-five degrees. The same principle can be used to eliminate glare from spotlights. These louvers eliminate the disadvantages of fluorescent light in room decor.

Installations. Although there are many more different types of

A built-in fluorescent fixture under a kitchen cabinet provides light for growing annuals, ferns and African violets from seed or cuttings.

Gottscho-Schleisner

fluorescent-light gardening fixtures on the market, real design progress is being made principally by amateurs and by professional interior architects and designers. Many growers have converted bookshelves and room dividers into magnificent decorative pieces by interspersing areas of books and art objects with stall light gardens—nothing more than fluorescent fixtures attached below the shelves.

Terrariums.   Since tropical fish aquarium manufacturers learned how to fuse the glass and eliminate the unsightly metal corner posts, we now have ideally decorative terrarium cases. With a fluorescent fixture set above the case, indoor gardeners can plant a colorful miniature landscape. Where pets are a problem, terraria afford perfect protection for house plants. For the more sensitive blooming exotics, they offer high humidity and protection against air pollution. They are ideal in a bookshelf, on a table, or in that unused fireplace. Needing little attention once the moisture is balanced, they are becoming increasingly popular.

Potting Mixtures.   Light gardeners are definitely committed to what is called the Cornell Mix and variations. This growing medium consists of peat moss, vermiculite and perlite in equal proportions. The mix is sterile, easy to handle and can be adjusted, by changing the proportions a bit, to accommodate almost any house plant. Garden-type soils, even when sterilized, are too heavy and, at the same time, dry out too quickly.

African Violet Hybridizing

PRISCILLA ALDEN HUTCHENS

HYBRIDIZING African violets is a fascinating hobby. In October 1949, when the growing of house plants under fluorescent light was in its infancy, I started an amateur project. Two 20-watt fluorescent lamps were fastened under the china cupboard in the breakfast room so I could grow my four African violets.

Soon propagation began. The first plant grown from a leaf cutting was good old Blue Boy, whose descendants still bloom continuously in my kitchen windows. Within a year a creative urge was stimulated. I wanted to grow plants from seeds. That's when the hobby began and the dining room was taken over as a plant room. Now the collection has over 300 African violet plants.

At present the plants are kept on movable carts equipped with two daylight 40-watt fluorescent lamps under each shelf. With an average room temperature of 70 degrees in the daytime, I use an electric floor humidifier to keep the humidity at 40 to 50 per cent. The temperature at night is not allowed to drop below 60 degrees. Under these conditions there is no rest period and the violets blossom continuously.

Before starting the hybridizing I try to set some fixed goal. Plants that grow best in my home surroundings are selected. I also consider size of blossom, color, shape and growth of leaves.

Pollinating is done on the warm, sunny days. The two yellow pollen sacs (anthers) are taken from a mature, well-developed blossom. The sacs are opened with a sharp needle and the yellow pollen is shaken onto a piece of black paper for visibility.

This pollen is touched lighly to the stigma (tip of the pistil) of the other parent. The pistil resembles a tiny antenna and remains on the stem when the blossom drops. Once I am sure that the pollen has adhered to the sticky surface of the stigma, I mark the mother plants with names and dates of crosses. The labeling is done with tiny jewelry tags tied to each individual blossom stem. If the pollination takes, the stem begins to swell in about a week. A seed pod is forming.

The parent plants are given the same care as the other plants. They are fed with an African violet food every three weeks, and the plants are allowed to continue blossoming.

In five or six months the seed pods begin to ripen. The large green pods shrivel and turn gray, and the stem dries up. The pods are then removed from the mother plant and allowed to dry in an open dish in the sunlight for at least a week.

To germinate the seeds I use a glass icebox dish with a cover. In it I place a mixture (about one and one-half inches deep) of vermiculite and ground sphagnum moss. Bits of charcoal are placed in the bottom for drainage. The mixture is dampened overnight with a very weak solution of a standard liquid fertilizer.

The next morning the dry seed pods are opened with a fine needle. I sift the pepper-fine seeds onto a piece of white paper and then over a section of the planting mixture. Each separated planting is marked with plastic labels. The top surface of these areas is gently pressed down, but the seeds are not covered. After covering the dish I put it in the center of the plant shelf so that the fluorescent lamps are about five inches above the lid. The lamps are kept on about twelve to fourteen hours daily.

The seedlings usually begin to show in about ten days, although some crosses from colchicine-treated parent plants start more slowly. As soon as a mass of tiny green seedlings appears in the dish, the cover is removed for about one-half hour a day to give the plants ventilation. Any large drops of moisture which form on the inner side of the cover are wiped off. The growing seeds should not be overwatered but the planting media kept just damp to the touch. I apply a little weak plant food solution, just a few drops at the outer edge of the planting.

When the seedlings are about one inch high, they are transplanted to small porous clay pots containing a mixture of sterilized potting soil, vermiculite and ground sphagnum moss. A few bits of charcoal are placed in the bottom. Each seedling is lifted from the dish individually with forceps or toothpicks. Vermiculite is kept on the tiny roots for protection.

I pot each seedling singly and place them uncovered on the shelves. The rim of each pot is about six inches from the tubes. The young plants are given the same care as the mature ones and are watched for growth characteristics, type and color of blossoms.

Out of the thousands of seeds and hundreds of seedlings I have grown and crossed, only seven have been selected for registration with the African Violet Society of America. The first plant registered was Rose of Sharon, named for a striking resemblance to the blossoms of the rose of Sharon shrub. This variety has a rich orchid bicolor, single blossom, with dark green, waxy, quilted foliage.

Pilgrim Maid has a demure China blue semi-double blossom with dark red petioles and large, dark green girl (scalloped) leaves. Double

Three-tiered carts supplied with fluorescent lamps
provide space for growing many African violets.

Gottscho-Schleisner

Rose of Sharon, a sport of Rose of Sharon, has large, double, orchid
blossoms and dark green, quilted leaves with deep red undersides.
Pink Popcorn is a deep pink, true double, with dark green leaves, red
on the underside. Since pink is a recessive color, many crosses had to
be made to develop this plant.

Christmas Rose has large, snow-white single blossoms, with big
yellow anthers. The flowers are set off by large, dark green, shiny girl
foliage. Double Christmas Rose, from the same seed planting, has
large, double, true white blossoms on shiny, dark green, girl leaves.

So the hobby expands. The shelves on the plant stands are full of
parent plants carrying fat seed pods. There are new seedlings to watch.
Some are double pinks with girl leaves, and some are colchicine-treated
seedlings. But it is most important to be selective in culling out any
inferior seedlings. Finally, though this hobby may bring rosettes, rib-
bons and trophies at flower shows, its greatest reward is in the development of new plants.

LEFT: Sturdy leaf is cut from African violet with sharp knife.

Nan Tucker

BELOW: Leaves are inserted in vermiculite and kept moist for rooting.

Nan Tucker

When roots form on the leaf tip, new young plants begin to appear. The young plants are potted in loamy soil when large enough to handle.

Nan Tucker

(317)

Starting with Seed

OLIVE E. ALLEN

The true "green thumb" house plant grower will want to raise a few plants from seed, even though it may take longer than obtaining additional or new plants from cuttings. House plant seed started in fall will not produce large plants until next fall. Some seedlings can go into the garden in spring from which cuttings may be taken in fall.

Seed can be sown in a small home greenhouse or little window greenhouse. At the very least, the grower needs a sunny window with proper warmth, humidity and space to grow seedlings.

As a starter, a package of mixed coleus seed will produce plants with foliage in rainbow colors. To obtain plants that display different colors, prick out all sizes of the little seedlings. Some seeds germinate more slowly than others, so that many fine colors will be missed if only the large or first-to-germinate seedlings are pricked out.

Impatiens, Jerusalem cherries and Christmas peppers are fairly easy to start from seed. Whether seed is sown in fall or in January from the berry of one of the Jerusalem cherry plants, it will provide berried plants for the Christmas holidays the following year. When impatiens are grown from seed, many of the flowers will be in colors different from any that the florist will have in the spring.

Geraniums, of course, can be grown from seed. They germinate easily and can be pricked out into small two-inch pots to live on a window sill. They do not make much growth during December and January. From one package of geranium seed, I have had both single and double flowers in all shades of red, pink and white. However, some of the plants raised from seed were "blind" and the others took a long time to reach the flowering stage. Many geraniums grown from seed tend to become leggy, even though pinched back.

Since it is difficult to buy plants of primroses other than the magenta-rose flowering sort, home seed sowing will give extra rewards. There is a beautiful salmon-pink primrose of which seed is available.

This variety is a bit hard to grow, but I did have several nice flowering plants for the following Christmas. Dainty fairy primroses (*Primula malacoides*) also can be grown from seed.

When a friend presented three or four coffee seeds from South America and said they would make good-looking house plants, these also were planted. Two seeds germinated but only one seedling lived. This is now a thrifty, shiny-leaved green plant, four years old. It grows slowly and so far has not shown any signs of flowers or buds.

The black-eyed susan or clock vine (*Thunbergia alata*), which has round, apricot blossoms, often with a dark eye, is worth sowing. It makes a pretty indoor frame for a window, or it can be grown outdoors in summer as an annual. Sow seeds in pots in October or early November for flowering vines by late winter. The vine needs lots of sun and grows rapidly.

The bright blue-flowered browallia can be started indoors from seed. Again, it takes time to grow flowering plants. Seed of *Browallia speciosa major* will provide showy specimens for hanging baskets. Another rather old-fashioned flowering plant—abutilon or flowering maple—also might be sown for color in winter.

Damping-off disease often affects the tiny seedlings in the pot or flat in which they have germinated. Dark, damp, cool days increase the danger of an outbreak of this disease. To avoid damping-off, use only clean sterile soil, vermiculite (my preference) or peat moss as the seed-starting medium.

Small seeds are pressed in lightly; large seeds are covered one and one-half times their size. The growing medium is kept moist, never wet or soggy. A pane of glass (propped up occasionally for ventilation) will keep the soil moist. When the seeds start to sprout, remove the glass and give the young plants plenty of light.

As soon as the second pair of leaves appears, the seedlings should be pricked out into two-inch pots of soil (one to a pot). The soil should be composed of one-third compost, one-third sand and one-third peat moss or humus. Plants must not be allowed to dry out, but they also should not be kept soggy. They use all the sun available during the winter months and need a little fresh air each day.

At night, when the temperature outdoors is low, a section of newspaper can be slipped between the pots and the window pane to provide insulation and protection from cold. An occasional syringing of the leaves will remove dust as well as add humidity to the air.

(319)

Air-layering for House Plants

WALTER SINGER

AIR-LAYERING, a popular method of increasing woody plants, is adaptable for house plants. It is particularly valuable when foliage plants outgrow their proper proportions or become leggy. This often is true of dracaenas, ficus and dieffenbachias.

Actually, there are two ways to improve an overgrown house plant. Either the top can be cut off and rooted in sand or the plant can be air-layered. Air-layering is preferred by the average home grower. Controlled temperature and humidity (as found in a greenhouse) are necessary for the cutting method to be successful.

Air-layering has had some refinements in recent years, but its purpose is unchanged. Briefly, the idea is to encourage root formation high on the leggy stem at the base of the foliage crown.

Although a stem will often form roots with no special treatment, an incision into the bark layer (cambium) incites the plant to root faster. When this cut is made the plant's water and nutrient (sap) channels are interrupted. In order to restore its food supplies the plant sends out new roots at the point where the incision is made.

Of all the types of bark cuts, a ring cut is effective for most house plants. This cut is made with a razor-sharp knife. Make it three-quarters of the way around the stem, two and one-half to three inches below the lowest leaves of the foliage crown atop the bare stem. The cut should be about one-half to three-quarters of an inch wide and only deep enough to go through the bark—not the woody part of the stem.

To spur rooting a hormone rooting powder can be brushed on the cut. However, this step is not absolutely essential to success.

After the cut is made, pack or wrap it with damp sphagnum moss. This layer of moss should not be more than one and one-half to two inches thick. To keep the moss around the cut and to assure consistent

A pebble tray provides moisture for a window-sill collection of geraniums, philodendrons and ivies.

Gottscho-Schleisner

moisture, wrap it with a piece of polyethylene film or a sheet of mimeograph plastic. Both ends of the material, top and bottom, should be tied firmly with rubber tape, string or twistems, so that air does not have a chance to dry out the moss.

Check the moss occasionally for dampness. Untie the top of the wrap and, if necessary, remoisten the moss. Don't forget to retie the wrap. During the rooting process the potted plant should be in a warm and shady place, out of drafts.

Under normal conditions a house plant air-layer will be rooted sufficiently within seven to ten weeks. Some species will take longer than others, depending on the type of plant and time of year. Early spring (February or March) is usually the best time because this is

(321)

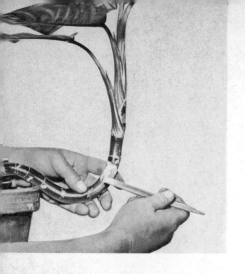

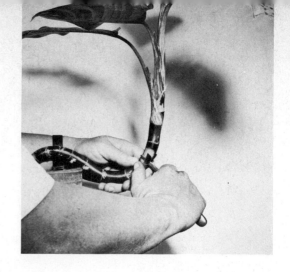

TOP RIGHT: An ungainly dieffenbachia can be air-layered by first removing a portion of the bark with a sharp knife.

TOP LEFT: Hormone powder is applied to the cut to speed rooting.

LEFT: Damp sphagnum moss and polyethylene film are used to wrap the cut area.

BOTTOM LEFT: Roots should form in seven to ten weeks. Plastic is removed.

BOTTOM RIGHT: Without disturbing the root ball, the new plant is set in sandy soil.

Walter Singer

when nature starts plants on a new growing period after the winter dormant season.

When the air-layered plant produces a thick mass of roots (they may push out of the plastic), it is time to take off the wrap. Cut off the top with a sharp knife or pruning shears just below the rooted part of the stem.

Do not leave a stubby, bare section of stem below the root mass because this will interfere with potting. It is advisable to leave the moss around the root ball, to avoid disturbing or damaging the new roots.

The rooted air-layer is placed into a flower pot. Handle it as any rooted cutting which requires a closed, humid atmosphere. The indoor gardener should use a little more sand in the potting soil mixture than he would use ordinarily.

The pot should be not more than one and one-half to two inches larger in diameter than the root ball. In most cases, a three- or three-and-one-half-inch pot will be sufficient. Overpotting in too large a container may slow the plant's growth progress.

For most types of leggy and bare-stemmed house plants, the preceding method of air-layering will be best. With some, however, a slightly different incision should give better results. This applies especially to plants with thin stems on which a ring cut would be rather difficult to make.

In such cases, a notch cut is recommended. With this method, the utmost care and precision must be observed to prevent breaking the stem. The cut is made upward into the stem a few inches below the crown of leaves. It should be about one to one and one-half inches long and should extend one-third to one-half of the way into the stem.

The notch cut must be kept open so that it does not grow together before roots form. Insert a pebble or small wooden wedge into the cut. Then pack the area as recommended for a ring cut. Because the stem is delicate, support it with a stake.

With either method of air-layering, there are extra dividends. Don't throw away the bottom part. It usually will shoot out again and may become an even bushier plant.

Also, healthy pieces of stem can be rooted. Choose sections with blunt buds or "eyes" and lay them sideways in a sand-peat moss mixture that is kept damp. When leaves push up and roots form, these little plants are cut apart and potted.

Fun for the Young

WALTER SINGER

YOUNGSTERS can get more from the kitchen than three square meals a day. They can raise a window-sill "garden" of plants that are propagated from everyday food items. This phase of a child's education has added value when winter's inclemencies put a premium on indoor diversions. Plants can be grown from seed, tubers, plant tops or roots.

A common house plant is grown from the seed of the alligator pear or avocado. With a little help this rather large seed will produce a handsome foliage plant. In the bottom of a four-inch flower pot place a few pieces of broken crockery; if the pot has a drainage hole, one piece will suffice. Fill three-quarters of the container with regular potting soil and the remainder with clean sand. Insert the avocado seed, pointed end up, so that about one-third of it is above the sand. Keep the sand damp, but not wet.

The avocado seed may also be rooted in plain water. Set it in a shallow saucer or else use toothpicks to suspend it in a glass so that the thick end just touches the water. The seed should be kept in a

RIGHT: Pineapple top is cut off at the "neck."

FACING PAGE, LEFT: It roots quickly in sand kept moist.

FACING PAGE, RIGHT: When sufficient roots form, the pineapple top is planted in soil.

Walter Singer

dimly lighted place for six or seven weeks, or until the long tap root emerges. This is the signal to move the plant into the light. A pale green shoot will appear shortly. At first the leaves will be small and pointed, but after the seedling is potted in soil, growth will be rapid.

Another delicious fruit from the tropics, the pineapple, will make an equally fascinating plant project for the youngsters to grow. On top of the pineapple fruit is a dense rosette of leaves called the crown. With a sharp knife, slice this off right at the line where it begins to grow on top of the fruit. For best results do not cut higher or lower.

Expose the cut to the air for a day or two so that it dries; a fresh, bleeding cut may decay. Then, with youthful help of course, press the cutting firmly into a shallow flower pot filled with clean mason sand.

At first the cutting is kept in diffused light, away from drafts. It should root in about five to eight weeks. During this time the sand must never dry out. When the pineapple crown is well rooted, pot it into a sandy soil mixture. Don't forget the drainage at the bottom of the container. Then place the pot in bright light, to bring out a red sheen on the pointed leaves. Pineapples make handsome house plants, just as do the pineapple's cousins, the bromeliads.

There is a little trick which will induce pineapple tops—in fact, all bromeliads—to flower. Dissolve five grains of calcium carbide—the crystal used for the old ethylene lamps—in one quart of water. Fill the center of the dense rosette of leaves with this solution. Let it remain for twenty-four hours, then drain off the excess. In about five to six weeks start watching for surprising results.

What vine could be more interesting than that produced by a sweet potato? The stems grow vigorously, even in plain water, and in little time they will be long enough to train around a window. A hyacinth jar is an ideal container. Place the tapered end of the sweet potato in the jar so that just the tip is under water. Pieces of charcoal in the water will keep it sweet and discourage odor and decay.

Shoppers at the grocery may come across some ginger roots. These, too, will come to life if suspended in water. The foliage is handsome—a shiny dark green—and compares favorably with any foliage plant. Yams, squash, onions and the like may also be tried.

Many plants in addition to the avocado may be started from seeds. Among these are fruits such as dates, grapefruit and oranges, and vegetables such as fresh peas, lentils and so forth. The youngster may not get abundant germination, but even a few bright plants will be a rewarding thrill.

Plant the seeds (after drying them off) either singly or, if small, in groups. Use small flower pots filled with a sandy soil mixture. The seeds should be covered with a layer of soil equal to the thickness of the seed. If the seed is very large, such as the date-palm seed, plant only one seed to a pot, preferably a four-inch pot. When the seedlings have made some growth or if they appear to be crowded, they can be transplanted into individual pots.

Woodland Terrarium

BARBARA B. PAINE

BUILDING a woodland terrarium is a practical and inexpensive way of bringing some of the outdoors indoors. One composed of evergreen plant material from the woods is so simple to assemble that even a child can undertake the project with some supervision.

A small area of woodland should provide enough varied evergreen plant material for a dozen simple terrariums. The plants should be

A woodland terrarium features plant material in a natural setting.

Barbara B. Paine

abundant enough so that the few picked—each with a little of its own soil—will never be missed. Needless to say, conservation laws should be checked first. Also, obviously, permission should be obtained before collecting plant material on someone else's property.

First, of course, the terrarium builder will need to obtain a container, such as an old goldfish bowl. A glass cover for it can be cut to order at a hardware store. The cover should fit loosely enough to allow some air to circulate. At one time open dish planter arrangements were popular, but they are not as satisfactory.

A rectangular shape is best for easy viewing, but a round container will do. Tiny terrariums five or six inches square can be enchanting, although the larger sizes are easier to plant. Also necessary in building a terrarium are a few small stones or bits of broken flower pot, some coarse sand or fine gravel and a few pieces of charcoal.

The beginner should go to the woodlands in the fall to gather evergreen material while the ground still is unfrozen. However, he should delay the expedition until the foliage of deciduous plants has turned color or dropped so the evergreen species are unmistakable.

Equipment for the collecting expedition includes a pan to be filled

(327)

with rich woods soil and leafmold, a trowel, a knife and either cellophane bags or a roll of waxed paper. When digging up the plants, keep as much of the soil around the roots as possible. Wrap up each plant separately, for the less moisture lost between picking and replanting time the better will be the plant's chance of survival.

Two main items in every woodland terrarium are mosses and seedling evergreen trees. Half a dozen varieties add interest. Pine, spruce, juniper, cedar, hemlock and laurel are all excellent among the seedling evergreens. A point to remember: four to five inches tall is the maximum height of plants for the average living-room-sized terrarium.

The hobbyist may want to use one small evergreen creeping plant in the terrarium. Depending on which is more abundant in his locality, he may look for either wintergreen or partridgeberry. Pick the plants only in areas where they grow in profusion, and then only take one short segment of stem and its roots.

A few "tidbits" will accent the terrarium. Lichens, with their little red knobs of spore cases, small moss-covered stones or oddly shaped rocks are attractive. Twigs with turkey-tail fungus growing around them, or some tiny hemlock cones will heighten the woodland landscape effect. An acorn or a maple seed will probably germinate and grow if planted and kept moist.

To plant the terrarium, first of all, scatter a few stones on the base to insure good drainage. Cover these with sand to an over-all depth of

Close-up of terrarium plants shows mosses, seedling evergreens and pieces of bark.

Gottscho-Schleisner

one to two inches; taper off just short of the edges so that the sand will not show in the final result.

Next, to keep the soil sweet, the sand should be covered with a thin layer of charcoal. If the charcoal comes in pieces, press bits into the sand.

A layer of an inch or so of damp rich soil from the woods, brought right to the wall of the terrarium, finishes the foundation. For contours—tiny hills and depressions—build up the foundation with more soil and thoroughly decayed leafmold or humus.

As in flower arranging, the larger, more important items—plants and rocks—are set in first. No plant leaves should ever touch the glass. Although the seedlings won't grow much, they need adequate room.

Beginning terrarium makers often tend to overcrowd the plants. After the seedlings are in, distribute the mosses and disguise the spaces in between with leafmold. Last to go in are the "tidbits"—a hemlock cone, an acorn or lichens.

Water the plants lightly with a bulb sprayer and put on the glass cover. The terrarium is now completed. Terrariums last better if kept in a cool room out of the sunlight. Watering is needed only once every three or four weeks. If the glass mists over, remove the top for a few hours to allow the plants to dry off.

Grow It in a Bottle

JOAN LEE FAUST

WHAT could be simpler than gardening in a bottle? All you need is a clean container, some stems from a green plant and water.

The idea is not new, of course, but with a little encouragement, some ingenuity and know-how, horticultural adventures can happen.

Dr. Henry M. Cathey, of the USDA Crops Research Division, is so enthusiastic about the idea that he says, "You can grow prac-

tically anything. All you have to do is follow a few very simple rules."
First, the container. It can be anything—clear glass, antique bottle,
smoked-glass bottle, ceramic vase or beverage bottle. The bottle must
be clean. Scrub clean inside and out with hot soapy water. To enhance
the decor, the bottle can be covered with paint, contact paper or
decoupage, but it's not necessary.

Next, the plants. Any plant that grows from a fairly sturdy stem
will do. There is a long list—about twenty-six different kinds of plants.
Here are some of his favorites: myrtle, geranium, oleander, wax begonia, fuchsia, impatiens, coleus, aucuba, dracaena, gardenia, pothos,
African violet, hibiscus, tradescantia, cissus, ivy, philodendron, Chinese
evergreen, fatshedra, zebrina, sansevieria, peperomia and even gesneriads.

The preparation of the plants is important. Slips should be cut
from healthy, sturdy plants. They should be long enough to extend
into the container for support. All leaves that would be below the
water line should be cut off.

Before the stems are placed in the water, they should be rinsed
clean to be free of any dirt or sticky resin residue. Several stems of
various kinds of plants may be grouped together—whatever pleases
the fancy. Then the container should be placed in light. Most of the
plants will do very well in reduced light. Bright sunlight encourages
the growth of algae.

It is only because clear glass encourages the growth of algae that
sometimes colored glass bottles are used But the clear glass does not
in any way affect the root growth of the plants.

Charcoal was once recommended to absorb the breakdown of
impurities caused by plants in water, but research has shown that the
benefit of charcoal is negligible.

Once the bottle garden has a good start (roots), it is helpful to
supply growing nutrient in the form of liquid fertilizer. It should be
used only at one-quarter to one-fifth the rate recommended on the
package—no more.

Now, this is the important part: sanitation. The bottle garden
should be cleaned inside and out once a month. This means emptying
out the bottle, scrubbing it inside and out with hot soapy water and
rinsing well.

The plants should also be scrubbed. Leaves should be rinsed off
well and the stems gently scrubbed with soap and water and rinsed

well. Then put the whole garden back together again with a fresh supply of water.

Algae growth tends to be rapid in bottle gardens, especially when fertilizer is added. This monthly scrubbing and cleaning out is the key to the whole success story.

If gardeners grow tired of the plants they are raising in the bottle gardens, these rooted cuttings can be planted in soil. A design with new and fresh foliage stems can then be worked out.

Water Jug Terrarium

ROBERT C. BAUR

LARGE water jugs found at auctions and antique shops convert into spacious bottle gardens. So do acid jugs, five-gallon pickle jars and kerosene bottles.

Thoroughly clean them before beginning. Most bottle stains are removed by an overnight soaking in a strong solution of laundry bleach.

Fingers are out, so planting must be done with a few long-handled tools. The handiest are a wooden dowel, pointed on one end, and a bamboo stake with a bent paperclip attached to the end to serve as a pruning hook. To pour in soil and gravel, fit a plastic funnel into the cardboard tube saved from a gift-wrapping roll. Sometimes the tube must be cut and taped to fit the opening. A kitchen shears and bottle brush will also be helpful.

Other planting accessories include sterilized general-purpose potting soil, a box of aquarium gravel, a package of dried decorator's moss or living sheet moss procured from a terrarium supplier, some shredded florist's sphagnum, a hunk of charcoal and a thermos bottle cork.

When the jar is dry, line the bottom with moss, forming a cup to contain the soil and to aid in absorbing moisture. The moss cup should be about one-fourth the height of the bottle.

Dried moss should be moistened and squeezed nearly dry before use. Cut the sheet moss into strips small enough to poke inside, with the green side pressed against the bottom and sides. Overlap the ends with the dowel so there are no gaps.

For drainage pour some aquarium gravel through a funnel tube and spread it about the moss cup in a thin layer.

Next, with funnel and carboard tube pour in soil almost to the top of the moss liner. Dry, finely sifted soil pours easily. Drop in several pieces of charcoal to keep the soil from smelling sour.

Planting is done with the dowel. Use the point for making holes, the blunt end for pushing, placing and covering roots.

Make a shallow depression where each plant is to go, and place it root first in the opening. Then press the dowel against the base of the stem and push it inside. A simultaneous shake or tilt of the bottle should drop plants where you want them. Don't be discouraged by an occasional miscalculation that entwines two plants. Untangle them with the bamboo pruning stick and push the errant plant into its proper position.

Small plants will slip neatly inside, but others may need some root or leaf pruning. You can avoid smudging the jar's inside walls by washing the soil from large root balls. Poke roots into the soil, cover and pack them firmly. Anchor top-heavy plants with pebbles or support them with a smaller plant.

Plan the planting carefully, providing contrast with variegated foliage and different leaf patterns. Starting with the taller plants in the back, work forward, reserving miniatures and sprawling vines for the foreground.

Rather than overcrowd, fill in the gaps with leftover moss strips or wads of moistened sphagnum. Finish the landscape with patches of aquarium gravel, small pebbles and bits of driftwood. Frogs or other ceramic woodland creatures must be small enough to drop inside. Wipe away mud stains and moss flecks with the bottle brush, bent to the contour of the bottle. Then, after a light sprinkling, just enough to moisten the soil, cork the bottle and the garden is on its own.

Natural light, preferably a bright window that receives little or no direct sunlight, is essential. Or twelve to fourteen hours of artificial light can be supplied daily. Average 70-degree room temperature is just about right for bottle gardens; don't worry about nightly thermometer drops.

The bottle garden is self-maintained by recycling evaporation moisture and condensation. Water only if this rain pattern fails to bead the inside of the glass. Dry plants are the result of a loose cork or insufficient water to start the moisture cycle functioning.

Cloudy glass usually means nothing more than a temperature change. If the situation persists, it may indicate a moisture buildup that can cause mold and plant decay. Remedy this by removing the cork until the glass clears or the interior dries out.

Window plants will grow toward the light unless you give the bottle an occasional turn. Deciduous native ferns will go through their natural seasonal process of dying down and sprouting new fronds. Otherwise yellowing foliage could mean overexposure to sunlight or a need for ventilation.

Snare out dead leaves or unwanted growth with the bamboo pruning stick. Twist the stem until it breaks, taking care not to uproot the entire plant. As you acquire the skill with dowel and pruning stick, you will be able to remove and replace whatever you wish without disrupting the landscape.

Snails or aphids are wiped out with a damp cotton swab fastened on the dowel with a rubber band. With occasional pruning, cleaning

Antique water jug converted into a bottle garden.

Robert Baur

and replacing, the five-gallon garden will continue to grow for many years. Moisture-prone, shade-inclined plants are suggested for bottle gardens. Avoid brittle leaf stems that will break in the bottle neck. Choose plants that share similar growing needs and conform to the size of the bottle.

Twelve-inch plants are proportioned to a nineteen-inch bottle, but smaller plants allow for expansion. Especially suitable are small-leaved miniatures from wild-flower nurseries: ferns, mosses, seedling conifers, shinleaf (*Pyrola*), *Lycopodium*, spotted wintergreen, rattle-snake plantain, partridgeberry, and white wood sorrel.

Baby tears, crinkle-leaved peperomia, creeping fig, creeping loose-strife, Kenilworth ivy and *Selaginellas* are other small plants suggested for fillers and foreground display.

Color is supplied by aluminum plant, dracaena, croton, dieffen-bachia, chlorophytum, tradescantia, strawberry begonia (*Saxifraga*), syngonium, pothos, hoya and ivy such as Glacier and other small green-and-white-leaved types.

Good foliage plants in smaller form are arrowhead, boxwood, Pteris and maidenhair ferns, grape ivy, kangaroo vine, palms, prayer plant and wandering Jew.

Bulbs Will Bloom Indoors

RUTH MARIE PETERS

Few house plants equal the gaiety of hardy bulbs which are potted in fall and forced into bloom indoors during the winter months. New ideas for forcing make it possible for even city apartment dwellers to enjoy spring bulb blossoms in winter.

Little bulbs such as snowdrops, scillas, muscari, chionodoxa and crocus can be brought into bloom just as easily as tulips, daffodils and hyacinths. Both the little and major bulbs are handled the same way. They must be potted early enough to allow a good root system to form (about ten weeks) before the actual flower-forcing begins.

The usual root-development method is to bury the pots outdoors in a trench or coldframe. This still is the best method when there is enough garden space or when there are a great number of pots to be rooted for forcing.

However, recent experience has shown that any dimly lighted location which will have a steady temperature close to 40 degrees will serve. The apartment dweller or home owner with a small garden can set a few pots of bulbs in bushel baskets or packing boxes filled with peat moss. These can be put in a poorly lighted place and filled to the top with soil, peat moss or sand. Pots can also be stored for rooting in a cold garage or unheated attic, without being buried in anything, just so long as the temperature will stay at 40 degrees.

The little bulbs are ideal for this method. A small pot will hold many bulbs, and a bushel basket will store several small pots.

Another new idea simplifies the forcing of hyacinths. Small pots of bulbs can be slipped into plastic bags to keep the soil evenly moist. Pull the bag over the pot from the top down, leaving six or seven inches of empty bag at top to give the future shoots room to grow. Overlap the bag at the bottom and secure with a rubberband. Place the pots in a cold closet, basement or attic.

When hyacinths are handled this way, there is no set number of weeks for rooting and forcing. Simply remove the bag and bring each pot into the light when shoots reach the top of the bag.

The best way for the amateur to be assured that all flowers will open simultaneously is for him to plant only one variety of bulb in each pot. To get a good display, set the bulbs close together so they almost touch.

Florists use a double-layer method to obtain a full pot of bulbs. The bottom layer is set on an inch of soil, with the space between the bulbs equal to the diameter of each bulb. Enough soil is placed around this layer of bulbs to almost cover their tips. The second layer is then planted, with the bases of the bulbs set in between the noses of the bulbs on the bottom.

For bulb forcing, it is best to use bulb pans—red clay pots which are wider than they are high. The drainage hole in the bottom of each pot should be covered with a flat stone or piece of broken flower pot.

Next add a layer of gravel or pebbles (a half-inch for a three-inch pot, one inch for a five- or six-inch size). A quarter-inch layer of sand,

Narcissus bulbs are set just below soil level in pots.   *Nan Tucker*

Tulips, daffodils and hyacinths can be forced into winter bloom indoors.
                                                              Nan Tucker

vermiculite or sphagnum moss over the pebbles will also keep the potting soil in place.

A general potting mixture of equal parts of garden soil, sand and leafmold or peat moss is adequate. Pot the bulbs so that their points are at or just below the final soil level. Label each pot.

Pots that are stored in a trench or coldframe are covered with six inches of soil. This layer is then covered with salt hay to keep the soil from freezing.

Give each pot a thorough watering before putting it away. If the weather is dry, give additional water as needed to keep the soil moist.

When ten weeks have passed, root growth should fill the pot and even show through the drainage hole. To be certain that the root mass is adequate, tip the soil ball from the pot. Roots should encircle the ball of soil.

Bulbs that are well rooted can be brought indoors into a cool (50- to 55-degree) temperature. Light from a north window is best for a day or two until the pale shoots turn greener. After this the pots can be moved to a sunny window where the temperature will be no higher than 60 degrees by day, 50 degrees at night.

Tulip bulbs that are potted up and stored in early October should be ready for forcing by mid-December. Later potting will give later bloom. Some varieties need more time than others. Little is gained, however, by potting earlier than mid-September, for even the earliest-forcing varieties should not be brought in before December 1. Flowers should open in two or three weeks.

Among the tulips recommended for forcing are the following single early varieties: Brilliant Star, scarlet; Duc de Berlin, red edged yellow; Duc van Tol Scarlet, scarlet; Duc van Tol White Maxima, white; Golden Glory, yellow; Mon Trésor, yellow; and Proserpine, deep rose. Two highly rated Mendel tulips are Early Queen, deep rose, and Olga, violet-red edged white.

Varieties which should not be forced before December 10 include Attraction (single early), orange-scarlet; King of the Yellows (single early), yellow; Scarlet Cardinal (double early), dazzling scarlet; and Willemsoord (double early), carmine-red edged with white.

Catalogues list additional varieties for forcing. For a novelty, try the species tulip, *Tulipa praestans* Fusilier, a bright vermilion-orange. The bulb bears two to four flowers on a stalk. It can be forced into bloom in a cool (55- to 60-degree) room after February 1.

Daffodils (*Narcissus*) need a somewhat longer rooting period. Two good yellow trumpet varieties for early forcing—after December 15—are Forerunner, bright yellow, and Magnificence, golden yellow. For forcing after January 1, try Allard Pierson (poetaz), Early Beauty (yellow trumpet) and Early Perfection (poetaz), all with white perianth and yellow cup. The yellow trumpet variety Golden Harvest is golden yellow; the incomparabilis variety Helios has a yellow perianth and flushed orange cup. Also worth trying are the dainty miniature species like *Narcissus bulbocodium*, *N. cyclamineus* and *N. triandrus*.

For early forcing of hyacinths, in time for Christmas, obtain prepared bulbs. Untreated bulbs need several weeks of cold treatment, as previously described. Recommended varieties are City of Haarlem, yellow; Duke of Westminster, deep purple; Edelweiss, white; Grand Maître, deep lavender-blue; Jan Bos, dark red; King of the Blues, dark blue; and La Victoire, rose-crimson.

Equally good are Lady Derby, bright salmon-pink; L'Innocence, white; Myosotis, light blue; Ostara, Eton blue; Perle Brilliant, porcelain blue; Pink Pearl, clear pink; and Queen of the Blues, azure blue. The city or suburban gardener should also try the small French Roman and cynthella hyacinths. They are not as full as the large hyacinths, but are more graceful.

Greenhouses for Growing

OLIVE E. ALLEN

With a greenhouse it is possible to garden all year long. Small home models are becoming more popular every year. It is not uncommon to see one nestled against a dining room window, connected to a toolhouse, or standing in the back yard.

There are plastic-covered or glass greenhouses available, but to my way of thinking the only choice is glass glazing, if a permanent structure is wanted. Plastic film material is cheaper, true, but it will last just so long at best. There is no doubt about the fact that glass on the roof and walls makes a much handsomer-looking, sturdier, more weather-tight and longer-lasting greenhouse.

Glass greenhouses come in two types—the lean-to and the free-standing. Both have their own distinct advantages and limitations.

A lean-to is actually just half the size of a regular even-span house —split lengthwise down the middle. Thus it is more reasonable in cost than the even-span house.

Also in favor of the lean-to, for maximum year-round gardening convenience, is the fact that it is usually attached to the home. The owner can enter it without exposure to the elements, a major advantage in winter.

A lean-to unit is easier and less expensive to heat than the free-standing greenhouse. It obtains warmth and protection from the building to which it is attached.

On the other hand, the free-standing greenhouse is the better buy. There is more bench growing space, more shelf space, more room for hanging baskets and more glass area through which essential sunlight can enter.

A greenhouse should be located where it will receive at least three hours of sunlight each day, more if possible. Winter shade from trees nearby should be avoided, but it is an advantage to have deciduous trees in the vicinity. They are not winter sun barriers, for they lose their leaves in fall. However, their foliage will shade the greenhouse effectively during summer.

An even-span greenhouse may have two glass ends, one with a door included. It may have one end up against a garage or house wall.

In any case, the hobbyist should start with as large a greenhouse as possible. He will soon find that it is becoming crowded, especially in spring, when there never seems to be enough room for all the flats of seedlings. All greenhouses may be extended with extra sections, but it is far cheaper to start with a larger one than to have to add more sections to a smaller-sized unit a few years hence.

At the present time, home greenhouses may be purchased in either aluminum or redwood framework. Some greenhouse companies offer both types of construction. Each material has its advantages.

The makers of all-aluminum greenhouses claim that their units are lightweight yet sturdy, need no upkeep, will not rot or corrode and admit the maximum of light. The advocates of redwood, on the other hand, claim that in winter in cold climates, aluminum conducts heat out of the greenhouse. Wood is a poor conductor and thus saves fuel by keeping heat in.

The firms who favor redwood claim that wood does not expand and contract as much as aluminum when there are changes of temperature. Thus a wooden framework is said to put less strain on the glass.

Whether an aluminum or redwood frame is chosen, the greenhouse usually will be purchased prefabricated (knocked down and ready to assemble). Some models come with glass all the way down to the ground. However, the unit that is placed on a two-foot concrete, brick or stone foundation is better where winters are severe.

This important foundation should be built according to specific plans furnished by the greenhouse company. The work should be completed before the greenhouse arrives.

Two people can erect a small prefabricated greenhouse in a day. It is ordered in sections, usually four, five, seven or eight.

The sections are erected and bolted together and then the glass is

A lean-to greenhouse is accessible and less costly to heat.

Lord and Burnham

A free-standing greenhouse can be placed to take advantage of the sunlight.

Gottscho-Schleisner

slipped into special grooves and fastened down—no putty needed. Gable ends—either all glass or with a door—are also bolted in place as specified in the instructions.

The cost of the framework and glass of an aluminum, free-standing, two-bench greenhouse varies slightly with different manufacturers but is approximately $750 to $964 for a twelve-foot unit. A lean-to of the same length, with only one bench, is about $150 less.

On the other hand, a redwood greenhouse of approximately the same size costs between $500 and $775 for the free-standing type. The price is usually about $100 less for the lean-to.

Most models of home greenhouses may be purchased with either hand-operated or automatic ventilators. Automatic ventilators with thermostat and ventilator motor cost anywhere from $115 to $260 for a twelve-foot-long greenhouse.

Benches may be constructed of redwood or of cement board with galvanized steel pipe supports. Two benches of redwood cost between $120 and $190 for a twelve-foot house, whereas cement board would be around $200. Extra partitions in a house are about $200 each.

Heating costs depend to a great extent upon the situation of the greenhouse and the winter temperatures. A small lean-to often can be heated by an extension from the existing heating system of the home to which it is attached. If this cannot be arranged, the greenhouse must have a system of its own.

An electric heater can be used for a small house, an oil- or natural gas-fired hot-water heating system for a larger house. Heaters cost from $250 up. Other valuable accessories such as thermometers, shelf brackets and shelves, humidifiers and so forth may be obtained, as needed, from most suppliers.

Plants for Pleasure

JAMES U. CROCKETT

A SMALL greenhouse can capture the breath of spring or the romantic fragrances of the tropics. Plant choices are just about unlimited.

The beginner will need plants of a permanent nature to form the background of his greenhouse garden. Other types may be selected for a profusion of bloom or interesting habit of growth. The plants should be grown in pots rather than in benches or open soil beds. Pot culture not only restricts too rampant growth and aids flowering but it provides portability as well.

Amateur greenhouse growers must determine where the warm and cool parts of the greenhouse are before deciding where to place the plants. Windswept corners are apt to be several degrees cooler than areas protected by the bulk of a house. The application of a shading compound to part of the roof will cool that area and provide special growing conditions. By matching plant needs to the micro-climates found in most small greenhouses, the thoughtful enthusiast will discover that a surprisingly wide variety of plants can be grown.

Surely the queen of winter-flowering shrubs for the home greenhouse is the camellia. The exquisitely formed pink, red or white blossoms long have been corsage favorites. They are produced freely from October until April.

No home greenhouse should be without at least one Chinese hibiscus. These easy-to-grow shrubs flower throughout the year, bearing huge pink, white, yellow or red blooms. Azaleas also make marvelous plants for home greenhouses. Those types which are not hardy outdoors usually are the ones with the largest and prettiest flowers.

Oleander blossoms when quite small. The white, red, pink or near-yellow fragrant flowers are produced month after month. As a truly exotic tropical shrub, grow the magnificent tibouchina, commonly known as the glory bush. The velvety flowers, of the most intense blue-purple imaginable, are produced nine months of the year.

Close to the top of any list of favorite long-blooming pot plants must be the cyclamens. In the cool end of a greenhouse they will easily flower without ceasing from October until April. Buy sturdy plants from the florist when they are in bloom so that a color choice is possible.

Both the fairy primrose (*Primula malacoides*) and *P. obconica* will bear a host of pink, white or lavender flowers month after month if grown in a cool location. Then there are everblooming geraniums and the spikes of brilliant orange crossandra flowers that open against glossy evergreen foliage. Crossandras need a warm, partly shaded location.

Trailing lantana, especially the lavender-flowered variety, never seems to stop blooming. Grow it in a hanging basket to display its beauty to the fullest. Another lovely everblooming plant for hanging baskets is the browallia. The most effective species is *Browallia speciosa*, which has large, deep blue flowers. Browallias and lantanas do well in either sunshine or light shade.

Nearly all the exotic plants that lend a tropical effect to a greenhouse do best under warm, humid, partly shaded conditions. Monsteras with their enormous perforated leaves, as well as many kinds of philodendrons, make luxuriantly growing vines for a shady greenhouse.

(343)

To add color, grow scarlet, pink or white anthuriums, mottle-leafed dieffenbachias and multi-hued caladiums. For a bold foliage effect, choose the Australian umbrella tree or the dwarf Chinese banana, and hang a staghorn fern on a shady, damp wall.

Spanish moss, a true air plant (epiphyte), will thrive if hung anywhere in a greenhouse. It does not need soil. As a curiosity, grow a pineapple plant. Many species of *cryptanthus, aechmea, billbergia* and *vriesia* (all bromeliads) grow well as hanging plants in a lightly shaded greenhouse.

Orchids are intriguing and will thrive in the warm end of a shaded greenhouse. The beginner might try a few flowering-sized plants of hybrid cattleya orchids. Hang them from roof bars so that they will have good drainage and air circulation.

Routine under the Glass Roof

OLIVE E. ALLEN

MAINTAINING a home greenhouse full of sturdy plants and flowers is rewarding but not always easy. The new greenhouse owner has a lot to learn about watering, ventilating, heating and insect control. He must take into consideration the day-to-day weather, sun-exposure of the greenhouse and the types of plants he is growing.

Automatic heating units and ventilator openers are a great aid to the greenhouse owner who must be away a good part of the day. Both systems are operated by thermostats located inside the greenhouse; they assure an even temperature and a supply of air. The automatic ventilator openers are fine for sunny weather but they should not be relied upon completely during a spell of dark, cold winter days.

The smaller the greenhouse, the less air space there is, so ventilation is important. Plants need fresh air constantly, but not drafts. Ventilators should be opened a crack in the morning, even on the coldest day. Later on, if the sun shines brightly the vents should be opened wider. A sudden clouding over of the sky will mean that the vents must be closed. At any rate, the vents should be closed by late afternoon.

Greenhouse temperature levels are determined by the preferences of the plants being grown. Certain kinds require a warm house (above 60 degrees at night), and others do best in a cool house (45 degrees at night). Many kinds of plants can be grown where night temperatures range from 50 to 55 degrees. Temperature requirements of various foliage and flowering plants are listed in house-plant catalogues and greenhouse books.

Hot-water heat is the best kind for the small greenhouse. It is steady and dependable and does not fluctuate up and down as quickly as steam heat. When the greenhouse is within 125 feet of the boiler in the home, heat can be piped out directly.

Where this is not feasible, the greenhouse must have its own heating system; it can be oil fired, gas fired or electric, operated by a thermostat. With these units, some kind of auxiliary power is advisable in case electricity is cut off by a storm. Hand-fired coal heaters are more bothersome (close attention is especially important in cold weather), but they are not dependent on electricity.

Every home greenhouse should be equipped with a temperature alarm. A bell, located in the house, is connected to a dry-cell battery and thermometer in the greenhouse. The bell rings if the temperature drops below or goes above certain designated points. This is a worthwhile device to help prevent serious plant losses from sharp changes in greenhouse temperature.

Watering is one of the most baffling chores for the beginning greenhouse grower. When, how much and what to water are learned from experience and observation.

In general, watering should be done in the mornings, when the temperature is rising—never at night. There may be some sunless days during the winter months when nothing will need to be watered.

Most amateurs are likely to overwater rather than underwater. Plants that are resting need little or no water. Pot plants need more water than those grown in benches.

Once in a while the grower should make a spot check of watering conditions. Knock a typical plant out of its pot and examine the soil at the bottom. If the top is moist but the bottom appears dry, the potted plants are not getting a sufficient amount of moisture. Sometimes, on sunny days, pot plants will have to be watered two or three times.

Always water gently and with water that is not too cold, if possible. Water should not fall on plushy leaves like those of African violets, or on soft ones like those of begonias. For these plants it is better to use a watering can rather than a hose.

Sanitation and cleanliness are essential parts of maintenance. A brand-new greenhouse, with fresh soil and clean pots, will not need much attention at first. Old dirty pots, used soil and plant refuse mean trouble. Also, insects and mold seep into wooden boards in benches. These should be treated with preservative to prevent rot.

Decayed matter is a haven for slugs, snails and centipedes. Slugs can devour a whole pot of fine young petunia seedlings in one night. Lime scattered under the benches will help to control these pests. Since they work only at night, slugs often can be hand-picked from plants. Poison slug bait containing metaldehyde also is useful.

The best way to control plant pests is to prevent them from getting started. A spraying every two or three weeks with nicotine sulfate, rotenone or pyrethrum will go a long way in controlling insects. None of these chemicals, applied either as sprays or dusts, will be harmful to the plants or the grower.

Experience has proved malathion to be most effective in controlling most greenhouse insects, but great care must be taken when using it. Rubber gloves and a gas mask are recommended for greenhouse use of malathion. Mites can be controlled with a miticide spray.

A hand sprayer will be adequate to use in a small greenhouse but it pays to buy a good one made of non-rusting copper or brass. The undersides of leaves as well as the juncture between stems and leaves must be sprayed.

Plants or cuttings to be grown in the greenhouse should be selected with care. By all means, swap cuttings and plants with friends, but first be sure their plants are healthy and disease free.

Greenhouse gardeners often find it hard to resist trying first one, then another greenhouse plant, but too many plants cannot thrive in limited space. Plants that are crowded become stunted and they are not easily sprayed, fed and watered. If the grower allows enough space between plants for good circulation of air, chores will be easier and many troubles prevented.

PART IX

AROUND
THE GARDEN

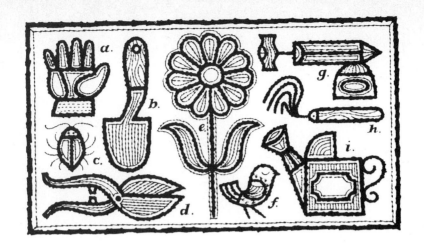

The Four Seasons

JOAN LEE FAUST

SPRING

March

THE sky uses modest colors. White streaks of snow sieve through dull blue. From out of dusty gray come silvery streams of rain.

When bright blues appear with cottony clouds, jasmine, Cornelian cherry and witch hazel match the yellow of the sun. Even though the grass is lazy, snowdrops, snowflakes and crocus push through. Early tulips spice the brown earth with flashy colors. There is a stir; the sap is rising. Growth has begun.

Spring arrives. All the showy shrubs of late summer—rose of Sharon, hydrangea, clethra and hypericum—are pruned now, as are trees. The lawn is limed, fertilized and seeded. The mower is sent for repairs. Trees are fed. Holes are spaced eighteen inches apart and kept in regular circles to the outer spread of the branches. Each twelve-inch hole is filled with about one-quarter pound of fertilizer.

The soil is too cold to dig. Those who doubt it will find heavy clods this summer that never break up. The urge to sow seed is satisfied in window-sill planters where snapdragons, petunias, lobelia, cabbage and tomatoes get their start.

April

SPRING comes into her own in April. Each day brings blossoms anew to spread upon the landscape. Forsythias and daffodils offer yellow. Cherries, single and double, add a dash of pink. Snowy white magnolias pose gracefully on gray branches. Fruit orchards in flowers of pink or white nestle like morning fog on the rolling hillsides. Some are settled in the valleys.

Spreading over the ground are white arabis and candytuft, cheerful doronicum and the happy faces of pansies. Early primroses bloom on the path that leads to the brook. Hepaticas, bloodroot and violets bestir the hush in the woods.

There is much to be done in the garden. The sun and wind warm and dry the ground for digging. Rosebushes are pruned lightly to remove any winterkill. Protective mulches are taken off the shrubs and perennials. Thin bands of fertilizers worked around them supply needed nutrients.

Woody plants are moved. Spinach, lettuce, raddish, carrots, beets and other hardy vegetables are planted. Cabbage and broccoli are placed in the rows. Seed of hardy annuals—larkspur, sweet pea, cornflowers, scabiosa and alyssum—can be sown. Strawberry plants arrive from the nursery just in time for setting out. Chrysanthemums and fall asters are divided to foster better bloom.

The sun moves higher, days are longer. Greenhouse temperatures rise. Vents open wide, but they close snugly at night. Jack frost still is about.

May

PERHAPS it is the dogwood trees decked with layers of creamy flowers or the loud colors that azaleas splash on the land. It could be the stately tulips or iris. Even the old-fashioned hawthorn by the door. Maytime has many symbols and each one cherishes his own.

(350)

Scents of lilacs fill the balmy air. Fat buds of peonies become magnificent flowers. Dainty deutzia and bleeding heart bloom in grandma's garden. Sometimes the viburnums spread new petals.

Everything moves outdoors in May. Tomatoes are set near tall poles for climbing. Squash and peppers are put into place. Zinnias, marigolds, portulaca, petunias, snapdragons fill window boxes, tubs and borders. Daylilies are planted but it is too late to divide any perennials. Shrubbery planting is finished, except for container-grown shrubs, which can be planted any time.

The soil is warm enough to put in tuberous begonias, caladiums, ismene, gladiolus, fairylilies and other tender bulbs. Hardy bulb foliage is ripening to form the flowers for next spring. It can be disguised with low-growing annuals and perennials.

Rosebush spraying begins; mulches control weeds and hold moisture. The smallest garden pool has room for a pygmy waterlily. Lawn mowers are kept busy.

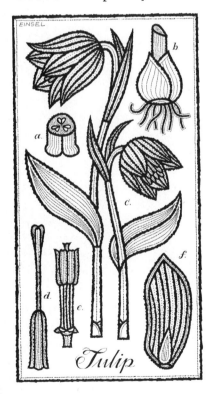

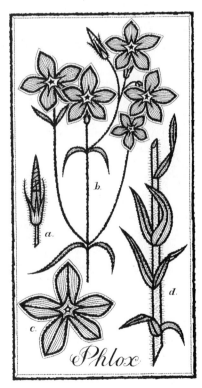

SUMMER

June

ROSES are everywhere. Sand dunes are bright with wild ones. Public parks have graceful arbors hung with flowers of yellow, red, pink or white. Floribundas enclose a terrace. Tree roses hold bouquets high in borders. Rows in bloom line the garden and tiny miniatures mark a stepping-stone path.

June invites the delphiniums, rhododendrons and laurels to share her days along with iris, platycodon, veronica, columbine—nearly all the perennials in the catalogue. Elegant lilies stand serene. Mockorange spills its fragrance. Annuals begin to show color. Alyssum is early, so is stock. Pink, red and white phlox are sparkling bright.

There is seeding to be done where the first crops of spinach, beans, radish and lettuce were growing. Replace them with succession crops or try late summer vegetables. Teeny fruits hang on the trees. To assure a good crop thin them out. Trees can support only so many to harvest.

All the house plants are vacationing outdoors. Tropical foliage plants earn places in the shade. The sound of the mower whirring across the grass interrupts the lazy afternoon. If the blades are sharp, the lawn will have a neater trim.

Biennial seed is fresh for sowing in a nursery bed. Tropical water-lilies may be safely planted in deep pools where there is plenty of sunshine. Weeds are growing; keep after them.

July

SUMMER has sounds. Quite early in the morning happy birds welcome the new day. The insects make their music and a startled grasshopper startles a hiker wading through a field of daisies. Hives are full of clover honey manufactured by the busiest bees.

Nature has settled to a steady pace. Flowers bloom as they will. Some are bold and brassy like early marigolds, zinnias, celosias, snapdragons, phlox, heliopsis and trumpet creeper. The muted plumes of astilbe and white lilies of hosta provide cool respite in the shade.

Evergreen leaves and shady grass make a hideout for the gardener's nap. If the borders are mulched and the rosebushes sprayed, a nap is in order. However, there may still be faded flowers to cut off the phlox to keep it from going to seed. Perhaps the hedge has grown a bit straggly but it can be sheared with an electric clipper in the cool of the evening.

If showers be slight, weekly soakings of trees, shrubs and flowering plants are needed. Lack of water makes a lawn become dormant and strawlike. It will surge back to growth when the rains come in fall.

Raspberries wait to be picked. Faded rhododendron blooms are snapped off branch tips to prevent seed pods.

August

ROSES are undaunted by the heat. Floribundas and even some hybrid teas are unceasing in their offerings of bloom. Flowers may not be plentiful but nonetheless they are there.

The shrubs share center stage, with rose of Sharon playing the lead. Minor roles are filled by tamarisk, potentilla, gordonia and beautyberry. The Chinese scholar tree pushes out its delicate petals. In spots the earth becomes hard and cracked where the sun has drawn up all the water.

It is time to plant again. Iris need first attention. Old clumps are divided. New Oriental poppies are settled. The last of the cabbage for fall harvest is planted and some lettuce can be sown for salads.

Adventurous putterers will find perennial seed aplenty and a small plot serves as a nursery. Bulbs are ordered for late fall planting from colorful pages of catalogues. The autumn-blooming crocus will bloom in September if tucked in conspicuous spots. Gladiolus and dahlias come into their prime. Show exhibitors choose their champions.

The scraggly old lawn at last gets attention with a thorough feeding. The new lawn is planted after a proper seedbed is prepared. Herbs and flowers are gathered and hung to dry.

AUTUMN

September

GOLDEN rays of sunshine fill the blue sky. Evenings are cooler and the earth wakes each morn refreshed.

Roses stage a comeback. Sycamore trees are early to drop their leaves and a playful breeze whirls them about. Purple-blue asters begin to appear and the earliest chrysanthemums open gold, yellow, maroon, pink or bronze petals. The late peaches are picked from the trees and juicy pears are ripening. Annuals keep up their parade of bright colors and delphiniums put on a stately show.

September is the planting month when fall begins. First on the agenda are the bulbs. Everything from the tiny snowdrop, scilla and crocus bulbs to the husky species tulips and bulbous iris are planted. Later in the month and on into October the daffodils, hyacinths and tulips will be planted. Perennials settle themselves quickly if set in the ground now. And evergreens have a few months to push down roots if they are moved into place.

The lawn is green and luscious. The new lawn seeded last month is ready for its first cutting when the blades are three inches high.

For tasty flavors in winter a few small herbs can be potted for the house. A small parsley plant will thrive inside, too. Tree and shrub seedlings can be tended in a home nursery. Take cuttings of border plants.

October

THE air has a spicy tang. Cheeks are rosy. Everyone steps lively. High overhead, nature outdoes herself with her most brilliant staging ever.

Sunlight catches a scarlet oak and the rays bounce off the golden Norway maple. Autumn leaves blend with the evergreens to spread a panorama never forgotten. Apple trees are hung with balls of red, red fruits. Bright orange firethorn berries delight the birds and decorate the espaliered branches trained along the terrace wall. Throughout the land little fruits bear the symbol of harvest. There are tiny violet beautyberries, black winterberries, red fruits of the viburnum and curious red rose hips.

There are many chores to be done. Hardy bulbs are planted where the soil is well drained. A few are saved for potting and forcing in late winter. Deciduous trees and shrubs are set in place as leaves fall. No fertilizer is applied until spring. There is time for last-minute lawn seeding and patching. Dahlia tubers and gladiolus corms go into the storage bins. Rugged root crops, beets, and carrots are pulled up.

There will not be many more times to mow the lawn, and after the final cutting the faithful machine can be cleaned and stored. Leaves, leaves, leaves ever falling keep the compost pile growing. Seldom, if ever, are they burned.

November

GRADUALLY a quiet hush descends upon the land. Trees have lost their splendid colors, and the twisty, bold branches poke out in all directions.

Even the busy squirrels are lazier now—their winter cache is filled. Most of the birds have gone for the winter, but sparrows, chickadees, grosbeaks and nuthatches and perhaps a few robins stay on. Pines, fir, spruce, rhododendron and laurel provide welcome greenery on the hillside.

All the outdoor tasks gradually draw to a close. Rosebushes have arrived from the nursery and are planted. A six to eight-inch mound over their base will protect them through the winter. Lily bulbs are set in place. Round clusters or neatly arranged rows are marked off for the latest tulips. Lily pools that are deep can be left filled through the winter. Shallow ones may need protective covering.

Flocks of birds sitting in the trees watch the feeder installation with eager anticipation. Straggly old canes of the climbing roses are cut to the ground and other unruly ones are tied back to the trellis. Hardwood cuttings can be buried in a sand pit.

Chores completed, the tools are well oiled and then stored. Indoors, seed of house plants can be planted in clay pots.

WINTER

December

IT is too chilly to linger long outside. The ground is frozen hard and everywhere trees, shrubs, perennials are at rest as winter settles on the land.

Mulches of straw, salt hay or peat moss are piled over the perennial beds and newly planted trees and shrubs. Here and there a burlap windbreak protects a cherished plant.

The first snow may fall. Birds are regular customers at the feeders and noisy squirrels try to invite themselves, too. The red berries of holly spark spiny evergreen leaves, and maybe a Christmas rose blooms where it is sheltered.

Indoors there is great activity with trays of house plants lining many windows. A thin layer of pebbles, kept moist, provides needed humidity. In the basement there is a complicated set-up of lights, trays, moisturizers and tiers upon tiers of house plants. A tidying-up of the tool shelf means tossing out old seed packets. Spray bottles are clearly marked, placed out of a child's reach. Fertilizer bags are high and dry.

Post cards are sent for catalogues. And by the roaring fireside the family gathers to string popcorn and cranberries to trim the Christmas tree. A pretty wreath hung on the door bids all a cheery welcome during the holidays.

January

THE new year begins. Nature tidies her carpet with a fresh dusting of snow. Puffs of it land on the limbs of the spruce and the pine. Shaggy oak leaves cling to bare branches. Rhododendron leaves are curled tightly as if huddled together against the cold.

Indoors, gardeners relax in easy chairs with piles of catalogues upon their laps. A pencil and pad nearby keep track of all new things to be tried. A dollar-and-cents column is checked against the budget.

Ready reference books, worn thin when chores call, can be laid aside. Now is the time to peruse some of the personal books, which carry tales of plant hunters' adventures. Gardeners can travel far and wide and learn the flora of new lands as each volume is explored.

It is a good idea not to relax completely during January. Oftentimes there are sudden thaws toward the end of the month. Harsh winds and high sun can dry out evergreens unless mulched. Tender kinds must be shielded from the wind. Applications of anti-desiccant sprays are vital. If icicles form on woody plants, wash them down with a stream of water when the temperature is above freezing. Whacking them breaks limbs. Put up snow fences to steer snowdrifts. Repellents keep deer from nibbling bark.

February

WITCH HAZEL pokes out wiry yellow tufts as soon as there is a hint of mild weather. Hazel will be joined by the yellow corylopsis bells and maroon parrotia. Pussy willow could show its furry heads. The brave skunk cabbage may decide to emerge from its swampy resting place.

The sound of the hammer is heard from the workshop as the new gate is pieced together. The broken rose trellis gets new crosspieces and a coat of white paint. Fat envelopes filled with seed orders await the next trip to the post office.

House plants look tidy. Yellowed leaves and faded blossoms are picked off regularly. The foliage plants are shined with spray. Potted tulips rooted in the coldframe are coming into bloom. A bunch of daffodils brought home from the florist hints that spring is coming. The impatient cut a few branches of forsythia, flowering quince or dogwood to bloom indoors.

Those who do not find enough to keep them busy indoors can go outdoors on an inspection tour. Fences and gates can be checked for repairs or any repainting. Bands of tent caterpillar eggs on fruit trees, bagworm sacs on needled evergreens, are pruned off and burned. The coldframe is put in order to sow seed of hardy alpines. Grapevines are pruned. Shade trees are examined for broken limbs.

List of Authors

ALLEN, OLIVE E.: long-time contributor to *The New York Times* garden pages and specialist in roses, perennials, and house plants

BARON, MILTON S.: Professor, Department of Urban Planning and Landscape Architecture, Michigan State University

BAUR, ROBERT C.: author, *Gardens in Glass Containers*

BETTES, RUSSELL M.: Assistant Professor, Department of Horticulture, Temple University, Ambler, Pennsylvania

BROOKS, MAURICE: retired, Professor of Wildlife Management, West Virginia University

BROWN, JUDITH-ELLEN: amateur gardener and freelance writer specializing in wild flowers

CALDWELL, JAMES L.: Extension Floriculturist, Ohio State University

CAPEN, BARBARA M.: landscape architect specializing in perennials and ornamentals, now living in Florida

CARLE, GEORGE A.: Department of Parks, New York City

CHRIST, ERNEST G.: Extension Specialist, Pomology, Rutgers University

CLARK, ROBERT B.: Taxonomist, Monroe County Parks Department, Rochester, New York

CLAYBERG, CARL D.: Assistant Geneticist, The Connecticut Agricultural Experiment Station, New Haven

CORNMAN, DR. JOHN F.: retired, Professor, Department of Floriculture and Ornamental Horticulture, Cornell University

COULTER, F. C.: retired, Director of Publicity and Public Relations for Asgrow Seed Company

(359)

CROCKETT, JAMES UNDERWOOD: author, *Time-Life Encyclopedia of Gardening*

DUICH, DR. J. M.: Professor, Agronomy Department, Pennsylvania State University

ELBERT, GEORGE A.: President, Indoor Light Gardening Society of America, Inc.

ENGEL, DAVID H.: landscape architect; author of *Japanese Gardens for Today*

ENGEL, DR. RALPH E.: Professor, Turfgrass Science, Rutgers University

FLEMING, BEVERLY: amateur gardener, specializing in vegetables and wild flowers

FOSTER, F. GORDON: author, *The Gardener's Fern Book*, and fern consultant, Brooklyn Botanic Garden

GERLACH, CARL S.: Professor, Department of Urban Planning and Landscape Architecture, Michigan State University

GOLDMAN, ALAN W.: advertising copywriter and consultant on azaleas and rhododendrons

GRASBY, NANCY: author, *Imaginative Small Gardens*; landscape designer

GRAYSON, ESTHER: co-author with her husband, F. F. Rockwell, of many gardening books

GREEN, MARY S.: freelance writer and horticulturist

HAISLIP, MARTHA PRATT: long-time contributor to *The New York Times* garden pages, whose hobby is roses and perennials

HARING, ELDA: author, *The Complete Book of Growing Plants from Seed*; amateur gardener specializing in perennials

HENDRICKSON, ROBERT: freelance writer with special interests in horticulture

HERSEY, JEAN: author, *The Woman's Day Book of House Plants* and *Cooking With Herbs*

HOWARD, FRANCES: author, *Landscaping with Vines*

HUNTER, BEATRICE TRUM: author, *Gardening Without Poisons* and *Consumer Beware*

HUTCHENS, PRISCILLA ALDEN: amateur African violet hybridizer

IREYS, ALICE RECKNAGLE: landscape architect; author, *How To Plan and Plant Your Own Property*

JAGSCHITZ, JOHN A.: Professor, College of Resource Development, University of Rhode Island

KORBOBO, RAYMOND P.: Professor, Department of Horticulture, Rutgers University

KOSAR, WILLIAM F.: retired, holly specialist, National Arboretum, Washington, D.C.; now residing in Corvallis, Oregon

LACEY, DONALD B.: Editor, *The Shade Tree*, Bulletin of the New Jersey Shade Tree Commissions, Rutgers University

LEACH, DAVID G.: author, *Rhododendrons of the World*; rhododendron hybridist

LEE, HAL: late founder and President of Rooftop Gardeners of New York; died 1959

LEES, CARLTON B.: Director, Massachusetts Horticultural Society; author, *Gardens, Plants and Man*

LEUTHARDT, HENRY P.: retired nurseryman specializing in espalier

LEWIS, CLARENCE E.: retired, Professor, Department of Horticulture, Michigan State University

MCKENNA, P. J.: late Assistant Horticulturist, New York Botanical Garden; died 1956

MEYER, KENNETH: late freelance writer and amateur gardener specializing in perennials; died 1966

PAINE, BARBARA B.: freelance writer and wild flower hobbyist

PETERS, RUTH MARIE: author, *Bulb Magic in Your Window*

PRICE, MOLLY: author, *The Iris Book*; long-time contributor to *The New York Times* garden pages

PULLAR, SARAH E.: former zoology instructor, Smithsonian Institution's Museum of Natural History; lecturer for Smithsonian Associates; now Mrs. Raymond Gagné

RADKO, ALEXANDER M.: Eastern Director, United States Golf Association, Green Section

REBHAN, JOHN R.: landscape design consultant

ROCKWELL, F. F.: co-author with Mrs. Rockwell of many garden books; Garden Editor, *The New York Times*, 1933–1943

ROSS, MARY-ELLEN: nurserywoman specializing in house plants

ROSS, RUTH ALDA: former staff member, garden news, *The New York Times*

ROUSCH, IRENE: amateur rosarian active in the American Rose Society

SECKMAN, MARY C.: long-time contributor to *The New York Times* garden pages, specializing in roses and perennials

SINGER, WALTER: late staff photographer, New York Botanical Garden; died 1971

SLATE, GEORGE L.: retired, Professor of Pomology, New York State Agricultural Experiment Station, Geneva, New York

SMITH, ALICE UPHAM: landscape architect; author, *Trees in a Winter Landscape* and *Patios, Terraces, Deck and Roof Gardens*

SMITH, NANCY R.: author, *Garden Smartly* and *Garden Full of Flowers*

STRAKOSCH, WINIFRED H.: landscape designer; former Director of the Children's Garden, Brooklyn Botanic Garden

SUTCLIFFE, ALYS: late horticulturist, Brooklyn Botanic Garden; died 1969

THOMAS, G. L., JR.: author, *Garden Pools, Water-lilies and Goldfish*

THOMASSON, R. R.: late Assistant Director, Cooperative Extension, University of Missouri; died 1966

THOMSON, RICHARD D.: author, *Old Roses for Modern Gardens*

TIRRELL, RUTH: amateur gardener specializing in vegetables and fruits

TRUEX, PHILIP: author, *The City Gardener*; now residing in California

VOS, DR. FRANCIS DE: Director, Botanic Garden of the Chicago Horticultural Society, Glencoe, Illinois

WESTCOTT, DR. CYNTHIA: author of many books, including *Anyone Can Grow Roses* and *The Gardener's Bug Book*

WYMAN, DR. DONALD: retired horticulturist, Arnold Arboretum; author, *Wyman's Gardening Encyclopedia* and many other books on woody plants

Sources of Plants and Supplies

The following list consists mainly of those nurseries that sell directly by mail to individual customers. Because of increased handling costs, nominal charges are made for most mail-order catalogues.

BULBS

Antonelli Bros. (tuberous begonias)
2545 Capitola Road
Santa Cruz, California 95060

Daffodil Mart
Gloucester, Virginia 23061

Champlain View Gardens (gladiolus)
South Hamilton, Massachusetts 01982

P. de Jager & Sons, Inc.
South Hamilton, Massachusetts 01982

Grant E. Mitsch (daffodils)
Canby, Oregon 97013

Oakhurst Gardens (rare)
P.O. Box 444
Arcadia, California 91006

John Scheepers, Inc.
63 Wall Street
New York, New York 10005

Mary Mattison van Schaik
(imported Dutch bulbs)
Cavendish, Vermont 01542

FRUITS

Bountiful Ridge Nurseries
Princess Anne, Maryland 21853

Kelly Brothers Nurseries, Inc.
Dansville, New York 14437

Henry Leuthardt (espalier)
East Moriches, New York 11940

New York State Fruit Testing
  Cooperative Assoc.
Geneva, New York 14456

Stark Brothers Nurseries
Louisiana, Missouri 63353

GARDENING SUPPLIES

House Plant Corner
Oxford, Maryland 21654

Walt Nicke
Hudson, New York 12534

Shoplite (fluorescent fixtures)
Nutley, New Jersey 07110

HOUSE PLANTS

Alberts & Merkel, Inc.
Boynton Beach, Florida 33435

Buell's Greenhouses
Eastford, Connecticut 06242

Cook's Geraniums
Lyons, Kansas 67554

Edelweiss Gardens
Robbinsville, New Jersey 08691

Fischer Greenhouses (African violets)
Linwood, New Jersey 08221

Kartuz Greenhouses
Wilmington, Massachusetts 01887

Logee's Greenhouses (begonias)
Danielson, Connecticut 06239

Merry Gardens
Camden, Maine 04843

Tinari Greenhouses (African violets)
Huntingdon Valley,
  Pennsylvania 19006

PERENNIALS

American Perennial Gardens
Garden City, Michigan 48135

Interstate Nurseries
Hamburg, Iowa 51640

Schreiner's (iris)
Salem, Oregon 97303

Sunny Border Nurseries
Kensington, Connecticut 06037

Wayside Gardens
Mentor, Ohio 44060

White Flower Farm
Litchfield, Connecticut 06759

Gilbert H. Wild & Sons
  (peonies, iris, daylilies)
Sarcoxie, Missouri 64862

ROSES

Armstrong Nurseries
Ontario, California 91764

Howard Rose Company
Hemet, California 92343

Jackson & Perkins Company
Medford, Oregon 97501

Kern Rose Nursery (old-fashioned)
Box 33
Mentor, Ohio 44060

Star Roses
West Grove, Pennsylvania 19390

Tillotson's Roses (old-fashioned)
Brown's Valley Road
Watsonville, California 95076

Melvin E. Wyant
Johnny Cake Ridge
Mentor, Ohio 44060

SEEDS

Breck's
200 Breck Building
Boston, Massachusetts 02210

Burnett Brothers, Inc.
92 Chambers Street
New York, New York 10007

W. Atlee Burpee Company
Philadelphia, Pennsylvania 19132

Henry Field Seed Company
Shenandoah, Iowa 51601

Joseph Harris Seed Company
Rochester, New York 14624

Nichols Garden Nursery
Albany, Oregon 97321

George W. Park Seed Company
Greenwood, South Carolina 29646

TREES AND SHRUBS

Adams Nursery
Westfield, Massachusetts 01085

Mayfair Nurseries,
Nichols, New York 13812

Miller Nurseries (nut trees)
Canandaigua, New York 14424

Musser Forests, Inc.
Indiana, Pennsylvania 15701

Corliss Brothers,
Gloucester, Massachusetts 01930

Oliver Nurseries, Inc.
Fairfield, Connecticut 06430

Stern's Nurseries,
Geneva, New York 14456

Weston Nurseries, Inc.
Hopkinton, Massachusetts 01748

WATERLILIES

S. Scherer & Sons
Northport, New York 11768

Three Springs Fisheries
Lilypons, Maryland 21717

William Tricker, Inc.
Saddle River, New Jersey 07458

WILD FLOWERS

Gardens of the Blue Ridge
Ashford, McDowell County
North Carolina 28603

Mincemoyers
Jackson, New Jersey 08527

Putney Nursery, Inc.
Putney, Vermont 05346

Vick's Wildgarden, Inc.
Gladwyne, Pennsylvania 19035

Further Reading

GENERAL REFERENCES

BUSH-BROWN, LOUISE and JAMES: *America's Garden Book.* New York: Charles Scribner's Sons; revised edition, 1966

CROCKETT, JAMES UNDERWOOD: *The Time-Life Encyclopedia of Gardening.* New York: Time-Life Books; 1972

TAYLOR, NORMAN (ED.): *Taylor's Encyclopedia of Gardening.* Boston: Houghton Mifflin Company; 1961

WESTCOTT, CYNTHIA: *The Gardener's Bug Book.* Garden City, N.Y.: Doubleday & Company; 1964

WYMAN, DONALD: *Wyman's Gardening Encyclopedia.* New York: The Macmillan Company; 1971

LANDSCAPING

CARLETON, R. MILTON: *Small Garden Book.* New York: The Macmillan Company; 1971

FOLEY, DANIEL J.: *Gardening by the Sea.* Philadelphia: Chilton Book Company; 1965

IREYS, ALICE RECKNAGLE: *How to Plan and Plant Your Property.* New York: M. Barrows and Company; 1967

LEES, CARLTON B.: *Budget Landscaping.* New York: Henry Holt & Company; 1960

MCDONALD, ELVIN, and POWERS, LAWRENCE: *Low-Upkeep Book of Lawns and Landscape*. New York: Hawthorne Books, Inc.; 1971

NEHRLING, IRENE and ARNO: *Easy Gardening with Drought-Resistant Plants*. New York: Hearthside; 1968

MORSE, HARRIET K.: *Gardening in the Shade*. New York: Charles Scribner's Sons; revised edition, 1962

TRUEX, PHILIP: *The City Gardener*. New York: Alfred A. Knopf; 1963

TREES, SHRUBS AND VINES

CLARKE, J. HAROLD: *Getting Started with Rhododendrons and Azaleas*. Garden City, N.Y.: Doubleday & Company; 1960

HALLER, JOHN M.: *Tree Care*. New York: The Macmillan Company; 1957

HOWARD, FRANCES: *Landscaping with Vines*. New York: The Macmillan Company; 1959

LEE, FREDERIC P.: *The Azalea Book*. Princeton, N.J.: D. Van Nostrand Company; 1958

LEACH, DAVID G.: *Rhododendrons of the World*. New York: Charles Scribner's Sons; 1961

WYMAN, DONALD: *Ground Cover Plants*. New York: The Macmillan Company; 1956

——: *Shrubs and Vines for American Gardens*. New York: The Macmillan Company; revised edition, 1969

——: *Trees for American Gardens*. New York: The Macmillan Company; revised edition, 1965

YOSHIMURA, YUJI, and HALFORD, G. M.: *The Japanese Art of Miniature Trees and Landscapes*. Rutland, Vt.: Charles E. Tuttle Co.; 1957

ZUCKER, ISABEL: *Flowering Shrubs*. New York: Van Nostrand Reinhold, 1966

ROSES

ALLEN, R. C.: *Roses for Every Garden*. New York: M. Barrows & Company; 1956

JENKINS, DOROTHY H.: *The Complete Book of Roses*. New York: Bantam Books; 1956

THOMAS, RICHARD: *Old Roses for Modern Gardens*. Princeton, N.J.: D. Van Nostrand Company; 1959

WESTCOTT, CYNTHIA: *Anyone Can Grow Roses*. Princeton, N.J.: D. Van Nostrand Company; 4th edition, 1967

WILD FLOWERS

COURTENAY, BOOTH, and ZIMMERMAN, JAMES H.: *Wildflowers and Weeds*. New York: Van Nostrand Reinhold Company; 1972

MATHEWS, F. SCHUYLER: *Field Book of American Wild Flowers*. New York: G. P. Putnam's Sons; revised edition, 1955

PETERSON, ROGER TORY, and MCKENNY, MARGARET: *A Field Guide to Wild-flowers*. Boston: Houghton Mifflin Company; 1968

SEARS, P. B., BECKER, M. R., POETKER, F. J., and FORBERG, J. R.: *Wild Wealth*. New York: Bobbs-Merrill Company, Inc.; 1971

TAYLOR, KATHRYN S., and HAMBLIN, STEPHEN F.: *Handbook of Wild Flower Cultivation*. New York: The Macmillan Company; 1962

HERBS

FOX, HELEN M.: *Gardening with Herbs for Flavor and Fragrance*. New York: Dover Press; 1970

SIMMONS, ADELMA GRENIER: *Herb Gardening in Five Seasons*. New York: Hawthorn Books, Inc.; 1971

BULBS

BAUMGARDT, JOHN PHILIP: *Bulbs for Summer Bloom*. New York: Hawthorne Press; 1970

LAWRENCE, ELIZABETH: *The Little Bulbs*. New York: Criterion Books; 1957

REYNOLDS, MARC, and MEACHEM, WILLIAM L.: *Complete Book of Garden Bulbs*. New York: Funk & Wagnalls; 1971

ROCKWELL, F. F., GRAYSON, ESTHER C., and DE GRAAFF, JAN: *The Complete Book of Lilies*. New York: Doubleday & Company; 1961

WISTER, GERTRUDE S.: *Hardy Garden Bulbs*. New York: Dutton; 1964

ANNUALS, PERENNIALS

BAUMGARDT, JOHN PHILIP: *Hanging Plants for Home, Terrace and Garden*. New York: Simon & Schuster, Inc.; 1972

COON, NELSON: *Gardening for Fragrance: Indoors and Out*. New York: Hearthside; 1970

CUMMING, RODERICK W., and LEE, ROBERT E.: *Contemporary Perennials*. New York: The Macmillan Company; 1960

SMITH, NANCY R.: *Garden Full of Flowers*. New York: Charles Scribner's Sons; 1965

WILSON, JAMES: *Flower Gardening for Beginners*. New York: Van Nostrand Reinhold; 1970

FRUITS AND VEGETABLES

Agricultural Extension Bulletins. State Universities.

FOSTER, CATHARINE OSGOOD: *The Organic Gardener*. New York: Alfred A. Knopf; 1972

HERITEAU, JACQUELINE H.: *How to Grow and Cook It Book of Vegetables, Herbs, Fruits and Nuts*. New York: Hawthorne Books, Inc.; 1970

RODALE, ROBERT: *Basic Book of Organic Gardening.* New York: Ballantine Books; 1971

HOUSE PLANTS

BALLARD, ERNESTA DRINKER: *Garden in Your House.* New York: Harper & Brothers; revised edition, 1971

CRUSO, THALASSA: *Making Things Grow, A Practical Guide for the Indoor Gardener.* New York: Alfred A. Knopf; 1969

FREE, MONTAGUE: *All About House Plants.* New York: Doubleday & Company; 1946

GRAF, ALFRED BYRD: *Exotic Plant Manual.* East Rutherford, N.J.: Roehrs Company; 1970

HERSEY, JEAN D.: *The Woman's Day Book of House Plants.* New York: Simon & Schuster; 1965

LANGER, RICHARD W.: *The After Dinner Gardening Book.* New York: The Macmillan Company; 1971

GREENHOUSES

BLAKE, CLAIRE L.: *Greenhouse Gardening for Fun.* New York: M. Barrows Company; 1967

CROCKETT, JAMES UNDERWOOD: *Greenhouse Gardening as a Hobby.* Garden City, N.Y.: Doubleday & Company; 1961

POTTER, CHARLES H.: *Greenhouses: Place of Magic.* New York: Dutton; 1966

LAWNS

CARLETON, R. MILTON: *Your Lawn: How To Make It and Keep It.* New York: Van Nostrand Reinhold; 1971

SCHERY, ROBERT W.: *The Lawn Book.* New York: The Macmillan Company; 1961

VOYKIN, PAUL: *The Perfect Lawn, The Easy Way.* New York: Rand McNally, Inc.; 1969

Index

Page references in parentheses refer to
illustrations in the text

(i)

A Note about the Editor

JOAN LEE FAUST, the garden editor of *The New York Times*, was born in Shamokin, Pennsylvania, and grew up there and in Bethlehem. A graduate of Michigan State University with a degree in floriculture, she was an instructor at the Brooklyn Botanic Garden for two years before joining the staff of *The New York Times* garden department as a reporter. In 1956 she was named editor of the garden pages, one of whose regular and most attractive features is Miss Faust's own weekly column, "Around the Garden."